ROUND THE WORLD YACHT RACE
THE BRITISH STEEL CHALLENGE
1992/3

CREW

UEFA EURO

BATTLE OF VS. THE AGES
FOREMAN
April 19, 1991
TRUMP PLAZA

Daily Telegraph
Michael Calvin
columnist
F45

CHAMP
SPLIT 19

CALVIN
Michael
DAILY TELE

N A-252

119th
OPEN GOLF
CHAMPIONSHIP
ST ANDREWS 1990

PRESS

Admit to Press Centre,
Clubhouse,
R&A Club Tent
and Course

NO DOGS OR
CAMERAS

Kodak

FA Cup Final
2010

WIMBLEDON 1981

NAME MIKE CALVIN
WESTMINSTER PR
NEWSPAPER
F.20
CENTRE COURT
SEAT No.

~B~~~~~~
~~~~~~P Q
~~
~

MICHAEL CALVIN SUNDAY MIRROR

Seat. 97

Michael
Calvin
Sunday Mirror

Grafo Matex
012697

KVALIFIKACIONA UTAKMICA ZA EURO 2012 - GRUPA G

CRNA GORA - ENGLESKA
TheFA

WEMBLEY STADIUM

5/10

PRESS 2

Also available at all good book stores

9781785316470

9781785313929

9781785315466

9781785312632

9781785317583

9781785317576

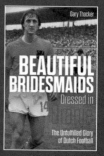

9781785318467

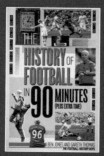

9781785318399

9781785315534

WHOSE GAME IS IT ANYWAY?

WHOSE GAME IS IT ANYWAY?

Football,
Life,
Love
& Loss

MICHAEL CALVIN

First published by Pitch Publishing, 2021

Pitch Publishing
A2 Yeoman Gate
Yeoman Way
Worthing
Sussex
BN13 3QZ
www.pitchpublishing.co.uk
info@pitchpublishing.co.uk

© 2021, Michael Calvin

Every effort has been made to trace the copyright.
Any oversight will be rectified in future editions at the
earliest opportunity by the publisher.

All rights reserved. No part of this book may be reproduced,
sold or utilised in any form or transmitted in any form or by
any means, electronic or mechanical, including photocopying,
recording or by any information storage and retrieval system,
without prior permission in writing from the Publisher.

A CIP catalogue record is available for this book
from the British Library.

ISBN 978-1 78531 884 9

Typesetting and origination by Pitch Publishing
Printed and bound in Great Britain by TJ Books Limited.

Contents

For: Marielli, Michael, and Jesse.

Chapter One

Father and Son

THE HANDMADE wooden box had lain neglected in a corner of a garden shed for many years. It was covered by a latticework of spider's web and a dark, tar-like substance that once, presumably, had a preservative quality. Two ancient plant pots, containing shrunken, dehydrated soil, were perched on top, and added to the sense of abandonment and decay.

It was an unlikely family heirloom, a chance discovery. The box, 35 inches long, 15 inches deep and 14 inches in height, opened to reveal an array of woodworking tools. There were chisels with finely worked wooden handles, a range of saws, blades still sharp despite the rust, two types of plane, a combination square, marking gauge and faded yellow spirit level.

All were embossed with the name F.C. Goss, in what had evidently once been tiny golden capital letters.

Frank Charles Goss was born in 1898, one of five children raised by John Goss, a builder, and his wife Elizabeth. He was known as a placid man, and, by repute, never lost his temper. Carpentry was a trade that suited his quiet diligence and seemingly inexhaustible patience. When times were tough, he worked as a clerk at what was then called the Labour Exchange to earn extra money.

Oliver, his only son, was born on 23 June 1922.

Olly, as he was known, was an athletic, resourceful and intelligent child, who had obviously inherited the genetic tendency to gentility. He became my father-in-law and, in 45 years, I never saw him agitated. He had an innate ability to relate to people, regardless of age or social class. His generosity of spirit was remarkable.

He first clapped eyes on me when called back to the family home from a party with friends by his daughter Lynn, my girlfriend, who would later become my wife. I was 17 and had passed out, trousers around my ankles, in his downstairs toilet after raiding his drinks cabinet. Somehow, he resisted the temptation to throttle me before driving me home and dumping me on the doorstep.

Frank passed away in 1971, without enjoying the long and fulfilled retirement he had planned for, and unwittingly left behind a multi-layered mystery. Why, inside the lid of that box, had he pasted the fixture lists for three Watford teams for the 1932/33 season? What subliminal message did those pieces of water-scarred text from an official club journal represent?

How did the minuscule photograph of an unnamed player, above the fixtures for the seven-team London Professional Midweek League, fit into the equation? Who was he, and why was he sufficiently significant to warrant such an intimate platform? Did it signal anything deeper than an affinity with a humble club?

If only it were as simple as deciphering the scores written, in pencil, beside the schedules for the first team, which finished in comfortable mediocrity, 11th out of 22 in the Third Division South, and the reserves, 11th out of 24 in the London

Combination. When the box was discovered, the initial phase of the pandemic was raging. Olly was approaching his 98th birthday and in lockdown at his care home in Devon.

He was suffering from an accelerated form of vascular dementia. The curtains across his memory were being drawn; though he had retained his easy-going nature, his lucidity was intermittent and unpredictable. And yet, because of the emotional intensity of his connection to football, something stirred when, on one of our daily telephone calls during enforced isolation, my wife asked him about watching and playing football.

He remembered the ritual of walking a mile with his father through the terraced streets of West Watford to the match. He was an outstanding youth footballer. He loved his dad's presence on the touchline, and his approval when he played well. Saturdays meant a treat at the sweet shop, the anticipation of the result and the drama of the game. He couldn't recall individual players, but he was hooked.

My children loved him unconditionally, and he loved them in return. Grandpa meant games and groan jokes. In retirement, he played football and cricket with them in the garden and on the beach. He shared stories of the pre-war footballers depicted on his collection of cigarette cards. They used his half set of Petron Impalas to hack golf balls into adjoining fields, which, in a sadly familiar act of vandalism by local planners, would be turned into a housing estate by 2019.

Late that year, my wife and I spent a 54-hour vigil by his hospital bed and were warned to expect the worst. When he astonished doctors by emerging from a coma, his first thought was to ask me how Watford had got on the previous day. They had lost 8-0 at Manchester City, conceding five goals in the opening 18 minutes.

When I told him I declined to answer on health and safety grounds, he laughed gruffly. His eyes shone with the sardonic acceptance of fate that identifies the true fan, too often treated like a Victorian scullery maid by those who control the modern game. I passed over the Sunday paper; the booming back-page headline consisted solely of the scoreline. He nodded, chuckled and changed the subject.

The box had been found at his bungalow. His handwriting on the sliding wooden top of his father's chisel set suggested that the tools were a form of inheritance, but mention of the photo triggered no immediate memories. How did it relate to those Watford teams who plied their trade when he was in his last year at primary school? A lifetime's allegiance to his local club was already established: were there hints of identity in his early childhood heroes?

Admission to Vicarage Road in 1932 cost a shilling (five pence), including 20 per cent entertainment tax. Dad and lad Goss had a new, steeply banked concrete terrace on which to stand behind one of the goals. It was built, over the summer, by manager Neil McBain, trainers Peter Ronald and Alex Gillespie, and two players, Taffy Davies and Arthur Thurley.

McBain's extraordinary career began with Ayr United in 1914. He guested occasionally for Portsmouth in the First World War, where he served in the Black Watch before joining the Royal Navy. An elegant wing-half, known for his aerial ability and intelligence on the ball, he returned to professional football in 1921, when he was sold to Manchester United for £4,600.

He made his Scotland debut the following year, and moved to Everton in 1923, crossing Stanley Park to join Liverpool in 1928. He remains the oldest player to appear in an English Football League match, being aged 51 years 120 days when, as manager, he answered an injury crisis by playing in goal for New Brighton in the Third Division North.

He spent two years as Watford's player-manager from May 1929, and would remain in charge until 1937, when he was sacked for what was euphemistically called 'family illness'. A scratch golfer and regular punter on horse and greyhound racing, his fate was sealed when an unnamed player complained to the board that, when he asked for his £35 seasonal bonus, the manager told him, 'The bookies have had it all.'

McBain subsequently managed Leyton Orient, acted as Chelsea's chief scout and spent two years as head coach at Estudiantes de La Plata in Argentina. Most unlikely of all, he returned to Watford for a desultory three-year spell from 1956. His lifestyle was distinctive; he lived off fish and chips and insisted players wait on the team bus while he popped into a convenient pub for a drink on the way to away matches.

The jowly, bloated figure of that time, looking at the cameraman with suspicious, deeply hooded eyes, is in stark contrast to the dapper, self-confident individual in a cream summer suit with high-waisted pleated trousers, who poses casually in front of the main stand for an informal version of Watford's 1932/33 team photograph.

He stands to the left of his 18-strong senior squad, augmented by nine apprentices, sitting cross-legged in front of them. They were evidently fresh from a three-team, nine-a-side training session. A third of the players were bare-chested, a third wore white shirts and the remaining third wore roll-necked goalkeeping jerseys.

Goalkeeping was the bane of McBain's life that season. Ted Hufton, a former England international signed from West Ham at the age of 39 to be first choice, never really recovered from breaking a finger badly in the first pre-season match. He played only twice before retiring, and was never adequately replaced.

The shining light was Billy Lane, a forward who began his career at Gnome Athletic, originally the works team for an engine manufacturer in east London. He became notorious for verbally inciting opponents and liked to instruct his wingers to get early crosses in, so that he could 'let the keeper know I'm around'.

He had a great spring, so this strategy invited assault by shoulder, stray elbow and, in one case captured by the camera, his backside, which connected with the goalkeeper's chin. He scored a hat-trick in nine minutes against Clapton Orient, contributed 68 goals in three years and went on to manage Brighton & Hove Albion to their first title, the Third Division South in 1957/58.

Watford was not a happy club. The directors did not endear themselves to the players by demanding extra fitness sessions. Fans were accused of apathy by the chairman, John Kilby, owner of a local brewery. He threatened to resign after being confronted by a supporter, who advanced on the directors' box and, in the polite phrase used by the local newspaper, the *Watford Observer*, 'made use of an objectionable sign'.

I studied that black-and-white team photograph, seeking similarities with the head-and-shoulder shot in the tool box. I recognised Taffy Davies, whose tanned torso stood out amid so many pale bodies, but he was fair-haired. The player in the portrait had dark, luxuriant hair. My pet theory, that he was Billy Lane, looked the most plausible.

Lane was between Davies and his manager in the team picture. His hands were tucked respectfully behind his back. His baggy shorts were pulled up well above his waist. He had dark hair, but in summer trim. There was a passing resemblance to the player in Frank Goss's box, but it was insufficient to justify a leap to conclusions.

Lane was 28, and in common with many players of his generation, looked old before his time. Action shots, taken later that season, were indistinct. The only other archive photograph of him I could find was taken in 1961, when, as Brighton manager, he was welcoming a new signing, John Goodchild. His hair was shorter, curly, and he had a widow's peak. Dead end.

By the time that photograph, a traditional football club image of a transfer, was staged, Olly had returned from Canada and become a respected teacher in the Watford area. He would allow a Greek-Cypriot sixth-former named Georgios Panayiotou to perform at the school disco with his friend Andrew Ridgeley and another pupil, Shirlie Holliman. He was suitably unimpressed, but within months George Michael and Wham! were unleashed on the world.

Olly had served as a Royal Marine commando in the Second World War after training in Devon. His fitness was honed on speed marches and he learned survival skills such as weapons handling, map reading, small boat operations and demolition, both by day and by night. He was in the first wave during the Sicily landings and was deployed in advanced positions.

His missions were extremely perilous, often covert, initially in the advance through Italy, and then during the reclamation of France. He also served in Africa, the Netherlands and Germany. In common with many young men of his generation, he sought to bury memories of horror and heroism, since such reminders could only corrode the spirit. He opened up to me only twice.

The first time he told me about being the solitary survivor of an ambush, having crawled to the bottom of a ditch, beneath the bodies of friends and comrades, to avoid detection. Each marine troop typically consisted of 30-man sections, divided into three sub-sections of ten men, so the sense of loss was personal and acutely painful.

On another occasion, advancing along the spine of Italy, his troop rested overnight in a barn. To their delight, they discovered a large vat containing rough red wine, dispensed through a wooden tap at its base. It was only the following day, when one of the commandos climbed to the top of the vat, that they realised it contained decomposing bodies.

His medals, kept without fanfare in a drawer at home, suggested valour under fire and significant sacrifice that he didn't wish to share. In the words of a quotation beneath a memorial of a commando soldier in Westminster Abbey, 'They performed whatsoever the King commanded.' He remained in the Marines until the commandos were disbanded in 1946.

He used football as part of the healing process, alternating between Vicarage Road and Stamford Bridge when semi-professional playing commitments permitted. It was when we were putting his affairs in order in the shuttered spring of 2020 that we came across another fateful photograph. Again, it was dulled by time, and had been roughly cut out of what seemed like an official publication.

It was of the Royal Marine NCOs School football team in the 1945/46 season. The manager was front and centre, in full uniform, with his cane across his lap. The captain was seated to his right, his seniority signalled by the leather football – with the legend 'NCO's School F.C.' in white paint – pressed between his legs.

The figure to the manager's left offered the most persuasive solution to the mystery, and posed a follow-up question. He sat straight-backed, arms folded, gazing intently into the camera lens. His thick hair seemed longer than regulation length. His left sock had been darned and both toecaps on his football boots were scuffed. It was, unmistakably, Olly.

The player featured on the inside of the tool box was younger, probably in his late teens, but strongly resembled him. Had his father added it as an act of love or pride? Did it signal that Olly had been given a pre-war trial by his hometown club? We will never know, since club records do not extend to such detail, but I would love to think so.

The possibility, distinct but distant, was deeply moving and strangely empowering. Football had facilitated an indelible impression of intimacy, and erected a bridge across generations.

We all, as fans, have a truth to tell, a secret to share. This is as good a time as any to make my confession of cardinal sin: at around that time I had fallen out of love with football, the game that had enriched me, emotionally, spiritually and professionally since childhood. I maintained the pretence, played the role of devotee, but had been infected by its cynicism and opportunism.

Worn down by its negativity, venality and elitism, I reached the point where anger was exhausted, and was ready to surrender to apathy. I loathed the institutionalised bitterness and ignorance of social media, on which everyone has to have an opinion, however bigoted or uninformed. I despaired of football's hysterical high priests and its bloodless bureaucracy.

Pondering the significance of that photograph, I knew I needed to reset.

What was it saying to me? How had the game spoken to me as a child? What did I forget to learn along the way? When had football's human touch grown cold? Why did I fall in love with the game, become consumed by its theatre, and allow myself to be distracted by its imperfections? Was it too late to reconnect with the boy who once fantasised about football on an isolation ward?

I was that boy, struggling to bridge the chasm between adolescence and adulthood. Nearly half a century after I recovered from tuberculosis, the world entered quarantine. Our notion of normality has subsequently been mottled by time and circumstance like an old headstone in a country churchyard. The pandemic, and the political incompetence and amorality it exposed, has left vivid scars.

Olly Goss was one of the victims of the grotesque lie that Boris Johnson's government 'threw a protective ring around care homes'. He passed away just before 6.30am on Thursday, 7 May 2020, having been infected by a fellow resident who was carrying the Covid-19 virus when released from the local hospital without a test.

We spoke every day when he was sufficiently lucid, but were unable to comfort him in person. That lack of contact, a simple privilege we had underestimated, was haunting. He remained stoic, gentle, and was loved by the orderlies who suffered from shortages of protective clothing. His last words to me, on a Facetime link the day before he passed, were 'Thanks for your support'. I often wonder what he meant.

He had touched so many people, spiritually, yet we had not been allowed to touch him, physically. Many wanted to pay their respects; only ten mourners were permitted to attend his funeral on a perfect summer's day caressed by an onshore breeze from the western reaches of the English Channel. We smuggled 13 into what we intended to be a celebratory service in a sanitised, impersonal chapel in a modern, featureless crematorium.

The farewells were fond, but he deserved so much more.

Why should sport matter in such circumstances? What is the importance of the surrogate family it provides, the equality of allegiance it promises? Should it be sustained as a communal activity, a social lubricator? Can it continue to act as a safety valve and an emotional conduit? Will its universal language ever be spoken again, lyrically, loudly, cogently and, above all, passionately?

The boy in that sanatorium in 1973 had no conception of how football, in particular, would shape his life. It has taken him to more than 80 countries, and set him on the perilous path of coming into contact with his heroes. His experiences will, hopefully, illuminate and educate as, much older and not appreciably wiser, I set out to make my peace with the game.

In the words of Jürgen Klopp, 'Your football has to be mirrored by your soul.'

It can still be a Beautiful Game, if that is readapted as a meaningful phrase instead of a convenient cliché. The riddle of that tool box is a parable, of sorts. When football is the enduring expression of an unbreakable bond between father and son it is, indeed, a matter of life and death. It's personal, not a business.

Love will find a way. It always does.

Chapter Two
Fantasy Football

I NEVER got to know the name of the old man they took away in the middle of the night. He left traces of his humanity, a discarded dressing gown, a bottle of barley water and the bowl into which he hawked his sputum, writhing in an uncoordinated frenzy on thin cotton sheets, but his presence was erased by the morning. We had exchanged little more than self-conscious greetings when I was admitted to a two-bedded room on an isolation ward at Harefield Hospital in the countryside outside north-west London. My enduring impression of him is of sallow skin, with the consistency of clingfilm, stretched back across his face and scalp. He was bald, with tufts of what I guessed had once been fair hair at the temples.

I vaguely remember the commotion in the early hours. Urgent, silhouetted figures tended him before wheeling his bed away. Nurses told me not to worry when they returned on the drugs round before breakfast; it would be several days before one confirmed that the man had died due to internal bleeding in his lungs. Tuberculosis bacteria destroy infected tissue and leave a thick, cheesy substance through an inflammatory process called caseation.

Back then, in early September 1973, the disease carried connotations of the Victorian workhouse. Doctors explained I had probably carried a latent infection for a couple of years. It was picked up quickly once it became active, though it required the closure of my school, Watford Boys' Grammar, for the day for a further round of testing. I felt tired and suffered night sweats, but put it down to the stress of my O levels.

I was whisked into a sanatorium just as I was gearing up for another season with the council estate team, Holywell Youth. We used jumpers and trackie bottoms for goalposts because the nets had been taken down for the summer, when some pitches were colonised by cricketers. Our goalmouths remained bare; boys are as bad as birds when it comes to ruining attempts to germinate grass seed.

I had been bombarding the local paper with unsolicited reports from youth football for several years and bought my first album, *Hunky Dory* by David Bowie, with a record token, first prize in one of their occasional sports quizzes. I had just celebrated my 16th birthday, and thought I had places to go and people to see. In hindsight, the hospital was my finishing school.

Harefield, initially established as a temporary convalescent centre for ANZAC troops in the First World War, became a sanatorium in the 1920s because the site, one of the highest in Middlesex at 290 feet above sea level, offered fresh air and sunlight, natural aids to recovery. It was essentially a complex of small houses connected by long corridors; wards like mine, opened in October 1937, fed on to large open spaces.

We were encouraged to use balconies outside each room. I had reason to be grateful for advances in medical science, most notably the development of a so-called 'triple therapy' of drugs in the early 1950s. As a relatively minor case, I would be released three months after consistently testing negative.

No one was permitted to visit me, apart from my dad, who cycled five miles from home once a week, but at least I knew where I stood, or, to be more accurate, lay. When my school friends arrived (a group, incidentally, that included Lauren Fox, the future partner of Luther Blissett, a footballer whose career would be interlinked with mine), they were only allowed to speak to me through a closed window.

It all sounds impossibly dramatic, but there was mundanity to the process, born of acceptance. In later life I would come to value the single-mindedness I developed in isolation, the sense of concentration on the present, the reassurance of order and the acceptance of risk. In true football style, I was quite literally taking each game as it came.

I wasted no time mourning my ill-fated fellow patient. His bed would never be occupied during my stay at Harefield, possibly because the staff wanted to protect me from further premature trauma, but probably due to the decline in the incidence of TB. That allowed me to spread out, and turn the room into a den. If I couldn't physically watch football, play or report on it, I could still do so in my imagination.

I created my own fictional football league, amending the First Division for the 1973/74 season by replacing Leeds United with my club, Watford, who, in the real world, would finish seventh in the Third Division, thanks largely to 26-goal Billy Jennings, the possessor of a magnificent golden mullet who was sold to West Ham.

The exclusion of Leeds was an unashamed act of schoolboy vindictiveness. I disliked the sour-faced perfectionism of Don Revie, who talked of going through the season unbeaten (their run ended after 29 matches, though they would win the title by five points from Bill Shankly's last Liverpool team). I thought their trademark sock tags, in particular, were pretentious.

Time softens, and mortality stimulates memory. There was an understandable warmth and conviction about the obituaries for Norman Hunter and Paul Reaney, victims of the coronavirus. Hunter, in particular, was an emblematic member of a team built in the irritating image of their captain, Billy Bremner. He had become a familiar friendly figure in the press box.

They marched on together, after a fashion. The iconic photograph, taken by *Daily Mirror* photographer Monte Fresco, of Tottenham's Dave Mackay, sleeves rolled up, snarling and pulling the shirt of a submissive Bremner towards him like an amped-up Popeye, summed up the spirit of the age in which the game seized my attention.

Bremner, it transpired, had deliberately kicked Mackay on a twice-broken leg. Had that incident taken place today, it would have generated red cards, a month's online inquest, a blizzard of tribal whataboutery and wild accusations of media bias. Back then, it was settled by a schoolmasterly dressing down by referee Norman Burtenshaw.

As young fans, we thought it was great fun, the equivalent of a bar room brawl in the Westerns we watched on Saturday morning at the Essoldo Cinema, next to a carpet shop. We would breakfast on ice cream tubs, and lunch on vinegar-soaked chips at Fry Days, fifty yards from Watford's ground, into which we sneaked via the adjoining allotments.

I had arrived in hospital with the latest edition of *Shoot!* magazine, costing seven pence, which I duly cannibalised. I pored over ghosted columns by Alan Ball, Kevin Keegan and Bobby Moore, and extracted full-page photographs and the centre spread, a team photo of Sunderland with the FA Cup, won at Leeds' expense that May.

Derek Dougan of Wolves and Martin Chivers of Spurs made the early version of my wall of fame, which might have been a short-lived enterprise but for Juventus captain Pietro Anastasi. Matron, who raised initial objections to potential damage to the paintwork by Sellotape 'borrowed' from the nurses' station, seemed quite taken by his Spaghetti Western ruggedness and chest wig.

Perhaps it was the memory of her acquiescence, the colourful nature of his nickname, Petruzzu'u turcu, (Pete the Turk in Sicilian), or the pleasing cadence of his surname, when repeated theatrically, but I subsequently tried to follow his career. Having scored the goal that won Italy the 1968 European Championship, he faded away at international level after the 1974 World Cup.

He retired in 1982, after spells at Inter, Ascoli and Lugano, and was celebrated as a folk hero by fans who identified with his humble southern Italian roots in an era of significant social tension between North and South. He was a particular favourite in the Fiat factories that formed part of the business dynasty created by the Agnelli family, owners of Juventus.

It was only by chance, scanning the English version of the club website that I learned of his death, aged 71, in January 2020. The obituaries applauded his 130 goals for Juventus, in 303 appearances over eight seasons, and recounted the story of him as a ball boy in Catania, begging for a photograph with his hero, John Charles. 'An unforgettable champion has left us,' it intoned.

There is something poignant about the death of any athlete, since they are frozen in their prime by the cryogenic act of memory, but his passing was particularly touching. He spent the last two years of his life imprisoned in his home and his body by motor neurone disease, which stripped him of the athleticism and adventure that defined him as a player.

A hospital might not be the most comforting place to contemplate one's mortality, but I had light relief. Crucially, that edition of *Shoot!* magazine contained free League Ladders, cardboard tabs of club names designed to slot into pre-printed tables from the major English and Scottish leagues. We collected these tabs in the early weeks of each season, and treated them with a reverence reserved for holy relics.

Our Super Sundays consisted of poring over the previous day's football results, and updating our ladders accordingly. Left largely to my own devices, and showing rare prescience in foreshadowing the 24/7 coverage of the next century, I resolved to stage imaginary matches in a full 42-round league season notated in an exercise book which had the school crest on its front cover.

In academic terms, I was not entirely faithful to the spirit of the school's motto, *Sperate parati* ('Go forward with preparation'). My tutor, overseeing remote study of A levels in English, Politics and Economics, might have expected greater attention to the detail of my course work. As far as classrooms were concerned, it was out of sight, out of mind.

I was reading *Oliver Twist* at the time because I loved the vivid nature of Charles Dickens' reportage. His eye for detail – Poor Law victims receiving 'periodically small quantities of oatmeal; and issued three meals of thin gruel a day, with an onion twice a week, and half a roll on Sundays' – was an unconscious education.

My day was delineated by duty of sorts. It began with an appraisal of two newspapers, the *Daily Mirror* and *Daily Mail*, which fired my ambition in different, distinctive ways. The *Mirror* was my newspaper of choice, an educated tabloid that honoured the campaigning disposition of Hugh Cudlipp, the first great editor of whom I was aware.

His great innovation in the 1960s was the 'shock issue', a carpet bombing of the reader's conscience in indignant text, booming headline and photographic montage. Cudlipp pledged to 'destroy taboos and foment controversy' by highlighting such enduring problems as cruelty to children, neglect of the old, pollution, social alienation and the iniquities of mass unemployment.

His message was amplified by John Pilger, a reporter who humanised his subjects and wrote with compelling clarity and an icy rage. My other journalistic hero, Ian Wooldridge, was the reason I pored over the sports pages of the *Daily Mail* each morning. He had written with such perception and empathy about the Munich Massacre the previous year that I began the ritual of cutting out his columns to remind me of how much I had to learn.

Woolers, as he was known to barmen, fellow travellers and sporting icons across the planet, would become a quiet mentor and consistent inspiration. He survived the Cresta run at St Moritz, as did I some years later in a shameless act of homage. He ran with the bulls at Pamplona, boxed Ugandan dictator Idi Amin and had the moral courage to condemn apartheid, from within South Africa, when it was at its height.

Cricket was his first love, yet his ability to puncture pomposity was employed in all sports, especially football. The game commanded attention, despite the lack of blanket television coverage to which we have become accustomed. Its drama might have been artificially induced from my hospital bed, but it was surprisingly easy to recreate with nothing more than three dice, a vivid imagination and a working knowledge of First Division teams.

I developed my own version of Rubstuds Socca, a game developed to help the promotion, originally undertaken in the 1950s by Tom Finney, of packs of twelve rubber studs and nails, which were hammered into the soles of football boots. It had two dice, which I supplemented with a third, 'borrowed' from an unattended Monopoly set.

The green dice was thrown to simulate an attack. If it landed on a square marked 'pass', you rolled again. If it came up as 'throw in' or 'robbed', you had to hand it to your opponent. If it showed 'shooting chance', 'free kick' or 'penalty', you were permitted to roll the red dice, which dictated the outcome of the attack.

The makers knew we craved goals – two of the six sides of the red dice carried the legend 'GOAL. Rubstuds Always Scores'. A 'corner' led to another roll. The three other outcomes, 'clearance', 'miss', or 'save', ended your turn. Since the game required two players, I simply allocated two clubs to that particular 'match', which I timed at ten minutes each half.

The plan was to record the scores in the notebook, write a brief commentary on that round of fixtures and compute the table, which would be transferred to the *Shoot!* League Ladder. It quickly became apparent that this was a desiccated version of reality, since it inevitably lacked the dimension of a player's character and achievements.

That was where the third dice, and a copy of the 1972/73 *News of the World* football annual, summoned hastily from home, came in. I chose four players from each club – two were strikers, each given two squares on the dice. The other two were usually wingers or attacking midfield players; they had one square each. The quartet would be the goalscorers.

I based my choices on the previous season, when a total of 1,160 goals were scored in the First Division, peculiarly the same total as in 1971/72. Pop Robson, who would score 265 times in 674 league matches for five clubs in a 23-year career, was leading scorer with 28 for West Ham. It was a time of change: the Charlton brothers retired, and the influence of Ajax's total football was beginning to be felt. Young forwards such as Micky Channon, John Richards and Malcolm Macdonald came to the fore.

My game was inescapably random and the notebook has, sadly, been lost. My final hope of retrieval, a clearance of the family house's attic after my parents passed away within nine months of one another in 2015, ended with the promising discovery of a red plastic holdall commemorating Nottingham Forest's second European Cup win, but it contained nothing more exciting than a batch of old match programmes.

I am, therefore, reliant on memory for the fine print of my fantasy season. Wolves, mid-table in real life, were champions, and finished a point ahead of Everton. Stan Bowles, of QPR, was leading scorer, though I can't remember how many goals he was credited with. Arsenal, Leicester and, I think, Coventry, were relegated. Watford finished fifth which, of course, undermined the credibility of the entire exercise.

Yet it was innocent and, in its way prophetic, since the simple act of combining the imagination with technology and statistical analysis has spawned a huge global industry. Fantasy Football is a $7bn business in the US; the leading fantasy football game in the UK, based on the Premier League, is played by 6 million people.

Simulated football has evolved from vicarious entertainment to an ersatz contributor to professional football, in which clubs use scouting data gathered by the team behind Football Manager video games, which enable users to indulge their inner Jürgen Klopp. The 2020 edition was supplied free, online, for two weeks in order to encourage gamers to self-isolate during the Covid-19 outbreak.

My rudimentary indulgence passed the time in rehabilitation, and was as therapeutic as the walks I was eventually encouraged to take around the lake in the grounds, which included a memorial garden to the ANZAC soldiers. When I was allowed to leave hospital, just before Christmas after a 14-week stay, I was a worldly, infinitely more focused character.

I still had a fleeting stigma to overcome – a former girlfriend's parents refused to let her see me – but I had confirmed my ambitions and expanded my horizons. I would work in football. Only how, and when remained an issue. The air was fresh and I had been renewed. The world was alive with sudden possibilities.

Chapter Three

From Playground to Pithead

AN UNOCCUPIED football pitch has the mystery of a silent stage. Stories are told in hints and whispers. An unrepaired gouge in the turf, logically caused by an uncompromising tackle in damp conditions, poses unanswerable questions about perpetrator and victim. Remnants of white tape, flapping lazily from a naked goal frame, are as evocative as Buddhist prayer ribbons.

There are fewer such sights in an age of austerity, where council-tended pitches have been priced out of existence or purloined by developers during the steady decline of the grassroots game. Childish joy, derived by all ages and both sexes, has instead been monetised in five-a-side centres with LED floodlights, the latest generation of artificial turf and, in some cases, roof nets to ensure the ball never goes out of play.

For children of the Sixties, football was as free and as omnipresent as oxygen. We ran around in the infants' playground, following what was usually a small plastic ball of the type sold on holiday seafronts like a frantic shoal of fish pursued by predators. Things got serious, in a football sense, when we were transferred to our primary schools.

I attended Holy Rood, a Roman Catholic school established in Watford town centre by Dominican sisters in 1893. Our games acquired shape and structure even though they remained chaotic; when we played a rebounding game called Wally, we had to calculate the uneven bounce off the flint walls of the schoolyard, built from the same stone as the adjoining Gothic church.

I picked up little life lessons along the way. Three and in was a selfish scramble. No one really wanted to be the goalkeeper, but that was the fate of the boy who won by scoring three times. I went through a sly phase, when I attempted to score only twice so I stayed longer on the pitch, but invariably couldn't help myself.

I would consistently underestimate the consequences of ignoring the unwritten rule banning goalkeepers from deliberately letting shots in to truncate their time between the jumpers. That got me into more than one fight, unhelpfully orchestrated by squeals of 'bundle', which attracted the attention of Miss Rigby, a teacher whose training had evidently been undertaken in a juvenile prison.

A severe lady with pinched features, tightly permed dark hair and thick black-framed glasses, she did not exert her authority gently. The inevitable whack across the knuckles with a wooden ruler was designed to ingrain a sense of dread, yet it did not deter us when it came to the psychodrama of Wembley, where the last boy who hadn't scored a goal in a particular round was eliminated.

It was a cheat's charter, perfect preparation for the cynicism and chicanery of the professional game. Goalhangers would claim the last touch with shameless disregard for the truth. Handball, punished by a penalty for all other survivors, was applied by mob rule; contact was rarely within the same postcode as the victim's outstretched hand. Disputes were vigorous, prolonged and physical, resulting in another painful session with the Handmaiden of Vengeance.

Away from school, I was beginning to sample the delights of the King George V Playing Fields on the Holywell estate, but the first full-size pitch I can recall with any clarity was some 320 miles north in the Cumbrian port of Whitehaven, my dad's birthplace. It became a place of pilgrimage in adulthood because of its spiritual power.

I last visited on a filthy January day in 2018, when I attended the funeral of James, my last surviving uncle. It was an extension of remembrance. The bleakness of its clifftop setting, emphasised by an onshore wind that whipped white horses across the Solway Firth from Scotland and the Isle of Man, blew half a century away. My mind's eye envisaged endless pick-up matches involving my brothers, cousins and assorted local kids.

We stole out through a hole in the wooden fence at the bottom of our grandparents' overgrown garden, and played with a heavy plastic ball purchased from the corner shop, which was perched on the top of Kells Brows, dizzyingly steep scrubland that led down to the town. It was also the source of our half-time drinks, stoppered bottles of sarsaparilla and dandelion and burdock.

The pitch was literally in the shadow of the pithead. Haig Colliery was a working deep coal mine until its closure in 1986; we would be lulled to sleep in the back bedroom by the hum of its steam winding engines, servicing two shafts which sent men underground and four miles out beneath the sea bed. An ethereal glow, shed through the wooden slats of a fence surrounding a floodlit washing pool, set back just behind one of our goals, was our reading light.

Coal mining in Whitehaven dates back to the 13th century. It was initially supervised by monks from St Bees Abbey, who owned the village until the dissolution in 1539. Coal was exported, mainly to Ireland, from 1636. The footpath behind our pitch was referred to as 'The Wagon Road'; in the 19th century, coal was transported along it, on a narrow-gauge railway, to the harbour or train station, for distribution. We would use it to reach the beach, where coal was washed up, collected and cherished.

The human cost of that anthracite was profound. More than 1,200 men, women and children were killed in Whitehaven pits. Fourteen miners are still entombed in the tunnels of Haig Colliery. Named after Douglas Haig, the butcher general of the First World War, the workings were notorious for firedamp, methane. Three explosions killed 79 men between 1922 and 1931. Victims were so badly burned facially they were identified by their belts and trousers.

We used to walk down to the town past an abandoned lift shaft that acts as a tombstone to the 104 victims of the William pit disaster in August 1947, just before my dad moved south to look for work. A distant relative, Herbert Calvin, aged 40 with three children, was among the dead. Like Haig, the pit had a lethal liability to spontaneous combustion.

Thirty-five rescue teams made 105 attempts to reach survivors; only three, given up for dead, were found, 20 hours after the main explosion. John Birkett, an older miner, acted counter-intuitively, and persuaded two colleagues to walk away from the lift shaft, towards fresher air. With that running out, they wet their handkerchiefs, covered their faces and went back the way they came. They stumbled through a curtain of gas, which contained the bodies of around 40 miners, huddled in small groups in a sitting position, before reaching their rescuers.

This, then, was a deeply connected community that treated sport as a diversion and a source of intermittent pride. Whitehaven Miners FC, a junior club, produced Dean Henderson, the Manchester United and England goalkeeper, who grew up in Hillside on the other side of town. It was here, playing on any available stretch of scrubby grass, and on pitches adjoining cow pasture, that he developed the survivor's mentality that has defined his rapid progress in the professional game.

Kells was known as a hotbed of amateur rugby league; in football terms, the high-water mark was reached 11 months before the William disaster. Haig Colliery played their only FA Cup match, losing 3-2 at Frizington United in the preliminary round on 21 September 1946. Revived in the late Seventies, the club won only two FA Vase ties in six seasons before being disbanded.

Grandad, an imposing, broad-chested figure in belted trousers which extended to his armpits, was a boxing man. Thrown out of work by the 1929 stock market crash until the Second World War, he scavenged and fought, bare-knuckled, in pubs for pennies to feed his family. He had volunteered for the First World War aged 15, as William Colvin, a ruse enacted with the full knowledge of recruiting officers; his was a land unfit for heroes. A lifelong socialist, he remains my inspiration.

He was a man of contrasts, a compassionate disciplinarian who expected his meals on the table, to the minute, but who doted on my grandmother, a devout Roman Catholic who, at 4ft 10in, was more than a foot shorter. One story involving my dad, who was in a group of local boys who would take turns at being lowered over the cliffs to collect gulls' eggs from their nests, sums him up.

The collector had the right to take home the first 36 eggs; the rest were distributed evenly. All went well until, on one expedition, the rope snapped, and a boy fell to his death. My grandad was unaware the raids had restarted, secretly, until my dad returned with a basket containing the collector's three dozen, which could be sold for a halfpenny each.

He expected praise for supplementing the family budget; instead his father ritually smashed each one over his head. 'You mean more to me than money,' he told him. 'You cannot put a price on our family.' One of the eggs slithering down his face was rotten; my dad remembered that smell of putrescence until the day he died.

He was a rugby league man, who took us on an annual pilgrimage to Wembley for Challenge Cup finals. Payback came in the form of joining him on the bleak, open terracing at Whitehaven Recreation Ground to watch the Marras, a nickname taken from the local dialect for mates. Originally playing fields for miners in the Victorian era, it also staged football, boxing, speedway and whippet racing.

We were quickly introduced to the legend of another relative, Ralph Calvin, a prop forward who explained, 'I went into a hard school. I listened and did as I was told and it stood me in good stead.' A trawler owner and publican, he would eventually become club chairman, having helped it to stave off bankruptcy in the early Nineties.

Football still winked at us, invitingly, eight miles up the road. As a special treat, Dad would take us to Borough Park to watch Workington Reds who, at the time, were defying the traditions of a club whose history is charted in a series of three books entitled *So Sad, So Very Sad*. I was too young to realise it at the time, but I was being introduced to the game's ability to connect generations.

A form of football, recorded in the *Cumbrian Pacquet*, a newspaper which ran from 1774 to 1915, was first played in the town on 20 April 1775. Bill Shankly managed the Reds on a shoestring for 21 months until November 1955, answering the telephone and filling out players' pay packets after his weekly visits to the bank. He eventually tired of squabbling with his co-tenants, Workington Town rugby league club, and left to make his name at Huddersfield.

Keith Burkinshaw also served his apprenticeship as Workington Reds player-manager. His under-appreciated eight-year spell in charge of Tottenham, in which he won three trophies, ended in the first European final I covered for the *Daily Telegraph*, a penalty shoot-out win after extra time against Anderlecht in the UEFA Cup at White Hart Lane in May 1984.

An undemonstrative, deeply principled man, he had taken the decision to resign before the game due to his disenchantment with the board's commercially driven strategy. Suddenly aware of how ultimately ephemeral a manager can be, he took a bow in the centre circle as the old ground shook to its foundations. He would not be the last man in his trade to leave with the lament 'you want it to go on forever'.

Folklore, which insists he reflected, 'There used to be a football club over there,' as he left White Hart Lane with a backward glance for the final time, is often more poetic than accurate. In Burkinshaw's case, he merely nodded in implicit agreement when Ken Jones, the sports columnist, marked the moment by mentioning the Frank Sinatra song, 'There Used to Be a Ballpark', about the demolition of the legendary Ebbets Field in Brooklyn.

I've learned, over the years, that football is an echo chamber. Burkinshaw was in the side beaten 3-1 in the FA Cup third round by the Busby Babes, in front of a record crowd of 21,000 at Borough Park on 4 January 1958, a month before the Munich disaster. Nostalgia, aligned to modern technology, helped the club through an existential crisis. A film of the game was streamed online on 30 May 2020 to raise funds for the club's Covid-19 Survival Fund. Viewers from around the world paid £2, and received a facsimile of the match programme.

Burkinshaw was succeeded by Ken Furphy, whose Watford team would seize my youthful imagination. The Reds eventually became the penultimate club to be voted out of the Football League, facilitating Wimbledon's ill-starred entry in 1977, but their decline cannot be dismissed as an irrelevance. Ignore the tyranny of the league table, and concentrate on flesh and blood.

Football is nourished by its local heroes, its unheralded tragedies, its mavericks and its morality tales. These are as relevant in the backwaters of the game as they are in the gilded cages of the Premier League. They point to the fragility of the human condition, and the freedom of expression sport offers.

In Workington's case, they gave a Football League debut to Tony Geidmintis, aged 15 years, 247 days, on 3 April 1965. Many such juvenile leads fail to fulfil early promise, yet he played 328 times for them. His transfer to Watford in 1976 was the first I monitored as a local journalist; he would retire at 31 due to a heart condition that led to his premature death, aged 42.

Peter Foley, one of the earliest black professional footballers, made his Workington debut soon after Geidmintis. He cannot remember playing against a black player, and was subjected to chants of 'Zulu, Zulu' at away matches. He kept a young Kevin Keegan out of the Scunthorpe side for two seasons before winding down his career in non-league football with the Reds.

His enduring influence on football, developed initially as a trade union official at the Sellafield nuclear processing site on the Cumbrian coast, is crystallised by three decades as an anti-racism campaigner. Recognised by the award of an MBE, he still sees his primary role as 'getting the players to understand what racism is'.

Fans identify more closely with eccentricity than erudition. Johnny Martin was a Cumbrian cult hero, a left-winger who described himself as 'the poor man's George Best'. His party trick was to dribble past two or three opponents, sit on the ball and ask, 'Who wants it next?' In a variation on a theme, he once did so while drinking a pint of beer offered by a fan.

He made his debut in a pre-season friendly against Rangers, who won through a goal scored by a certain Alex Ferguson. Somehow, he avoided apoplectic opponents for five seasons in which he made 224 league and cup appearances. He played another 21 games on returning to the club for a season in non-league football, a year after retiring to run a Safeway supermarket.

He moved to Tenerife, was diagnosed with leukaemia in 2006 and passed away in 2013. We often talk in grand terms about a footballer's legacy, but his reputation confirms that the game is about more than grand designs and its glitterati. It can still be about fun, invention and mischief. He deserves to be remembered for his favourite story, told in a valedictory interview with Workington's weekly newspaper, the *Times & Star*:

'One game a supporter ran on to the pitch with a crown in his hand. The referee was going mad and told me to play the game but I ignored him. I got down on one knee and arose the King of the Derwent End. I ran towards the dugout holding my crown aloft. It was a great feeling because everyone was cheering and chanting my name. The ref gave me a yellow card for it, but do you think I was bothered?'

Martin, I decided, was my type of footballer. At the time I was enraptured by Stewart Scullion, Watford's Scottish winger, who had the hypnotic command of a snake charmer and the body control of a downhill skier. He was nigh-on impossible to dispossess, had a devastating change of pace and a low centre of gravity.

He was a Third Division player, as opposed to an established international, because he played with his head down; crossing the ball was an act of blind faith, rather than a repeated example of clinical precision. In modern terms there was no end product, but on a frigid late October afternoon in 1967 he scored the greatest goal I witnessed, live, until Diego Maradona's second against England at the Azteca Stadium in Mexico City in 1986.

Watford were playing Stockport County and would win 5-0. Since the teams were 12th and 13th respectively, it could not have been more of a mid-table scuffle. I stood on the shale bank to the left of the Rookery End, which Scullion was attacking. He beat five defenders in a trademark dribble and, equally typically, lost the ball as he attempted to round goalkeeper Alan Ogley.

Ogley immediately threw the ball out to full-back Freddie Goodwin. Scullion raced across to dispossess him, and beat four more defenders before side-footing the ball, right-footed, underneath the goalkeeper. When I checked the club's official history to confirm my boyhood memory, a photograph of the moment revealed a delicious detail I had missed all those years before.

The ball is a blur, and about to go beyond the sprawling Ogley. Scullion has his tongue out, a joyful sign of child-like concentration. What can an ageing boy do, but fall in love all over again?

Chapter Four

The Match

IT FEELS like Christmas morning. There is no tree, turkey or tinsel, but the present is a ticket for the match of our lives. Sent to bed early, our sleep swamped by anticipation, we are half-dressed before the promised 4am alarm call reverberates through the bedroom wall. The stair creaks, signalling Mum's descent to the kitchen, where she makes jam sandwiches and a flask of tea.

Dad pads across the landing, and checks we have enough layers on to deal with the pre-dawn chill. We head out, through the estate, where illuminated windows tell of similar rituals. By the time we approach the railway bridge, in the dip from which a pathway leads to the abattoir, we are part of a shadow army marching on Vicarage Road.

It is Sunday, 26 January 1969. Less than 12 hours previously, we had sat in front of the electric fire and watched *BBC Grandstand*. We shared David Coleman's ad-libbed astonishment as Watford, little Watford, plucky Watford, patronised Watford, held European champions Manchester United to a 1-1 draw in front of 63,498 at Old Trafford in the fourth round of the FA Cup.

Just in case we didn't believe the teleprinter – and we didn't – the familiar full face, thick moustache and clipped, slightly breathless tones of Denis Lowe confirmed the detail of schoolboy legend. I would eventually work with him, as the most junior reporter on the *Daily Telegraph*, and be too shy to confide that he was a totemic figure from my childhood.

In that era, satellite links from football grounds were in the realms of science fiction. Reporters like Denis and another future colleague, Ken Jones, would watch the first half of a match, dash into a waiting car, and be hustled into the studio for an 'in vision' report. The first rule of such reports involved praying for an early goal.

It arrived, in Watford's case, in the second minute. Stewart Scullion, playing off the cuff as usual, accelerated from a standing start across the pitch, executed a wall pass, and turned inside Bobby Charlton before taking a touch and shooting, right-footed from 30 yards. The body of Nobby Stiles, advancing but half-turned, shielded the flight of the ball from goalkeeper Jimmy Rimmer.

United equalised in the second half, a collision between Watford goalkeeper Mickey Walker and defender Brian Garvey resulting in a loose ball that Denis Law dispatched. The goal was frustratingly avoidable, but the mood was exultant when we joined the queue for replay tickets outside the old nurses' home, some 400 yards from the ground.

Two rivers of humanity flowed from different directions to the club offices, which would not be open for another four hours. We approached from the west. The other line stretched back towards the town centre. It contained many supporters who had joined up straight from Watford Junction station after disembarking from six football specials, on their return from Manchester.

The queues were benevolent; we were allowed to jump a few places to join other lads from the estate, and took turns to warm up in a flimsy plastic tent. A Third Division club like Watford needed every penny, but the act of attempting to buy a ticket was an expression of football's wider community, as opposed to the modern system, which nourishes touts and parasitic secondary ticketing firms.

Expectation is timeless, and free of charge. I would feel it again a couple of years later, when, together with my brother David and Stephen Payne, a childhood friend, I joined the queue for the juvenile enclosure at Stamford Bridge, where, for 15p, we watched Colin Bell score twice in two minutes to end Chelsea's defence of the FA Cup. Even now, 50 years later, Steve can still recall the pressure on his rib cage, pinioned against a crush barrier.

As 11-year-old experts, we reckoned Watford could get at Steve James, United's young central defender, and argued about the respective merits of Charlton, Best and Law. Bobby was my man from the moment he effectively launched England's 1966 World Cup campaign with a thunderous goal against Mexico in the second group match.

He swept down the middle of the pitch at Wembley before scoring, from around 35 yards, with the hardest shot I had ever seen. I couldn't stop talking about it on the top deck of the bus going to school the next morning. You could tell he was excited by the way he leaped in the air with both arms extended; he normally pushed back his comb over and accepted manly handshakes.

It meant I went through a phase of toe-punting my shots to see if I could generate his sort of power. Some hope.

Tea drained, sandwiches scoffed and still starving, the scale of sudden devotion became apparent as finally, reluctantly, darkness lifted. Football crowds have a formidable density, but this was different. The line stretched as far as I could see, but it was somehow more personal than being part of a mass of bodies, crammed into a shop-soiled ground.

We edged forward for three hours before handing over three shillings (15p) for a ground ticket. I put the ticket in the pocket of my anorak, and didn't move my protective hand, placed instinctively over it, until we had got home. Dad offered to place it behind a photograph on the mantelpiece for safe keeping, but I preferred to keep it under my pillow.

Modern matches, routinely over-hyped as 'huge', are diluted by the supposed need for specious comment. Their drama is often lost in the din created by the dim-witted instant expert. Back then, big games were savoured, like a special bag of sweets, sucked until the roof of the mouth stings. Since they were so relatively rare, their images and story lines were cherished for days.

The *London Evening News* whetted our appetite on the Tuesday evening by producing a 'Cup tie special' with a front page headline that read, 'Watford's Big Chance'. Didn't we know it? The sub-editors were in fine alliterative form, framing photographs of 'Scullion's Screamer' and 'Law's Leveller' from Old Trafford. In all, that front page contained 12 images, perfect scrapbook material.

A douche of reality was applied on the sports page, under the headline 'Hot Cuppa for Brave Watford'. John Oakley, a kindly man who covered Wimbledon for 53 years until his passing in 1999, wrote: 'Manager Ken Furphy believes his team will do it. So do all the Watford players and no one can doubt the opinion of the club's Cup-crazy supporters. Can they do it? At the risk of being lynched by Watford fanatics I rather doubt it.'

There had been another siege of the ground that morning, when 4,000 tickets, returned by United, were put on sale after initially being lost by British Rail. In hindsight, we should have paid greater attention to an afterthought, in bold six-point type, which revealed that local referee Eric Press had inspected the pitch after heavy overnight rain, and declared it fit.

Shatteringly, he was misguided. The replay fell victim to a foul winter, and would be staged the following Monday. Though the phrase wouldn't be coined for several decades, subsequent school days, in the first form at the Grammar School, suddenly stretched to infinity and beyond. 'Beery' Thompson, our florid-faced geography tutor who doubled as a football coach and cricket umpire, had no chance of rivalling David Coleman as our teacher of choice.

The familiar *Grandstand* theme tune signalled that class was in session. We watched 40 seconds of highlights from Old Trafford before Coleman introduced a ground-breaking, ten-minute film of Watford manager Ken Furphy's team talk before the first game. It was, for me, the equivalent of being offered a guided tour of Tutankhamun's tomb by its discoverer, Howard Carter.

Though obviously shot in a hotel meeting room – guests could be seen wandering by through ornate frosted glass windows – this was an unprecedented insight into the dressing room, the inner sanctum. Professionally, I have never lost my sense of privilege at being allowed access to such a private place. My respect for its rituals is rooted in childish awe.

I have never seen anyone smoke in a team talk, as one of Furphy's players did from the back row. Most wore thin club ties, and were seated soberly as the manager identified 'over adventuresome' full-backs and suspect defensive downward heading as areas of opportunity. Stiles, the toothless titan, was described as 'a tremendous professional' who could be pressured into using his weaker left foot.

What of the Holy Trinity? Tom Walley, a flinty Welsh midfield player, was encouraged to 'go and have a bite' at Best, provided he had sufficient cover. Charlton was identified as a playmaker from left-half, who had to be shut down at source. Furphy's warning about Law was prescient: 'It doesn't matter whether the cause is lost; this fella is following it in, all the time. He's pretty spring-heeled, to say the least.'

There was something soothing about Furphy's Cumbrian lilt. He ended with the following entreaty: 'This is the chance to show whether you can play or not. We get a lot of criticism about being Third Division managers, or Third Division players, right? You're playing against a First Division side, the European champions. You're going to see now whether you can play.'

I don't know about the team, who at least feigned concentration, but it got me going. I ran the mile and a half home from school, and wolfed down my tea, so that I could be there as the turnstiles opened, two hours before the replay kicked off. I came armed with a hand-knitted scarf and a heavy metal rattle, which could stun a rhino and wake the occupants of the graveyard just down the road.

The old bowl of the stadium, a gravel pit until 1922, quickly filled up. We wriggled to the front, to stand against iron railings with an uninterrupted view; those further up the banked terracing struggled to move independently. The record attendance, 34,099, is unlikely to be surpassed, but I still find it hard to romanticise the experience of succumbing to the collective power of the crowd.

This was 20 years before the Hillsborough tragedy redefined the notion of public safety, and introduced us to the nightmare of men, women and children never returning from a game of football. On this night, a crush barrier collapsed under the weight of humanity. Around 30 fans were ferried to the adjoining hospital for treatment. I have yet to find a report of the incident.

In truth, we watched it unfold with morbid fascination without losing sight of the main event. It seemed part of the drama of a big occasion, a backhanded compliment to a small-town club like the rickety television gantries, the packed press box and the daredevil kids who scaled floodlight pylons in search of a better view.

Such events are in the process of being airbrushed out of history. The biggest clubs have deemed FA Cup replays are an unwanted chore; if you believe their suspension for the 2020/21 season will be temporary, as proposed, give my love to the fairies at the bottom of your garden. Another financial lifeline has been cut; romance has been priced even more prohibitively.

As things turned out, it was just another tale of what might have been. The pitch was a mixture of sand and compacted mud, which froze after nightfall. The home crowd's noise lacked menace and impact; it had a pantomime quality more usually associated with the local Palace Theatre which, somewhat optimistically, was staging the *Gang Show* that evening.

United's performance was an object lesson in the professionalism of an elite team. Stiles, booed relentlessly but ineffectively, justified Furphy's prediction that he would act as minder to James, the raw centre-half. Law showed unusual defensive discipline, heading two corners clear before, on the half hour, he reverted to type.

Brian Kidd passed behind a retreating defence to Best, who crossed to the far post, where Law, coming in from the right, scored with a firm downward header from one of those spring-heeled leaps the Watford manager had mentioned in his team talk. Innocence dies hard in a pre-pubescent boy, but once Rodney Green's equalising 'goal' was disallowed for what seemed an imaginary foul on recalled United goalkeeper Alex Stepney, I feared the worst.

Perhaps that was the evening my mistrust of percentages was confirmed. Furphy estimated that Watford enjoyed 75 per cent possession. It was a random statistic, a damned lie, exposed by the scoreline. Law secured a fifth-round tie against Birmingham, five days later, by pouncing on a poor clearance to score his second goal, three minutes from time. That volley was our 'Dear John' letter.

Like any heartbroken fan, I obsessed about what could have been. Why had the referee taken Stepney's side at a key moment? What would have happened had Duncan Welbourne's volley from the edge of the box gone in after beating the goalkeeper, instead of ricocheting to safety off the underside of the bar?

Face it, kid. You loved, and lost. It might have been the first time, but it wouldn't be the last. You were about to be given a tantalising glimpse of your fate.

Chapter Five

Stairway to Heaven

QUITE WHY someone bothered to measure the length of Occupation Road is a mystery, but it extends 423 metres along the east side of Watford's ground. Overlooked by terraced housing, lined with garishly painted garage doors and littered by the occasional discarded sofa, it is barely wide enough to welcome the away team bus.

For a year, from July 1969, it was where I reported for work. The hours were great, but the pay was non-existent. I'd have happily sacrificed my paper-round money for the green rectangular pass, encased in a plastic wallet, which signalled the success of my application to be a ball boy for the club's first season in the Second Division.

The letter, on headed notepaper, and signed 'R.E. Rollitt, General Secretary, Watford Association Football Club Ltd', requested that I arrive at least 50 minutes before kick-off. It came the day after my school report, in which my form master suggested that 'I am inclined to suspect that the energy he shows to such good effect in athletics might usefully be applied to his classroom subjects.' No prizes for guessing which observation commanded greater attention, from me at least.

I was still intoxicated by the events of 15 April, ten weeks after that Manchester United match, when Watford secured promotion from the Third Division, their most significant achievement since winning the Southern League in 1915. We were on the pitch a fraction before referee Ken Markham blew the final whistle, sweeping towards the main stand and across the greyhound track.

Players took their bows on the front row of the directors' box, glugging champagne and drawing on thick cigars like gauche pools winners. Jimmy Hill, minor royalty, circulated with a TV crew. Jim Bonser, a notably parsimonious chairman, even allowed the floodlights to blaze for another hour, instead of switching them off within minutes as was his wont.

It was a release from generational mediocrity. Journeymen footballers were kings for a day and a long, long night. A small club was, for a heartbeat in its history, far bigger than the sum of its parts. Years before the corporate conceit of glass-walled tunnels for the premium punter, and the expensive apathy of Club Wembley hospitality, there was an innocent need to belong.

Only 40 glasses were smashed in the Supporters Club party, where players sang to the fans and professed undying love for the club. Managerial homage was paid to the tune of 'Grocer Jack', from *A Teenage Opera*: 'Ken Furphy, Ken Furphy. Is it true what mummy says? We're going to … Division Two-ooh-ooh?' In the town centre, fans dived into the High Street pond, shinned up flagpoles and threw tulips, wrenched from the Town Hall flowerbeds, at passing cars.

Less than three months later, I was in the inner sanctum, admitted to an endearingly shabby stadium through the 'Players' and Match Officials' Entrance'. This was a portentous title for two wooden doors, with green paint flaking at the sill, and a hole in the wall, measuring no more than three feet by two feet.

A steward waited within on an old kitchen chair; white envelopes containing complimentary tickets were stacked on a shelf. He surveyed my cardboard pass, as if for fingerprints, and waved me through with an imperceptible nod of the head.

The stairway to heaven was steep, and fell sharply towards a narrow walkway at the base of the wooden main stand. Directors and dignitaries walked straight on; I threw a left and turned into the first door on the right. It led past a groundsman's cubby hole, complete with kettle and tea cups that possibly helped Alexander Fleming discover penicillin, to another room, which saw service as a laundry.

This was the realm of Molly Rush, who doubled as tea lady and brought her Alsatian, Sabre, to matches. The room smelled like football, the mustiness of old socks offset by liniment and a soupcon of soap powder. There, on top of Molly's industrial washing machine, was our kit, faded bottle green tracksuits that had seen too many spin cycles. They chafed like a penitent's hair shirt, but, to this besotted boy, felt like the finest silk.

What to wear beneath? Unlike most of the other lads, I didn't possess a Watford shirt. Mum, practical to the last, had bought me a billowing, round-necked Manchester City shirt the previous Christmas because she was taken by its colour, light blue, and its growing room. I wore my Gola Wembley boots with screw-in white nylon studs, though I longed for a pair of Adidas World Cups, or George Best's side-laced Stylo Matchmakers.

Most of the working-class heroes in the dressing room next door wore Puma Kings. Since their average win bonus was only £4, the brand's popularity probably owed more to the generosity of the boot company's representative than any sense of style. They were black, of course. The acid trip colour schemes of the next century were not even a figment of the imagination; Alan Ball's white boots, launched the following season, were as flamboyant as it got.

I made my debut on 13 August ten days after my 12th birthday, in a League Cup first-round tie against Lincoln City. Watford won 2-1, with goals by Barry Endean and Stewart Scullion, and I threw the ball, several times, to the opposing full-back, Graham Taylor. Watford did not get their first league win until a month later, at the eighth time of asking. They defeated Tommy Docherty's Aston Villa 3-0 in what would prove to be a preview of a season-long struggle to avoid relegation.

A week before, on 6 September, I made my first away trip, in a neighbour's motorcycle sidecar, to see Watford lose 2-1 at Oxford. The Manor Ground, which closed in 2001 and is now the site of a hospital, seemed impossibly romantic. I paid a shilling for the programme and threw up on the way home because I had eaten a cheese sandwich that had simmered in the late summer warmth.

My cheese allergy wouldn't be recognised for years, though I subsequently stuck to Bovril, and Bovril-flavoured crisps on matchdays. We were allowed out to watch the warm-up, which generally consisted of players putting their cigarettes out long enough to amble around and launch scuffed footballs into the terracing.

My first job was to carry out boxes of metal numbers, to be placed on hooks at half-time on two scoreboards that extended from A to L down each side of the pitch. One set of numbers was white on a black background, the other gold. As surreal as it may seem, in this age of ceaseless information and online searches measured in milliseconds, I could hear the buzz as scorelines began to register with spectators.

If we turned up early enough, we could catch the players coming back from their lunchtime steak. Dietary regimes were distinctive. Tom Walley, a midfield enforcer who would go on to become a celebrated youth coach, trained on chip butties, collected under duress by apprentices from Fry Days. Johnny Williams, a left-back who would play more than 400 games between 1964 and 1975, was often spotted in a nearby greasy spoon, demolishing the full English.

I loved Williams. One of the youngest members of the team, he wore thin-lapelled suits and cultivated pork-chop sideburns, a fashion statement overtaken by a Mexican moustache in late autumn. He was scouted playing with his mates on playing fields on a council estate in Hemel Hempstead, and often stopped to chat, or sign the programme. He headed the ball with more force than was probably good for him, and played as if he needed a passport to cross the halfway line.

Full-backs drew me into the game, taught me its humanity. They were so close I could hear their grunts of exertion and casual obscenities, spat above the hum of the crowd. These were not lofty figures, captured for posterity by magazine photographs plastered above my bunk bed; they were flesh and blood. I could see their chests heave and their eyes dull, or blaze, dependent on the state of play.

Duncan Welbourne, a right-back who played every match for six and a half seasons, fulfilled my image of him, as a flick-knife-wielding Teddy Boy, by turning up in winkle pickers. He was our pantomime villain; fans would warn him whenever an opposing player was involved in nefarious activity. Vengeance was taken with an assassin's efficiency; the referee would turn around to see the transgressor in a heap on the ground.

Big Dunc would wink during a lull in play, job done. I knew it was for the crowd's benefit, but imagined it was personal. My affinity with him grew in adulthood, when I discovered he had been sold by Grimsby, for £1,300, on the day President Kennedy was assassinated, because he had been in hospital, suffering from tuberculosis. When I heard he had passed away, aged 79, in January 2019, I felt a surge of sadness that I never had the chance to share that I, too, was a member of the Sacred Order of the Sputum Bowl.

There were no sinecures for these stars. Welbourne managed Southport and worked in the commercial department until they could not even afford to pay him a pittance. He became a tunneller, toiling in dangerous conditions, in constant dampness, on major infrastructure projects such as Canary Wharf. Williams worked in an electrical wholesaler owned by a supporter of Colchester United, his only other club. He suffered from Alzheimer's, the curse of his generation of footballers, before passing away, aged 73, in late January, 2021.

Weakness, in football, takes on many forms. Proximity to the pitch offered hints of hidden strain. The anguish of a player in a rut, struggling to play himself into form, was tangible. The fear and pain of an injured player for whom the trainer's magic sponge wasn't working was visible. It was my first lesson in the fragility of a professional sportsman's career.

The inevitability of decline is confirmed intermittently, sometimes on the biggest occasions, always in the most public manner. So it was with goalkeeper Bert Slater, recalled that September for a home League Cup tie with Liverpool, his former club, after nine months' banishment to the reserves. He was 33, stocky and hard-faced, once a Scotland Under-23 international. He projected the resilience of a veteran, but his performance reflected inner turmoil.

Slater bizarrely turned a harmless Bobby Graham cross into his own net after six minutes and, following Keith Eddy's second-half equaliser from the penalty spot, somehow allowed Ian St John's shot to squirm through his legs for the winning goal. His thousand-yard stare, as he trudged past us on the way to an inevitable dressing room inquest, would become a familiar distress signal down the years. He never played professionally again.

Eddy's misfortune was also typical. He was Watford's captain. His economy of effort and intelligence of movement as a central defender would have distant echoes, in future generations, in the assuredness of Rio Ferdinand and Vincent Kompany. Tall, and fair-haired, he was the only Watford player to get a full-colour portrait in *Charles Buchan's Football Monthly*.

He had a natural air of leadership, declining to leave the team bus before an away game at Shrewsbury until he had finished a game of chess with Oli Phillips, my first sports editor at the *Watford Observer*. He would go on to captain New York Cosmos; when Pele missed a penalty in one NASL match, he returned to the dressing room at half-time to be told by Eddy: 'From now on, I'll be taking the penalties, my son.'

His season turned sour on 10 February 1970, a cold Tuesday night in Carlisle, when he sustained a knee ligament injury in a 5-0 defeat. It required an operation that cost him his place in the club's first FA Cup semi-final, against Chelsea at White Hart Lane, five weeks later. My mental image of him on that day is revealing in its clarity, intensity and longevity.

I was in a fleet of supporters' coaches, which left Watford at breakfast time. This was five years before the M25 opened, so we were stuck in a traffic jam in suburbia, somewhere near Enfield. A police siren announced the passage of the Watford team bus, picking a delicate path down the middle of the road. Our coach was pushed on to the pavement.

Our shouts of recognition, as the team bus passed by, could only have been a muffled, fleeting echo. Eddy was in a window seat, staring out forlornly at what must have seemed an endless sea of unfamiliar faces. He smiled thinly, smoothed down his club tie and held his right hand up towards the glass in a poignant gesture of gratitude.

Even in the hyper-conflated world of professional football it is not every day you are denied a distinctive form of immortality. That, to this boy at least, was conferred by being in this team, which I can still recite, unbidden: Walker, Welbourne, Williams, Lugg, Lees, Walley, Scullion, Garbett, Endean, Packer, Owen. Sub: Garvey.

Watford might have lost 5-1, setting up a knife-fight of an FA Cup final between Chelsea and Leeds United that was only decided by a replay, but this was the type of defeat that enhances reputation, and softens memory. The old White Hart Lane, atmospheric and elemental, became one of my favourite grounds. At first sight, it had a scale and impact beyond anything I had experienced. The stands seemed to scrape the sky.

The pitch on that afternoon, mainly compacted mud and sand, was fringed by dull, stubby grass. It was not the leveller we had hoped, even though the euphoria of Terry Garbett's first-half equaliser, a bobbling shot from the edge of the penalty area, is intensified by the passage of time, and the white lie of memory.

In such moments of brief hope, football reveals itself as an ally that cannot be trusted but will invariably be forgiven. I felt criminally underdressed in the circumstances, wearing a rosette, with a small silver-papered trophy at its heart, but that season's cup run confirmed my love for a competition that has been belittled and betrayed too often in recent years.

It began on 3 January that year, my brother David's birthday, with us listening to *Sports Report* on the kitchen radio, which regaled us with *Family Favourites* over Sunday lunch each week, before we could escape to watch *The Big Match*. Watford, granted the rare privilege of an automatic third-round place, won 2-1 at First Division Bolton Wanderers. Both goals were scored by Barry Endean, the folk hero signed for £50 while working as a welder.

Stoke, another top-flight team, were subsequently beaten at Vicarage Road by a 30-yard drive from Colin Franks, who lived just down the road. Fame, of a sort, arrived in the fifth round when a local photographer captured me hugging another ball boy, Keith Furphy, the manager's son, during a 2-1 win over Gillingham.

Keith eventually excelled in indoor soccer in the United States. He was small, straw-haired and a frankly irritating feature in team photographs, though he would claim his own giant-killing scalp seven years later, scoring directly from a corner as Wealdstone defeated Reading 2-1. On the Monday lunchtime, following the Gillingham win, we were brothers in arms.

There was a quiet stampede when the school bell sounded for lunch. A group of us had arranged to meet in the quad, to listen to the quarter-final draw on a small portable radio. The draw had the feel of a monthly meeting at a gentlemen's club, rather than the sub-reality TV of today's equivalent. We listened to the comforting click of balls encased in a velvet bag, and got what we wanted.

Liverpool at home. I couldn't wait to watch a legendary manager, who would be both lionised and rejected by the game into which he poured his heart and soul.

Chapter Six

The Man on the Wire

*'Ken Furphy wears Rocola Golden Tricopress
shirts in Bri-nylon. They have the famous one
piece Bluff-edge collar and he appreciates their
dedication to quality throughout. J.P. Taylor
always have a fine selection – not only for
Ken Furphy, his boys and supporters, but for
everyone who likes to call.'*

EVEN HALF a century ago, at a small, unheralded club that
lived from hand to mouth, the cult of managerial personality
flourished. This was an era in which advertising executives
drew on briar pipes rather than dabbled in the more exotic
substances allegedly ingested by modern counterparts, but they
understood football's power of endorsement.

Ken Furphy's association with sartorial elegance involved
an uncomfortably staged photograph of him in Bluff-edge
collar and tie, thrusting a white football at a visibly bemused
teenager under the headline 'Sound Advice'. It featured
on the front of a 16-page supplement on the eve of what
would be a definitive personal achievement, Watford's win

over Liverpool in the quarter-final of the FA Cup on 21 February 1970.

That defeat prompted Bill Shankly belatedly to break up his first great Liverpool team, which had dominated the mid-Sixties, winning the league twice and the FA Cup once in 1965. He delved into the lower divisions to find new heroes and develop a philosophy that blended political principle with the power of his personality.

The local newspaper pull-out and the match programme are time capsules which offer social and sporting insight. Motorists buying more than four gallons of petrol were promised quadruple Green Shield stamps. A 'low cost luxury' bathroom suite was offered for £55. Carpets were on sale for 49 shillings (£2.45) per square yard.

First prize in the Golden Goal competition was £20, and the club paid forelock-tugging homage to 'The Worshipful The Mayor', Alderman J.S. Oliver, for donating the match ball. Watford's squad was valued at £30,500; readers were breathlessly informed that Bill Shankly had 'a million pounds to pick from'.

The tie was duly condensed into cliché. Watford was 'the club with a yen for a place in the sun'. Shankly was 'a man for all seasons'. The editorial in the programme, which bizarrely gave prominence to the following month's match between the Football League and Scottish League at Coventry, implored fans 'to show Liverpool we have a Kop'.

Tickets had been slow to shift because of a price hike to six shillings (30 pence), but the crowd, glimpsed through a half-open frosted fanlight in our changing room, felt weighty with excitement. There was a sense of other-worldliness about the Liverpool players, at whom we gawped unashamedly. Shankly seemed strangely small and unassuming in their presence; Ron

Yeats, in particular, had the dimensions of a Marvel Comic superhero.

Keith, the manager's son, got the plum job operating behind the goal at the Rookery End, and would be picked up by the television cameras dancing like a demented urchin when Barry Endean scored the winner. I was positioned on the Shrodells' side, in front of a low-roofed stand, an eyesore which adjoined the hospital in which my mum worked as an auxiliary nurse. On shift when Gareth Southgate, a future England manager, was born there later that year, she passed on the good news to his Uncle Mick, who lived at the end of our road.

For all its technological marvels, and hanging juries made up of the great, the good and the think-they-were-better-than-they-were, modern coverage lacks the home-made intimacy of the game's early television treatment. There were far fewer camera angles, less distinct black and white images, but Barry Davies' commentary, in clipped tones which indicated he had gone through a Reithian elocution school, still sings across the ether.

Look hard and you will see me play a key role in the only goal of the game in the 64th minute. I collected the ball in front of a sign advertising Double Diamond (the slogan 'Works Wonders' now seems particularly apt) and quickly tossed it to Ray Lugg, a £7,000 signing who had a career day. He took a short throw to winger Stewart Scullion and moved into space to receive the return pass.

In a flash of virtuosity out of keeping with his status, and that of a pitch which had the consistency of bread mix, Lugg nutmegged Peter Wall, the covering full-back, and delivered an outswinging cross. Endean timed his run perfectly, left the ground with the grace of a Lancaster bomber and met it with a diving header. It was too powerful for goalkeeper Tommy

Lawrence, whose nickname, the Flying Pig, was suddenly explained.

Once I had returned to earth, I looked around and marvelled at the spectacle of collective insanity. Fans on a narrow ledge were clinging to the outside of the stand with one hand, while using the other to initiate joyous free-form semaphore. Watching strangers lost in the moment, and sharing the joy of a community celebrating its difference, was strangely life-affirming and enduringly influential. I wanted this to be my workplace, my artist's easel.

The calmest people in the place were those in grimy yellow round-neck shirts, with a hornet on the left breast, who trotted back to the halfway line in a purposeful huddle. As Furphy's pre-match ghosted column suggested, 'The greatest factor, after we have planned and practised our strategy, selected and blended the team, and presented them into the "arena of fate" at 3pm, is the will to win.'

Liverpool played with revealing desperation, as if they could not bring themselves to trust their talent and breeding. Yeats and Ian St John fouled so crudely they would have been sent off in today's climate. Wall simply caught the ball when it was being played in behind him as the game entered four minutes' added time; he also escaped punishment.

In late spring, I had been in the advance guard, leaping the fences to storm the pitch in celebration of promotion. Now, as the final whistle sounded with the ball at Terry Garbett's feet, just inside the Liverpool half, I found myself in the second wave, sprinting diagonally towards our sanctuary, a narrow entrance on the right of the lower tier of the main stand.

It was there, having fought my way through the scrum of players and supporters, that I saw a grown man cry for the first time.

A punctured balloon in human form, he wept bitterly as he slumped into a wire mesh fence beside the wooden hut that housed the Supporters Club. He wore his allegiance garishly: a Liverpool scarf, with the names of individual players woven into each section, hung over his shoulders and stretched towards his knees. Countless enamel badges, attached with such fateful pride, grated against the fence.

As he sank into the sort of regulation-issue donkey jacket worn by my dad, digging trenches for the Electricity Board, he confirmed a football fan's capacity for taking defeat personally. It was an act of self-flagellation that offered an early lesson in the game's ability to strip an individual's self-worth. Grieving so publicly was irrational, yet implicitly demanded by a deep-seated sense of tribal fealty.

Devotion precludes detachment. This was obviously something more profound than disappointment in his desperate act of worship; it was as if the fan had turned in on himself because he could not bear to comprehend the fallibility of his heroes. He felt somehow complicit in their embarrassment. In hindsight, his self-destructive adoration was the harbinger of modern excess.

Loyalty has mutated to such an extent that a vocal minority of fans of such clubs as Manchester City and Newcastle United indiscriminately attack those who question the ethical purity of their club's owners, or courtiers. It has been monetised by the fraudulent emotion of Fan TV. The balm of belonging has been infected in a way we could not have comprehended, back at the birth of the Seventies.

This was still an age of the great football staple, the plucky underdog, in this case Barry Endean. He was interviewed, post-match, by John Bean, a veteran Manchester journalist who called everyone 'matey' and, though regularly banned by Sir Alex

Ferguson, developed an uncanny ability to see out the manager's periodic rages. His party trick, sand-dancing on table tops, helped.

'I'd like to play in the First Division if I am good enough, but if I don't make the grade I'll be happy to get back to the North East,' Endean told him. 'It's more friendly back home, and the beer is stronger and cheaper.' It was that Everyman quality that appealed to me, as boy and man alike. In a Q&A for Jimmy Hill's short-lived *Football Weekly*, he listed 'fried eggs and chips' as his favourite meal.

A singular character, who left Everton, his first pro club, after four days due to homesickness, he was signed by Watford from a pub team. This was his 15 minutes of fame; he would never again be so prominent, though he eked out a journeyman's career for six more years. The club lost contact with him; other than the vague notion he became a builder in his birthplace, Chester-le-Street, he remained an enigma.

I set out to find him, as a formative hero, for a documentary I was making in 2019. Watford's former players' association had no record of him; it was only when Tom Boswell, my producer, tracked down his Singapore-based son, Barry Jr, on Facebook that the trail ran hot. In the event, his father politely declined our interview request; aged 74 and in retirement, he was conscious of his hearing difficulties.

It would have made a wonderful soft-focus ending for the film, but in a way, it is best that he, and other such figments of childhood imagination, remain preserved in the aspic of memory. I have revealingly mixed feelings about meeting Shankly just before his death in 1981, when he was promoting a double album of interviews conducted by the producer Barry Murray.

I couldn't help myself asking about that significant afternoon at Vicarage Road. 'A bitter day, son, bitter,' he answered in that familiar Ayrshire drawl, which pulled words and emotions along like a locomotive, towing coal trucks on a narrow-gauge railway. The facts of his ruthlessness spoke for themselves from the history books.

When Shankly joined Liverpool on Monday, 14 December 1959, they had just been beaten by non-league Worcester City. He described Anfield as 'a toilet' and shed 24 players in a year. The unanimity of purpose of his first great team was too strong for the virtuosity of such rivals as Manchester United and Tottenham, but he admitted Watford's win told him, 'I had a duty to perform for myself, my family, Liverpool Football Club and the supporters.'

Roger Hunt, a World Cup-winner, was eased out, along with such pivotal figures as Yeats, St John and Lawrence. Injury ended Gerry Byrne's career prematurely. A new generation, featuring the likes of Emlyn Hughes, Ray Clemence, Steve Heighway, John Toshack and Kevin Keegan, won the UEFA Cup within three years.

To me, brought up to respect benevolent socialism in a close-knit working class family, Shankly was football's Che Guevara. Just as Sir Alex Ferguson's catechism was created in the Govan shipyards, Shankly's playbook was suffused by the spirit of two years working underground in the Scottish mining industry that has vanished, along with Glenbuck, the pit village in which he was born.

Jürgen Klopp, his modern equivalent, must find common humanity and unifying character in a collection of multi-millionaire footballers who are, essentially, CEOs of their own global corporations. The club's current marketing strategy cannibalises Shankly's formative principles without placing them in proper context; its owners pay similar lip service to his significance.

'Team spirit is a form of socialism,' he would say. 'That kind of camaraderie is a basis for socialism. I am not a militant man. I'm not talking about politics in the true sense of politics. I'm talking life. I'm talking about humanity, people dealing with people and people helping people. By playing collectively they get individual honours.'

The album, signed by him in two pens (mortifyingly, the first one, blue, ran out after the first word of his message), has become a treasured memento. It acts as an oral history, since he brings the ghosts and the greats of the game to life in staccato sentences. His summary of his 16-year playing career, as a right-half for Preston North End either side of the Second World War, is memorably succinct: 'I was hard, like steel. I had the will.'

His eulogy for Tom Finney, in his estimation the greatest player he had seen, built to a crescendo: 'About five seven, five seven and a half, eleven stone. Sturdy-legged. Strong calves. They gave him natural lift and he was good in the air. Left-footed, quick, elusive. His close control was unbelievable. He could attack you from the front, facing you, and run past you. Just shake himself and be gone. He deceived you. Like all the great players he had a great awareness, not only of his ability, but your ability too. When he had the ball it was his. When he got to the byline, the game was his.'

Raich Carter would 'have scored a hundred goals a season' had he had been in the same team as Finney. He 'leathered the ball into the net'. Alfredo Di Stefano was 'a magnificent man, a big strong fella'. Other Real Madrid legends like Kopa and Gento were 'more showy and flashy, more twisty and turny. They seemed to be in a bigger hurry than Tommy. He was more composed.'

Shankly was at Wembley to watch the end of empire, when England were beaten 6-3 by Hungary in the so-called 'Game of the Century' in 1953. His recollection is forensically precise to the point of being focused on a single pass, from Ferenc Puskás to Nándor Hidegkuti, the deep-lying centre-forward whose movement into midfield exploited the inflexibility of the self-proclaimed masters:

'I was glad I was there because I remember the ball. I could see the markings on the ball as he was hitting it. It was propelling. As it was reaching its target, it was spinning like Jack Nicklaus had hit a golf ball, you know? You could see it reverse itself. When it reached Hidegkuti, it was slowing down, ready to control ...'

Shankly watched a training session at Melwood before Panathinaikos, managed by Puskás, beat Everton on away goals in the last eight, on the way to the European Cup final in 1971. His evocation of a finishing drill, from a central position on the edge of the 18-yard box, is tinged with awe: 'He hit it, left-footed, a foot inside the post 12 times in succession. He'd long finished playing, and he lashed it, a few inches above the grass. I wanted to see him doing that.'

Studying another generation, Shankly suggested Pele 'ranks amongst them all. Not only could he play but he was as strong as an ox. He was a light-heavyweight. Bone and muscle. He could run like a gazelle, like Eusebio, who was taller and quicker. Great players, oh yeah ...'

Jimmy Greaves 'scored the goals he should have scored. Side of the feet, didn't blast them. All he wanted to do was get the ball over the line. He was a (Wilf) Mannion, a (Peter) Doherty, a Len Shackleton, blessed with confidence.' Denis Law was 'brilliant in the air, good with his feet, quicker in the box than the rest of them because he didn't carry any weight.'

His summary had a raw lyricism: 'Every player should be taught what to do, in every situation. If the goalkeeper stays, do something. If he comes out, do something else. If the goalkeeper stayed, Jimmy would take it to him, sidestep him, angle himself and put it into the empty net. Thanks very much. Law and Greaves and Doherty: they knew what to do. The things that these men knew …'

So why, then, on the day we met, was it a faintly troubling experience? I was a novice writer on a dream assignment. I couldn't put my finger on it at the time, but he appeared diminished, in isolation from his legend. I knew of his compulsive generosity to Liverpool fans in retirement, the invitations to tea at his semi-detached house near Everton's training ground, and kickarounds with local kids, but there was something missing.

His spirit.

He was 68, exercised daily and neither drank nor smoked. His olive green suit might have drawn the colour from his face, but there were hints of the virility he exuded in his prime. It took many years before I thought to compare him with that man on the wire at Vicarage Road. Each was, in his own way, a victim of football's abiding cruelty. One's distress was anonymised by the crowd; the other's was excruciatingly exposed by his celebrity.

Football betrayed Shankly. He quickly struggled to keep up the pretence that retiring, after overseeing Liverpool's FA Cup win in 1974, was for the best. He was marginalised, belittled, and eventually rejected. Banned from Melwood, damned by comparisons between his teams, and those of his successor, Bob Paisley, he found the game did not give him a backward glance.

In late September, soon after his promotional appearance, he suffered a heart attack and was taken into Liverpool's Broadgreen Hospital. Such was his mystique, no one thought he would test one of his stage-managed admissions that 'I want to die a healthy man'. A second, massive heart attack killed him three days later.

A city mourned, a game grieved, and a nation pined for the simplicity of his example. But did it learn from the callousness football showed to one of its own? Events suggest not. As we all enter a new age, perhaps we should revise Shankly's legacy. He tells us, from the grave, to allow even the most prominent of his successors their humanity.

Cut them, and they bleed.

Chapter Seven

Nights in Pink Satin

KEITH TURNER, headmaster of Watford Boys' Grammar School, pulled a face that suggested I had defecated on the mahogany desk that dominated his study. As education's answer to Hyacinth Bouquet, his curtain-twitching, middle-class sensibilities were easily offended, especially by a council estate kid with ideas above his station.

He was known as 'Trog', short for troglodyte. The most popular dictionary definition refers to a cave-dwelling hermit, but the alternative explanation, 'a person who is regarded as being deliberately ignorant or old-fashioned', was more apposite. He viewed my decision to abandon my A levels to become a junior reporter on the *Watford Observer* as an act of ingratitude.

Mum had cried when I received the offer letter from Ernie Foster, the editor. Turner, a self-styled arts buff, treated it with something close to contempt. 'Calvin,' he intoned, 'this will lead to nothing.' When, as chief sports writer on the *Daily Telegraph*, I was cleared for ideological purity and invited back to the school to contribute to his valediction after 28 years in charge, I invented the excuse of a crowded diary. It was an act of pettiness of which I am not proud.

My most influential tutor turned out to be Oli Phillips, who wrote evocatively, passionately and intelligently about Watford for 58 years until 2018. He was my first sports editor, one of the last of an endangered species, a local journalist who cared about his community, amplified its voice and resisted all invitations to broaden his horizons.

A tall, soft-voiced man, he introduced me to the daily sports desk ritual, a canteen breakfast of tomatoes on toast, with the remnants of the frying pan drizzled (ok, slopped) on top. He was less successful in trying to convert me to the nasal poetry of Bob Dylan, whose musical legend, together with those of Pink Floyd and Radiohead, I still cannot comprehend.

Oli gave me my first byline, as Mick Calvin, for a report on the Husband and Wives' bowls on 17 July 1974. He offered me the scope to lay out, and fill up, my own broadsheet page, covering the Watford Sunday League. Though a closet workaholic, who only admitted to persistent anxiety in his final piece before retirement in France, he taught through a quizzically raised eyebrow rather than the theatrical monsterings administered in darker corners of Fleet Street.

His best lessons had a stark simplicity. I went through a stage of referring to Sunday teams as 'mediocre', usually after they had suffered double-figure defeats. Oli read the description, rolled the word around his tongue with a relish he usually reserved for real ale, and tossed a heavyweight edition of the Oxford English Dictionary across the desk.

'Look it up.'

I had been mistakenly using the adjective in the sense of a performance being dire. The dictionary definition 'of only average quality; not very good' was instantly imprinted on my brain. 'Make sure you know the meaning of a word before you use it,' he said. Message understood. I have seen some truly terrible teams down the years; none have been marked by the 'm' word.

Oli didn't quite own the football club, but in acting as Boswell to a succession of frankly mediocre managers, he acquired certain intellectual property rights. In 1973, he had unwittingly helped to secure Watford's long-term future by introducing the board to a long-time supporter, Reginald Dwight. 'Who the hell is he?' asked Ron Rollitt, who ran the place, as general secretary.

My future boss had spotted a line in the *New Musical Express* in which Elton John, Reggie's alter ego, spoke about how he had yearned for Watford to beat Chelsea in the 1970 FA Cup semi-final that had so enraptured me. When approached about potential investment in the club by Vic Lewis, the pop star's European manager, Oli suggested they play down their ambitions by paying £50 a year to become vice-presidents.

That gave them a seat in the main stand, a cup of tea at half-time, and access to a pay bar, without arousing the suspicions of the notoriously sour chairman, Jim Bonser. Elton was deferential and modest when they were introduced, excused his platform shoes and violet-streaked hair, and left the boardroom with a tiepin, scarf and tie.

The following Saturday, after watching Watford win 3-1 during an exploratory away trip to Rochdale, he established a journalistic tradition, of sorts, by playing bar billiards with Oli in the Supporters Club. They had bonded over a shared love of Buddy Holly; Elton's glasses, which resembled diamante-studded toilet seats when I played darts against him a couple of years later, were worn as a tribute to the ill-fated rock'n'roll pioneer.

He was invited to join the board after donating £25,000, proceeds from a fundraising concert at Vicarage Road that featured a cameo appearance by Rod Stewart. This wasn't a celebrity indulgence; when he missed the train on which the team travelled, soon after buying a majority shareholding for a rumoured £70,000 in 1976, he hired a private plane to get to Workington for a 1-0 win in the Fourth Division.

By that time I was being eased into the Vicarage Road rotation, and seeing football in a different light. As a fan, I was too busy hearing tunes of glory to listen to the whispers and moans that permeate struggling clubs. As a kid clinging to Oli's voluminous coat-tails, I was learning from the bottom up. A 1-0 loss, at Darlington on 30 August 1975, left Watford 92nd in the Football League.

Football's deeper satisfaction lies in the constancy of its more subtle attractions. Age is an equaliser; we identify with footballers who happen to be our contemporaries, since they grow old as we do. They might be complete strangers, but they go through a similar, if accelerated, cycle of aspiration, achievement, disappointment and decline. It is a strange, invariably invisible, bond that, because of the nature of my job, became personal.

I spent most of my first season with the Under-18s on Saturday mornings, covering a lad of the same age called Luther Blissett, who was ripping up the South East Counties League. Truth be told, I was initially intimidated, a sign of personal and professional immaturity since he was easy-going and unaffected by the buzz created by his obvious potential. As our respective careers progressed, I became quietly proprietorial.

I saw him score on his first team debut in a 2-1 home win over Swansea on 17 April 1976, in front of a crowd of 4,536 that reflected the disillusion generated by a futile season in the Fourth Division. I reported on his England debut, when he scored his only international goals, a hat-trick in a 9-0 win against Luxembourg at Wembley on the evening of 15 December 1982. I even saw him score on his home debut for AC Milan, in a 4-2 win over Verona on 18 September 1983.

Those were headline events that required the sort of context only time can provide. Blissett's football career, like many others, was a consequence of a chance conversation, and a powerful, private protestation of faith by a far-sighted coach, enacted upon by a manager who would have a fundamental impact on his life.

He was 15 when Paul Kitson, a former pupil, returned to Willesden High School to talk about signing his first professional contract with Watford. Kitson raised the prospect of players from the fifth form team undertaking open trials at the club, which were to begin at the end of term. The conversation in the Common Room gave sudden focus to an ambition fired by the 1968 European Cup final, and specifically, George Best.

Blissett's voice softens as he recalls: 'We talk quite loosely about what a kid's dream means, but seeing Best play all I could think of was: "This is what I want to do." The things he could do with the ball, gliding and floating above the ground, made me want to be him, on the field at least.' Seven fifth-formers put themselves forward for the trial. Three got through to the second phase, but only Blissett was taken on.

Kitson, the catalyst, reflected an alternative reality beyond my comprehension, as a young reporter. He was rapidly released, and played for 14 clubs in 19 seasons in indoor soccer in the United States, winning championships with Baltimore Blast before a brief managerial career stalled in Canada, where he died in 2005, aged 49, while conducting a coaching session for a youth team in Toronto.

He was of a generation of black footballers subjected to appalling racial abuse and institutionalised ignorance. Blissett felt the slights as powerfully, but learned from his example: 'Paul never turned away and took a breath. He dealt with it head on. I understood why he did that, but that wasn't the right way to deal with that particular subject at that particular time.'

He, too, would have made only the briefest impression on the professional game without the advocacy of youth coach Tom Walley. Aware that Blissett was earmarked for release after a single season, he persuaded Graham Taylor, the new manager, that the striker was 'worth a punt' because 'he scores goals and looks hungry to play'.

Taylor repeated his name three times when they first met – 'with a name like that you have got to be a star' – before instinctively taking his coach's counsel. 'Graham saw the traits Tom had spoken about,' Blissett remembers. 'He had a sense of humour, but my first impression was that I was in the presence of a leader.

'On a personal level, you could trust and believe in what he said to you. You need that trust and belief as a young player. He wanted all of us to feel part of the family he was creating. He instilled a responsibility to give back, 100 per cent, to others through our performances. He gave us a cause to commit to.

'Graham's first lesson was to be critical of yourself. He looked closely at the way you conducted yourself. That dictated how people saw and perceived you, not just as a player, but as a person. He expected honesty in how you assessed your game. I'd have people telling me I'd played well, since I had scored, but, deep down, I knew I had not hit the benchmarks I had set for myself.

'Playing like a kid, because you love it, can only take you so far. You must never allow anybody, or anything, to get between you and your principles. Graham stressed we were representing our team-mates, the coaching staff, the directors and the club, as well as the supporters who invested so much in our efforts. We were not take, take, take. We gave back through our performances.

'It was a series of life lessons. If you are going to be successful you have to understand how to conduct yourself when you lose. We cannot all be winners, all of the time. Don't beat yourself up when you fail. Don't beat others up when they make a mistake. We all make mistakes. Realise that the people around you have the same goals.'

Blissett, whose first kit was sponsored by Elton John's mother, Sheila Farebrother, maximised his ability. He spent a season in Serie A before returning for the second of three spells at Watford, ending as the club's record goalscorer, 186 in 503 appearances. His coaching career was intermittently frustrating, but he remains a hugely popular figure, with a social conscience in keeping with difficult times.

He was the central character in one of the most surreal football-related stories I can remember. His name was appropriated by hundreds of artists and activists who formed the Luther Blissett Project in 1994. The movement spread from Italy to the UK, Germany, Spain, Slovenia, Canada, the United States, Finland and Brazil over the following five years before its members decided to commit symbolic ritual suicide.

It spawned a best-selling historical novel, *Q*, which followed an Anabaptist radical across Europe fomenting unrest during the Protestant reformation in the first half of the 16th century. The four Italian authors, who took Luther Blissett as a nom de plume, now write under the name Wu Ming, which, as every schoolboy knows, is Mandarin for anonymous.

The real-life Luther bought the book, 'but after reading the first page and a half I wondered: "What's all this about?"' He remains quietly amused: 'The first time I heard about it I was sceptical. I didn't want to believe it. To think that someone, a group or a single person, could take on my name seemed ridiculous, but in a strange way it is something to be proud of.'

Reggie Dwight, of course, reinvented himself as Elton Hercules John. He found, in football, an antidote to excess that just about saved his life. The game gave him acceptance, without the distortion of his celebrity. It offered the sanctuary of common ground, away from the quicksand of global stardom. In return, he was unforced, authentic, grounded and, above all, grateful.

Though I had moved on from my two-tone tonic suit phase, I feared I was overdressed for our pre-arranged darts night at the Supporters Club. I was wearing my pride and joy, a navy blue velvet jacket with lapels that resembled an elephant's ears. I need not have worried; Elton, who usually favoured relatively sober suits on football duty, was in a pink satin number. He swayed alarmingly on the oche, due to platform boots that probably needed planning permission.

The chasm between awestruck, aspiring writer and indiscreetly balding rock god was quickly bridged by reminiscence and mutual experience. He was 29, 11 years older, so I hadn't seen his formative heroes. Centre-forward Cliff Holton was signed from Arsenal, where he had won a league-winner's medal, and unsurprisingly scored 48 goals in a single Fourth Division season. Sammy Chung dropped his original Christian name, Cyril, and went on to manage Wolves.

I had to admit I had never heard of the final member of Elton's Holy Trinity, Freddie Bunce. He was apparently a fast, tricky left-winger who played with his head down; local legend in the early Sixties insisted the club had built the Rookery End to prevent him running straight on into the adjoining allotments.

He would play for a season in South Africa before emigrating to Australia, where he died, aged 53, in October 1991.

I discovered I stood in the same section of the ground as Elton, after sneaking in. The Bend, a sloping expanse of shale, shored up by railway sleepers, featured the Marie Celeste Tea Bar, so named because it was frequently empty. His claim to have invaded the pitch after the Liverpool FA Cup win prompted my memories of being a ball boy, which in turn led to the realisation we both adored Duncan Welbourne.

Elton had fulfilled a lifetime's ambition, playing up front for Watford for the first 20 minutes of Welbourne's testimonial. After the match, he presented him with his gold disc for 'Goodbye Yellow Brick Road'. He also played solo sets in successive years, at the local Top Rank, to raise money for him and Johnny Williams, the other fabled full-back from my childhood.

Football reveals character, good and bad. He could afford the magnanimity of the gesture, but what registered was his consistent generosity of spirit, that spoke of the man behind the mass entertainment myth. When he became chairman, he made a point of ordering flowers for club employees enduring domestic difficulties. He did similar fundraising concerts for other players, like striker Ross Jenkins, but also for less celebrated figures, like Ron Rollitt, the general factotum.

Many years later, on an England trip to Budapest, I would see him play an impromptu post-match set of similar standards on a piano in a hotel lobby, for players, management and stray members of the hack pack. I was struck, then and now, by the significance of a superstar being so visibly star-struck by international footballers. This testifies both to the game's emotional impact, and the complementary power of dreams.

I came to appreciate another, equally surprising character trait during that darts night. His hunger to achieve, and respect for those with different outlooks and distinctive talents who did so, resonated with me. The music industry and professional sport eat their young; it takes a survivor's spirit and an improbable constitution to endure in each, past your 30th birthday.

That hidden hardness came to the fore in an interview he gave to Oli Phillips, on becoming chairman. 'This is not Elton's folly,' he told him. 'I am not a quitter. I got where I am by hard work, going hungry, travelling up and down the country without sleep in the back of a van. I will work hard to make this a success, but I expect everyone else to do so as well.'

There were to be no sinecures, no excuses. When his first season as chairman quickly turned sour, he refused to fund signings around the transfer deadline because 'I am not going to be blackmailed by players.' He sacked manager Mike Keen, who was set on releasing Blissett before Walley's intervention, and flirted with replacing him with Bobby Moore before recruiting Graham Taylor.

My football education accelerated suddenly, because I saw a club, and community, galvanised by the force of a manager's vision, principles and personality. Taylor was empathetic, inclusive, sensitive and utterly ruthless. This wasn't the modern-management model, shallow promotion of a personal brand through strategic soundbites and populist gestures. It was a refreshing reminder of the game's humanity.

I intend to dwell on the unfairness of his fate, in the context of our respective professions, later in the book. For the moment, I don't wish to sully the memory of his ability to set the mood of strangers, and sell the dream to unbelievers. His first season was a crusade; Watford won the Fourth Division by 11 points, having clinched the title with six games to spare.

Elton had given Taylor five years to get into the Second Division; he needed two. It took five seasons to rise from the Fourth to the First, where Sunderland were beaten 8-0, with Blissett scoring four. Elton, joining the players on an end-of-season lap of honour, was captured turning to them in wonder, having just heard that Watford had been confirmed as runners-up to the champions, Liverpool.

So much of life is squeezed out by record books and league tables. Such summaries of achievement are, at best, statistical shorthand. Football is a patchwork quilt of intimate memories and personal insights, ill-served by abbreviation. Strange things lodge in the brain.

I particularly remember a fleetingly frustrating FA Cup defeat at non-league Northwich Victoria in 1976, which the next home programme unconsciously excused by referring to them as Norwich. Watford had insisted on kicking off at 2pm because of the quality of their floodlights; Northwich fans flaunted candles.

Away trips on football specials entered folklore. On one particularly lively return journey from Hull, a fan known as Dingo, who stood at the Rookery End, stole several cases of gin from the platform. He walked down the train, swapping bottles of gin for beer. Suffice to say, the majority of passengers were legless when they reached Watford Junction, three hours late, in the early hours.

My final memory of life on the *Watford Observer* is of hitching a ride on another football special to watch Blissett score with two headers in a 2-1 League Cup win at Manchester United. I moved on to Fleet Street, and an agency run by Reg Hayter, a legendary figure who took post-prandial naps, head down on an ancient sit-up-and-beg typewriter, but managed to produce generations of leading sportswriters.

It was another world. I covered up to ten matches each week, at varying levels, and would occasionally be employed in the old Wembley press box, which was suspended from the roof, to read over punchy paragraphs of running copy, typewritten on half-sized sheets of paper by Frank McGhee, the *Daily Mirror*'s chief sportswriter. I didn't dare change a word, though I was tempted.

It would be many years, and a couple of thousand matches, before I began to experience anxiety dreams about live reporting. The plot is consistent: I am sitting in a press box, in an indeterminate country, watching two unrecognisable teams. Everyone around me is absorbed in their work, honing phrases, developing story structures and following events in that woodpecker way we have of glancing between game and computer screen.

My screen is as blank as my mind. The veil never lifts. Time is a tyrant. In desperation, on deadline, I pick up an ancient telephone, and dial the office. Surely my outdated speciality, ad-libbing a report to a copytaker, will save me. I usually wake when I discover there is no one on the end of the line, and I am making no sense.

Shot to bits, I hear you say. Perhaps, but Reg recognised the value of impudent ambition in his stable of spotty hopefuls. No assignment was too obscure, taxing or urgent. So, when he made me an offer I couldn't refuse, delivering a 2,000-word piece for ITV's *World of Sport* annual by close of play that day, I was expected to take it in my stride.

The subject was competitive frog jumping.

This, remember, was an age before Mr Google was a hack's best friend. My only lead was provided by Reg: he remembered reading a short story by Mark Twain, based on a contest in California. Disguising desperation, and inured to indignity, I put in a call to the press office at the US Embassy. The novelty factor saved me; one staff member came from rural Louisiana, and remembered being told of contests, dating back to the Depression. I was off, and running.

Ghost-writing Denis Compton's column for the *Sunday Express* involved a weekly visit to Valhalla, also known as El Vinos, the legendary Fleet Street watering hole. There, in mahogany-lined booths, I would convene with cricket's greats. Denis was regularly joined by his best friend, Bill Edrich, Richie Benaud, the peerless commentator, and Keith Miller, who admitted to bowling with greater hostility when suffering from a hangover.

Miller was once asked to reflect on the strain of professional sport, and memorably announced: 'Pressure? I'll tell you what pressure is. Pressure is a Messerschmitt up your arse.' When Donald Bradman, his captain, ordered him to bounce Edrich, England's leading run-scorer, out of the 1946/47 Ashes tour of Australia, he refused because 'I've just fought a war with this bloke.'

Benaud was only 15 when war ended, but he understood enough to frame one of his most telling principles: 'The *Titanic* was a tragedy, the Ethiopian drought a disaster, and neither bears any relation to a dropped catch.' He took up commentary after retiring in 1964, learning the value of brevity and the sanctity of silence from Henry Longhurst in golf and Dan Maskell in tennis.

The clan convened at the Lord's Test, in the old press box at the top of the Warner Stand. Denis, who fitted an alternative career as a winger for Arsenal around his 78 Test appearances, was respectful and charmingly disengaged. When I asked if he had any views on the topic of the day, he would invariably reply: 'I'll leave that to you, old boy. I'm sure you'll do a great job.'

Benaud, writing for the *News of the World*, pecked at a portable typewriter. John Arlott would be in the left-hand aisle, crafting poetry with a bottle of claret by his side. Len Hutton would be in the back row, making notes in pencil in preparation for his tea-time appointment with his ghostwriter. Fred Trueman would be circulating in a mushroom cloud of pipe smoke.

The figures in Watford's old wooden press box were not as celebrated, but they had their constituency. The Hospital Radio commentary team, led by Reg Stacey, often informed patients that they had been joined by Elton, listening from some far-flung place. The dynamics of the relationship between manager and chairman was shifting, subtly but significantly.

The pop star regarded Taylor as an older brother, and indulged his instinctive generosity. On hearing Taylor intended to buy his wife Rita a VW Beetle, he arranged for a new one, complete with bow, to be parked on their front lawn when the curtains were opened on Christmas morning. They played intensely competitive games of Monopoly, and Elton often joined family dinners.

A home truth was delivered on one such occasion, when Graham asked his wife to serve them dinner, as normal, but to leave the visitor's place empty. The manager, concerned about the level of his chairman's drinking, made his point by placing a bottle of brandy where the plate should have been. Gauging Elton's surprise, he told him: 'That's all you need nowadays.'

In football, harsh truths, powerfully applied, are ignored at your peril.

Chapter Eight

Playing with the Pros

THE ATHLETIC Bilbao winger, recruited from the *cantera* as a ringer for the Basque press team, was quick, had adhesive control and exuded the exaggerated self-confidence of youth. He was visibly pleased with himself and evidently a little too accustomed to praise to recognise the danger of his impulsive desire to impose his will on the opposing right-back.

He lined him up and saw only a man old enough to be his grandfather. The approach was slow, deliberate and almost mocking. Then, with a sudden drop of the shoulder, he slipped the ball through the defender's legs and sped away, with an admittedly impressive burst of acceleration. His near-post cross, well struck and accurate, was duly headed in.

That was the easy bit, since I was supposed to be marking the goalscorer.

Despite fielding a couple of ringers of our own, named Bobby Charlton and Geoff Hurst, we, the perspiring English, were on the way to a 6-1 defeat the veteran full-back took personally. 'Son,' he growled at the winger as he trotted past him, on the way back to the restart, 'do that again and I'll have you.' The young player made the mistake of smiling, and feigning incomprehension. He failed to read the full-back's eyes and the menace in his voice.

Around ten minutes later, the inevitable occurred. The winger accepted a pass and rolled his foot across the ball, examining his options before advancing with obvious intent. When he attempted to repeat the trick, the defender employed the nuclear option. His tackle was fractionally late and notably high; his boot made contact with his tormentor's shins, about three inches below the knee.

Jimmy Armfield turned his back, wordlessly, having administered a life lesson. Never attempt to embarrass a seasoned pro, especially if he is a stranger. Do not underestimate professional football's ritualistic code of respect. Placidity of temperament does not preclude or prevent retribution if it is defied. Even Gentleman Jim, the kindly soul who played the church organ, was dangerous when armed.

He was in his late forties at the time of that press match, a former England captain on the way to becoming a national treasure. He possessed an innate dignity, a down-to-earth manner and the soothing voice of a parish priest. He entered print journalism as a former Leeds manager, and left the BBC as one of its best-loved radio commentators. His death, aged 82, in January 2018, was widely mourned.

He was celebrated as the embodiment of what the game was in the process of losing. He was a balanced and empathetic observer, warm and wise, at a time when self-appointed trend-setters were jaundiced and ignorant, shrill and superficial. He had the perspective of the wartime evacuee, an appreciation of life bred by the ration book and the greyness of the 1950s.

He was of a generation that valued loyalty, and generated it in return. He was charitable, and inspired others to demonstrate their humanity. Ian Ridley, an award-winning football writer and author whose friendship with Jimmy was forged through their mutual experience of cancer, led a successful campaign to give him a World Cup-winner's medal as a non-playing member of Sir Alf Ramsey's 1966 squad.

Professional footballers are different from you and me, the uninitiated. They may be judged in competitive situations, but are best assessed dispassionately on the training ground, where entry involves accessing a circle of trust. It is there, in that privileged vacuum, that talent is expressed most naturally, almost thoughtlessly. It's a cynical trade, and some do the minimum, but others dance when they think no one is watching.

It is, as Xavi, the iconic Barcelona player, insists, a game of time and space. Players are close enough for you to gauge the weight of a pass, to appreciate the use of the contours of the foot in its delivery. Decisions are made quickly and movement off the ball has a synchronicity born of repetition and instinct. A manager morphs from a media stereotype into a teacher. His coaches circulate, offering caustic commentary and calm advice. Their lines of communication are broad.

Downtime is play time. My favourite moments involve the casual application of spontaneous skill: Dele Alli giggling at his dexterity in scoring with a mid-air, back-heeled flick from a corner and Trent Alexander-Arnold pinging 70-yard diagonal passes with the verve and accuracy of an NFL quarterback.

It can still be a game of joy and childish innocence. When the Liverpool full-back trained at Melwood for the first time during the early stages of Project Restart, he posted a seven-second clip on social media. In it, he flicks the ball up with his right foot and allows it to bounce twice before cutting across it, imparting the spin that allows it to swerve into the net, close to the far post, with a comforting thud.

'Still got it,' he wrote.

Another arresting image of that sunny day is equally adhesive. In it, a father was captured waiting outside the training ground, with his son on his shoulders, so that he could see over the surrounding wall. The boy had a red ball in his hand and a Liverpool bobble hat on his head. I couldn't see his face, but I'd bet it had a look of wonder because of his proximity to his heroes.

That spirit of the schoolyard has been institutionalised in Japan, where a New Year tradition involves three J. League stars taking on 100 children on a full-size pitch. They face ten goalkeepers and are subjected to a swarm of would-be tacklers, yet manage to manipulate possession and move into space where none seems to exist. The pros rarely lose and tend to score through cushioned headers; if they concede, it is usually an act of charity.

These boys can play.

Even the game's journeymen deserve genuflection. Their reflexes are sharp, their skills honed beyond the conception of park-pitch warriors. They have internal stop-watches, which reduce time to fractions of a second in the most pressurised of circumstances. The best players make the right choice, more often, at the right time, but all pros are self-contained and recognise their interdependence.

Each has an unspoken capacity to harm the other. They know when to leave a foot in, how to disguise their malevolence. Training matches can become warzones; I've seen close friends exchange punches and insults before they are separated by team-mates. Vengeance is rarely acknowledged publicly: that's why the mutually destructive feud between Roy Keane and Alf-Inge Haaland ultimately diminished both.

Those realities are downplayed by the modern fantasy packages, which offer ordinary mortals the chance to feel like a hero for the day. The opportunity to play alongside and against former players at important venues can have a charitable dimension (the Football Aid project has raised in excess of £2.2m for diabetes research) but invariably participation is a corporate perk.

I cannot complain. I have desecrated Wembley, lumbered around half a dozen Premier League grounds and been indulged across three continents while going through the charade of representing my country. For a leaden-footed, slow-brained MOT failure of a centre-half who rose no higher than the Fifth Division of the Watford Sunday League, that's absurd.

A journo's thick skin is a blessing, since there is no place to hide. Once, playing in a press match at the old Highbury, I heard Pat Rice, Arsène Wenger's assistant, shout 'Get your head up' as I attempted to carry the ball forward. By all accounts I obeyed instantly, snapping my neck back with such force I should by rights have suffered whiplash. The old pros along for the ride fell about laughing.

The sound I hear most often, in those all-too-vivid 3am nightmares, is the cackling of Jack Charlton, who decided, on a whim, to watch his younger brother, Bobby, play against the Swiss press in the shadow of St Jakob Park in Basel in late May 1981. A disconcertingly large crowd gathered in the sun on grassy banks; there was an edge to the atmosphere that foretold trouble at the following day's World Cup qualifier.

I was in my first year covering England and suffering from culture shock. We posed for a team photo, in the D at the edge of our penalty area, in a classic Admiral England kit. Two future England managers, Terry Venables and Howard Wilkinson, lined up alongside Bobby, who had circulated in the dressing room beforehand with earnest intent, offering individual encouragement.

If that was akin to watching Usain Bolt prepare for the dads' race at the village school, Jack had no intention of putting his World Cup-winner's medal on the table. This, he exclaimed to no one in particular, was comedy hour. He pointedly failed to disguise his bewilderment at my meanderings; I chose to take it as constructive criticism, a form of identification with a fellow toiler at the coalface.

I also chose to ignore the inconvenient fact we were three goals down by half-time.

The venerable Brian Glanville, who reported on the '66 World Cup for the *Sunday Times*, had earned a reputation as a 'robust' full-back over four decades, playing in Hyde Park for Chelsea Casuals, a team of itinerant writers and artists who, perhaps more accurately, were originally called the Chelsea Choppers. Jack decided he tackled like 'a rice puddin''.

If that was harsh, and not entirely fair, Bob 'The Cat' Harris, our goalkeeper, deserved praise, rather than ridicule, for plunging at the feet of an advancing Swiss striker. His save prevented us from going further behind, but his glasses came off second best. We were accustomed to the sight of Bob, on all fours in a goalmouth, scrabbling to check his bins hadn't been damaged beyond repair: he did something similar in a game in Spain. On this occasion, however, it was all too much for the future Republic of Ireland manager.

'A 'keeper playing in fookin' glasses … now I've fookin' seen it all …'

His brother, though, had greater faith. His half-time team talk felt as if it was stolen from a schoolboy's dream sequence. This was Bobby Charlton for heaven's sake, looking into our eyes and telling us that this match mattered. 'We can do this,' he urged. 'Keep your heads up. We score the next goal and it's a different game.'

If football was pre-packaged as soft-focus fantasy, we would prevail 5-4, with Bobby scoring the winning goal. It isn't, of course, (though let's not give modern broadcasters an idea) but that was precisely what happened. I swear the connection on Bobby's winning goal, a trademark 30-yard thunderbolt, was so pure it never made a sound; the shot had the effortless quality of a golf pro's 350-yard drive.

I picked up pace and ran, a rare exertion, to ensure I didn't miss the opportunity to shake his hand. This, I decided, would be a moment to tell the children about, provided they played their part in being conceived and safely delivered. The memory remains so vivid I've broken off from writing this to post the team picture from the match on the Family WhatsApp group.

Reality reasserted itself all too soon. England lost 2-1 the following day, their sixth match without a win. They were in danger of failing to qualify for their third successive World Cup. The FA's official Travel Club had been infiltrated by right-wing hooligans, who rioted. Tear gas was employed and the local police chief suggested: 'If we do not see them here again for 50 years, it will still be too soon.'

The tone of the next decade or so had been set. Ron Greenwood, the England manager, was ordered, by a pitiless red top headline: 'In the name of God, go now.' He was dissuaded from announcing his immediate resignation and stayed in Switzerland to prepare for the following Saturday's match in Budapest, when Trevor Brooking scored twice in a redemptive 3-1 win at the Nep Stadium.

This was the era in which teams stayed overnight, and flew back the following day. A civilised exercise for those on tight deadlines, but dangerous since the first editions of the Sunday newspapers, printed before the match, were on the plane. The inquest, staged on the assumption of another failure to reach a major tournament, was premature and brutal.

Players were not amused to see lines dramatically drawn through photographs of their faces, which signalled their redundancy. Greenwood admitted to 'a sense of shame' and told his team that he intended to announce his departure on arrival at Luton. He admitted that he could feel 'people looking at me as if I had committed some crime'.

A curtain stretched across the aisle separated the squad from the press, who sat uncomfortably in steerage at the back of the plane. It might as well have been made of six-inch steel. We were oblivious as, further forward, senior players, led by Kevin Keegan, Mick Mills and Brooking, talked Greenwood around.

In today's climate, in which information passes between players, agents, families and journalists with remarkable speed and intermittent accuracy, reports of the England manager's dramatic change of heart would have been on social media before the squad had emerged from baggage reclaim. The secret remained in house; no one knew of the machinations until after England narrowly failed to reach the final four in Spain the following year.

It was still a time of relative innocence since the press corps were given a lift on the England team bus when we arrived in Bilbao before the tournament, but the fault lines between players and those paid to record their exploits were gradually expanding. The Rotters, predatory news reporters who took pride in the mischievous connotations of their nickname, were moving into the game.

Having warmed up by triggering a chair-tossing brawl between English and American journalists at a John McEnroe press conference at Wimbledon, their shock tactics expanded at the World Cup. No news equals bad news: when it didn't exist it was simply manufactured, through a warped form of genius. The legend of Dead Dog Beach was born.

The epicentre of the so-called story was England's team hotel, Los Tamarises, selected on the advice of anti-terrorist officers because it was secluded and protected by a cliff face. This gave the Rotters their traditional pre-event tale, the Ring of Steel, which involved florid references to obsessive security surrounding the England team, and the threat posed by ETA separatists.

So far, so predictable. A false, but full-blown health scare was created by a photograph of a dead dog among rubbish on the beach overlooked by the hotel. It took time, and more than a few tinctures, to discover the truth. The unfortunate animal was found nearby as roadkill. An enterprising news reporter paid local kids to transfer it to the beach.

A front page splash, and Fleet Street folklore, beckoned.

The FA did enjoy a measure of revenge by burying an authentic story, the back spasms which threatened Kevin Keegan's participation. He borrowed the receptionist's Seat 500, drove 200 miles to Madrid and flew to Hamburg for treatment without any of the media being any the wiser. Yet, as that era passed, money multiplied and mobile telephones began to operate as judge and jury, attitudes hardened.

The thought of Bobby Charlton's equivalent, a David Beckham, playing in a press match is fanciful to say the least. Recently retired players in the modern era, with the exception of TV pundits like Jamie Redknapp, rarely deign to take part. For every Chris Waddle, a press team irregular who was well into his fifties when he played park football in Sheffield, there are countless former pros who have fallen out of love with the game.

I understand such reticence, because they are products of an introspective culture, in which emotions are distorted or diluted. Footballers are wearied by unsolicited opinion, delivered by those who have no appreciable level of expertise. Ask yourself this: how would you like to be criticised for perceived shortcomings by strangers who have no conception of how you do your job?

Perhaps this new age needs a new understanding. The public does not own players. They have families and feelings. The vast majority, in my experience, are well-rounded individuals. It is not their fault that social media has become so unsocial. Though it is unrealistic to expect a seismic change in attitudes, they do not deserve to be treated as prize exhibits in a human zoo.

In return, footballers must confront their own, deep-seated prejudices. Their show-us-your-medals response to independent scrutiny reflects a sour, self-defensive strain of professional arrogance. It will be difficult to break down since it is cultural rather than individual, but any understanding must be mutual.

Jimmy Armfield had an answer to anyone who sought to snipe from behind the barricades. Once, in the Stadium of Light's press room after yet another home defeat, Howard Wilkinson, Sunderland's manager, failed to contain his frustration at having his tactics and strategy second-guessed. 'How many England caps have you got?' he asked his inquisitors.

The silence was broken by a soft, unmistakable, Lancashire accent: 'Forty-three, actually, Howard.'

Chapter Nine

Behind the Curtain

MOSCOW BECAME a Potemkin Village during the 1980 Olympics, which opened the Soviet Union to global scrutiny for the first time since the 1917 revolution. The world was shown the façade, invited to share the quasi-religious experience of visiting Lenin's Tomb and the artistic splendour of the Bolshoi. Reality was hinted at in the bare shelves and leaking roof of the GUM state store on Red Square, and confirmed by the brutal suppression of dissent.

I was in a group of British journalists, attacked by police and plain-clothed KGB agents when Vincenzo Francone, an Italian gay rights demonstrator, attempted to chain himself to Saviour's Gate on the eastern edge of the Kremlin. A distinct click, whenever I dictated copy to London, signalled that the telephone was tapped; a *Daily Star* photographer, face blooded and teeth chipped during the assault, destroyed the television set in his hotel room because he was convinced it contained a listening device.

At 22, the youngest member of the British press corps, I grew up fast. I had travelled, as advised, with a detachable bathplug and Mars bars, in case the food was inedible, only to find the plumbing worked and the press cafeteria served caviar and Georgian champagne. I quickly bribed the Babushka, an elderly lady who sat in the hotel corridor, monitoring our movements with a security guard, with several pairs of stockings. They came in handy when David Emery, latterly sports editor of the *Daily Express*, goose-stepped, naked, past her in his sleep.

It was a time of mutual misapprehension and mistrust, when athletes were drawn into a nebulous war between East and West. The most politically charged sporting event since Hitler's Games in Berlin in 1936 began with an Orwellian opening ceremony in the Lenin Stadium, where a 103,000 crowd watched 22 soldiers slowly goose-step around the track before releasing white doves from their right hands.

The British audience was captivated by Sebastian Coe's soap operatic rivalry with Steve Ovett. They were a classic study in contrasts, track and field's equivalent of Ali and Frazier, Borg and McEnroe, Senna and Prost. Coe was a scientifically prepared media darling; Ovett, a loner but the more natural runner, with a long, almost leisurely stride, was a media nightmare.

Coe, shaking and close to tears, described being beaten by Ovett in the 800 metres, which he was expected to dominate, as the equivalent of attending his own autopsy. His rival, who had not spoken to the press for five years, sold three exclusive interviews to a Sunday tabloid which destroyed the sour stereotype he had done so much to sustain.

'I sometimes go to schools and see kids who can hardly walk,' he said, in the first interview, conducted as he celebrated with his family. 'To be blessed with the ability to run is enough. Olympic golds are secondary, really.' His wistfulness signalled the limitations of ambition. We were not to know it at the time, but that was his 'is that it?' moment.

Ovett finished third in the 1500 metres final. The iconic picture of Coe crossing the line as champion, head thrown back, eyes bulging and mouth open, before dropping to his knees, was used in more than 800 newspapers around the world the following day. On his return to London police closed the M4 for several minutes to allow him to escape a pursuing posse of press.

Given that level of hysteria, Olympic football was an unremarked curiosity to the majority of our readers. British participation in the tournament was prevented by the petty politics that blocked a combined Home Nations team. As so often, time-servers in committee rooms imposed their will on those who actually played the game.

The event was marginalised when six qualifiers, Argentina, Egypt, Ghana, Iran, Malaysia and Norway, joined the 66-nation boycott led by the United States in response to the Soviet–Afghan War. They were replaced by invitees, Venezuela, Zambia, Nigeria, Iraq, Syria, Finland and Cuba, who reached the quarter-finals despite losing 8-0 to the Soviets in the group phase.

Children had been sent out of the city, to summer camps, to avoid Western contact. Sullen lines of spectators walked under military supervision to underpopulated venues to bolster crowds. But football, the universal game, was resurgent. A record 1,821,624 spectators watched the 32 matches, despite a lack of quality; that represented 35 per cent of the attendance for the entire Games.

The rest day for the athletics programme ensured that attention was focused on the semi-final, which pitted the Soviets against East Germany. We had become accustomed to the eerie experience of walking from the Metro to the Lenin Stadium through a human corridor of unarmed Soviet soldiers, staring coldly, silently and immovably as if yearning to get their retaliation in first, but this felt different.

Flags flew on a wet evening, but there was little of the colour associated with other set-piece football occasions. A crowd of 95,000 was fused by molten greyness. Their restlessness was tangible, suggesting this was more than a struggle between hosts and holders. The propagandists had done their work effectively; the game was an extension of political tension. Leonid Brezhnev's communist mothership was on collision course with Erich Honecker's satellite state.

State-sponsored 'amateurs' from the Eastern bloc had dominated Olympic football since the Second World War, winning 23 of the 28 medals available between 1948 and 1980. Stalin used football sparingly as a symbol of national potency because of its capacity to cause embarrassment: the authoritarian subtext meant a formidable Soviet team was under huge pressure to succeed.

The 1980 team would have been picked apart on the open market. Rinat Dasayev, arguably the best goalkeeper in the world, played behind a defence that featured Aleksandre Chivadze and Oleg Romantsev. Right-back Volodymyr Bezsonov would play in three World Cups over a 13-year international career. Sergey Andreyev was the tournament's top scorer with five in six games.

Yet its fatal flaw was a lack of creativity, a one-dimensional approach that dictated the shape of a frantic, fast-paced match in which the Germans were content to rely on their defensive discipline under a barrage of high crosses. The Soviets forced 13 corners to their six, and attempted 26 shots, yet were beaten by a 16th-minute goal by Wolf-Rüdiger Netz.

Defeat was regarded as an enduring national disgrace: the team were subsequently jeered and whistled when they secured a bronze medal by beating Yugoslavia 2-0 in the third-place play-off. In what would be the GDR's last appearance in an Olympic tournament, East Germany lost to a solitary goal by Czechoslovakia's Jindrich Svoboda in a final that hinged on the 58th-minute dismissal of their playmaker Wolfgang Steinbach.

Six of that team, including Netz, had played for Dynamo Berlin four months previously, in the European Cup quarter-final against Nottingham Forest. The away leg, at Friedrich Ludwig Jahn Sportpark in East Berlin, was my first foreign trip as a journalist. It required a mandatory introduction to Brian Clough, who, in his pomp, was a mischievous, messianic figure.

I had resolved never to be intimidated by a subject's celebrity. I would respect their status without losing sight of our common humanity. They were, after all, flesh and blood. I had literally road-tested the theory the previous month by interviewing Muhammad Ali in the middle lane of Park Lane. He simply wandered out of the Hilton hotel, stopped the traffic and held court.

A photograph of the moment is above my PC as I type these words. He is smart, white-shirted and tilting his head forward slightly as if trying to hear my words in the scrum. I have a mullet, a juvenile moustache and a striped tie, tightened by a Windsor knot the size of a fist. He was campaigning to be permitted to return from retirement, despite concerns about his trembling hands, the first sign of Parkinson's disease. In my youth, I still believed in invulnerability.

Twenty years later, I was confronted by my naivety. I was in Auburn Hills, Michigan, covering the so-called Showdown In Motown, the craven two-round surrender of Polish boxer Andrew Golota in a heavyweight title fight against Mike Tyson, whose subsequent positive test for marijuana led to it being declared a no-contest.

Ali's daughter Laila headed the undercard, in her eighth professional fight, against Kendra Lenhart. He created the usual human earthquake as he was escorted to his ringside seat on the opposite side to the press benches. Some four years after the ravages of Parkinson's were revealed by his hesitant lighting of the flame at the Atlanta Olympics, it was a heart-rending sight.

Laila would fight for a further seven years and retire, unbeaten, after 24 contests of variable credibility. This would be one of only three of her fights that went the distance, but I have no recollection of her style and athleticism, other than a vague notion of her height advantage. I was, instead, mesmerised by the mute agonies of her father.

Ali literally could not bear to watch. He sagged forward in his seat, and spread his hands awkwardly across his forehead. He looked up only between rounds, when he mopped his brow with a white handkerchief. His legend offered no protection. He was a powerless father, worrying about his daughter.

Boxing, bloody hell.

'My dream is this,' he had said that day in London. 'I love challenges. I love controversy. This is befitting for me to try. I wanna hear the man say after the fight, when I come back, if I come back, "and ladies and gentlemen, four-time heavyweight champion of the world, Muhammad Ali." Can you imagine? Four-time champion? It was a hundred years before Floyd Patterson became the first man to do it twice. I can still dance. I was so supreme and so superior. Only age can make me equal to some people.'

The exchange seemed normal, despite its surreal circumstances, and tragic undertones. Why, then, I reasoned, should I be daunted by a mere football manager? I seized my chance while we waited in baggage reclaim at Schönefeld airport, another symbol, like Checkpoint Charlie, of a divided city. I announced myself with as much confidence as I could muster, and felt myself being drawn into the force field of Clough's personality. All it took was an arched eyebrow.

'Eh, big 'un,' he said, in those clipped tones that become irresistible to amateur impressionists after a pint or ten. 'Bit of advice. Don't be a shithouse. Too many shithouses in your game.' It was another important early lesson in reading between throwaway lines. Had he sensed my malleability? Was he playing up to his reputation? Or was there a more significant message?

Better men than I have been lost in the labyrinth of his mind. Those who loved him were unable to steer him away from the path to self-destruction. Yet the fact his words remain embedded in my brain, and represent a principle to which I have tried to remain true, offers a clue as to why he evokes such warmth and loyalty amongst his former players.

Clough was a master of the unexpected. A notoriously poor flyer, he caused chaos on the tarmac at Madrid airport the morning after Forest had beaten Kevin Keegan's Hamburg in the final that season by insisting on a group photograph with the press corps and the European Cup, in front of the club-chartered aircraft.

He loved us really, when it suited, and used the proceeds from exclusive interviews to buy electric wheelchairs for disabled children. He was loved in return: the Midlands press pack, principally John Sadler, John Wragg, David Harrison, Ray Matts, Dave Armitage and David Moore, were notably protective of him in his later years when alcoholism took hold.

That second European Cup final was another object lesson in his determination to be different to the point of perversity. Peter Shilton's preparations were completed on a traffic roundabout, which Clough decreed was the only suitable grass surface on which he could practice shot-stopping. He insisted John Robertson sit on his knee, like a portly ventriloquist's dummy, during the follow-up press conference.

The title defence reached critical mass in East Berlin because Forest had been beaten in the first leg at the City Ground by a 63rd-minute goal by Hans-Jürgen Riediger, Dynamo's so-called Golden Arrow, who scored 105 times in 193 games for club and country before his career was ended prematurely by a knee injury.

He contributed to the first five of Dynamo's ten successive Oberliga titles between 1979 and 1988, a tainted achievement that focused the hatred of what they represented, as the sporting arm of the Stasi. Erich Mielke, who as Minister for State Security controlled 85,000 domestic spies and 170,000 civilian informants, referred to them as 'my boys'.

Players were given privileged access to housing, allowed to ignore the ten-year waiting list for a car, the two-stroke Trabant, and were permitted to travel abroad. Most were paid at least three times the average worker's wage; those in the armed forces, promoted for good performances, earned even more. Crowds became hostile when they emerged from the team bus eating bananas, a rare luxury.

Team-mates and their coaches were encouraged to spy on one another, across East German sport. Their gold medal-winning rowing eight at the Moscow Olympics was, for instance, informed upon by their Stasi-trained coxswain Klaus-Dieter Ludwig, who acquired the nickname Lucky over 19 years at international level and eventually drank himself to death.

The weight of the state dragged down good men like Jürgen Gröbler, arguably the greatest coach in any British sport over the last half century. His record in rowing is unsurpassed; before surprisingly retiring as Team GB's head coach in August

2020, his crews had won medals, including 33 golds, in every Olympic Games at which they had competed since 1972.

I accumulated huge respect for his methods, though his ruthlessness in selection was increasingly out of sync with the modern trend towards consensus and conciliatory man-management. He took time to teach me the intricacies of his application of sports science, sharing a unique fund of knowledge originally acquired at East Germany's College of Physical Culture in Leipzig.

Having come to the UK after the fall of the Berlin Wall, he was revered by the athletes he transformed into champions, like Steve Redgrave, Matthew Pinsent and James Cracknell. He pushed them physically, imposing intimidating workloads that mirrored his background in the Eastern bloc, and understood their psyches. Trust was hard earned, but reciprocated. His love was tough, but had fleeting moments of tenderness.

Ultimately, though, when his personal Stasi file came into the possession of the *Mail on Sunday*, I had a job to do. I travelled on a rain-lashed morning in April 1998 to the British training camp at Hazewinkel, a lake near Mechelen in Belgium. My mood matched the bleakness of the setting, in which rowers were housed in eight rudimentary huts.

I feared I was about to ruin his life and have never forgotten the alarm in his eyes when, sitting around a small metallic table in an equally sparse cafeteria, he pored over photocopies of hand-written files, compiled by the secret police. They were, as I wrote at the time, largely 'an exercise in bureaucratic mundanity' but the implications were inescapable.

Gröbler became a Stasi informer in July 1974 and reported to two case officers, named only as Ratzl and Schoen. His code name, 'Jürgen', suggested they, too, were functionaries, filling time and forms with artificial zeal. No one associated with rowing was among 113 coaches being investigated by the public prosecutors' office in Berlin but, with allegations surfacing about rowers being administered steroids, maintaining silence was not an option.

Gröbler spoke quietly, in a tremulous tone: 'I know I cannot run away from my past. Some things that were going on at that time might not have been correct, but I can look everybody in the eye and not feel guilty. I am not a doping coach. I am not a chemist. It was my job to bring in medals, but to do that I had to be a diplomat in a GDR tracksuit. You must understand that thousands of people were contacted. I wanted to leave Germany because I wanted to prove I could succeed in a different system.'

No charges were ever brought against him, and context is important. Gröbler was one of 300 coaches and support staff in the GDR's international rowing programme, spread across 15 training centres. He was clever, ambitious and knew his family would be protected by his success. He followed, to the letter, rowing's officially sanctioned textbook, which called for 'comprehensive and systematic basic training' and 'party and class-conscious education of the oarsman into a socialist sports personality'.

Sport was embedded in the system, under Article 18 of the Constitution, as a 'fundamental right designed to serve the all-round physical and intellectual development of citizens', but the Stasi's influence was pernicious. Dynamo Berlin, set up originally for members of the secret police in 1953 and reconstituted in 1966, benefited from unilateral transfers of the best players from rival teams.

Mielke, who advised Franco's secret police during the Spanish Civil War and served Stalin murderously in the Great Purge after fleeing to the Soviet Union, used fear in its most basic form, so that it became self-perpetuating. He had decreed that 'football success will highlight even more clearly the superiority of our socialist order', so referees were terrified into favouritism.

Decisions were biased to the point of absurdity; one Dynamo goal was so obviously scored from an offside position the authorities banned its transmission on national television. A so-called 'penalty of shame' given in Dynamo's favour was so egregious the referee was banned for incompetence in a form of show trial designed to counter the club's reputation as *die Schiebemeister*, the cheating champions.

There would be more sinister implications of influence. Lutz Eigendorf, a Dynamo player who defected after a match in Kaiserslautern in 1979, died mysteriously in a car crash in March 1983. He had been a vocal critic of the East German regime in exile, and security experts concluded the accident was caused by a classic Stasi ploy, of blinding a driver with a bright light. Alcohol was found in Eigendorf's blood, though friends were adamant he had not been drinking.

The stadium at which Forest played, a bowl largely open to the elements, was bordered on its western side by the Berlin Wall and its Death Strip, the no man's land on which would-be escapees were shot on Mielke's express orders. It was a surreal setting and a freezing night; Shilton took the precaution of wearing tracksuit trousers as the pitch hardened.

Clough was swathed in a blanket as he watched from a touchline bench; some of us in a makeshift press box had used hard currency to illicitly buy army-issue hats with padded ear-protectors. Since telephone contact was haphazard, I took the precaution of ad-libbing a running report; fortunately, Forest were three up by half-time.

Ad-libbing is a lost art, as divorced from technologically dependent modern reportage as hieroglyphics. It essentially involved writing verbally, by framing sentences and story structures mentally. Dictating events, from minimal notes, as they occurred was an adrenaline rush; it enabled you to better reflect the rhythms, patterns and emotions of a match. In these circumstances, it was a professional life-saver.

Dynamo, who had begun their period of domestic dominance by winning the East German league by seven points the previous year, had been defeated only once that season. Forest had lost 1-0 to Wolves in the League Cup final on the previous Saturday, but, as so often during that period, proved to be irresistible. No wonder they believed in miracles.

Trevor Francis, criticised heavily for his performance at Wembley four days previously, gave Forest a 16th-minute lead from close range, after Larry Lloyd's free kick had been headed on by David Needham. He doubled the advantage in the 35th, turning sharply before scoring off the underside of the bar. John Robertson's penalty, converted three minutes later, provided sufficient insurance against a successful second-half penalty by Dynamo captain Frank Terletzki.

The world turns. Dynamo now play in the fourth tier of German football, the Regionalliga Nordost, which covers Berlin and the former East German states of Brandenburg, Mecklenburg-Vorpommern, Saxony-Anhalt, Saxony and Thuringia. They have a small, notoriously far-right fan base and have suffered multiple relegations and bankruptcies.

Mielke, their detested benefactor, wielded covert influence all the way to his grave. Arrested following reunification, he was jailed in 1993 for crimes dating back to the infamous Bülowplatz police murders in Berlin in 1931, when he acted as one of two assassins. Accusations of treason and embezzlement were left on file, and he only served two years before being released due to ill health, five years before his death, aged 92, in 2000.

Sports writers are used to jibes about working in the toy department, but the ubiquity of football, in particular, offers the opportunity to help provide a first draft of history. The pace of social and political change over the past 40 years has been profound and though this may seem obtuse, sport has a power to influence the most repressive regimes.

Poland was under martial law for two and a half years from 13 December 1981, when the so-called Military Council of National Salvation flooded the streets with troops, citizens' militia, tanks and other armoured vehicles. More than 10,000 members of Solidarity, the first anti-communist trade union, were rounded up. Approximately 100 were killed in disturbances.

It is sobering to consider that the horrors of the Second World War were as close, to them, as those times are to us today. Borders were sealed. Inter-city travel was forbidden without a permit. Media and postal services were censored. The secret services wire-tapped public telephones and bugged state institutions.

Western journalists were prevented from bearing independent witness, though the BBC's Polish service, alerted unofficially by the Foreign Office, distilled news transmitted through an open international telephone line to Istanbul, and an IBM computer link to Vienna from the mathematics department of the Polish Academy of Sciences. Both channels of communication had been forgotten by the regime's bureaucrats.

It was equally remarkable that something as relatively trivial as the European Under-21 championship should guarantee entry to a closed country. When Poland were drawn against England in a two-legged quarter-final in March 1982, the threat of exclusion from the tournament persuaded the authorities to bow to UEFA's demands that Dave Sexton's team be accompanied by accredited football writers.

I had followed the team as a means of acquiring contacts with players of my age. They were an eclectic bunch, typically full of life, hope and ambition. Fate would not be kind to some of them. Justin Fashanu was a gentle soul, hiding the secret of his sexuality, which would drive him to suicide. Tommy Caton, a precociously talented central defender, would go on to captain Manchester City, but pass away from a heart attack at the age of 30.

Gary Shaw won the league title and European Cup with Aston Villa, and would have been a generational superstar but for a serious knee injury. On the way out to Poland Gary Mabbutt, who was playing in the Third Division for Bristol Rovers, confided he was being courted by Tottenham, who he would captain for 11 of his 18 years at the club.

The tie provided perfect cover for the real reason for the trip, a first-hand account of life in a hermetically sealed nation. Within hours of us landing, local journalists had stealthily provided links to the underground opposition. It was assumed that we would be followed, so a rendezvous was arranged to fit in with a supposed tourist trip to Warsaw's old town on the morning of the game.

The setting, St John's Archcathedral, an ornate Roman Catholic church originally built in the 14th century, was plausible because it had traditionally attracted international visitors in more normal times. It was highly symbolic, since it was where Stanisław August Poniatowski, the last king of Poland, was crowned, declared the Constitution and was eventually buried.

Solidarity activists were waiting in the section of confessionals usually reserved for priests. A small group of us played the role of penitents and conducted our interviews through the central grille. They detailed the brutality of ZOMO paramilitary police, provided lists of prominent detainees and insights into the privations of daily life. Food shortages were tightening; families were struggling.

Tensions bubbled to the surface at that night's match. Spectators bellowed the national anthem, defiantly, at the massed ranks of soldiers and militia, deployed to deter protests at what Lech Walesa, the shipyard worker who had been jailed, as Solidarity's leader, described as a 'great crime that broke the unity of the nation'. It would be seven years before communist rule in Poland ended, along with the Cold War.

Given the weight of history, it almost feels impertinent to record that England, given a tenth-minute lead by Paul Goddard, won 2-1 through a late goal by David Hodgson. Two early goals by Mark Hateley in the return leg at Upton Park maintained a competitive momentum that took England to the title, at Germany's expense in the final.

Football had opened a window on the world as it was, rather than how tyrants wanted us to see it. Never dismiss it, or underestimate its impact. It remains a game without frontiers.

Chapter Ten

Milestones

A TELEPHONE on a formica-topped table beside a narrow wooden bed rang just after 9am in a cold, claustrophobic hotel room in the Polish city of Łódź. It was London calling an hour later than planned, a bonus since I had spent three hours on arrival the previous evening waiting for a connection and fretting over an impending deadline.

Through the static, Christine, my copytaker, gabbled the news that John Lennon had been murdered overnight at the Dakota apartment complex, his residence on New York's Upper West Side. Details were yet to emerge, but Mark David Chapman, a deranged fan, had been arrested by police, who rushed Lennon to Roosevelt Hospital. He was pronounced dead on arrival a little after 11pm, 5am the following day in my time zone.

He had been hit four times in the back by hollow-point bullets fired from a .38 special revolver. Chapman, who claimed to be inspired by Holden Caulfield, the fictional symbol of teenage rebellion in the novel *The Catcher in the Rye*, was eventually sentenced to 20 years to life imprisonment. In late August 2020, as Prisoner 81A2860 at the Wende Correctional

Facility near Buffalo, his 11th application for parole was rejected; he faced a two-year wait to try again.

In an instant, on that frigid morning, 9 December 1980, filing my preview of what appeared to be the formality of the second leg of Ipswich Town's third-round UEFA Cup tie against Widzew Lodz lost its urgency. The prospect of John Wark extending a remarkable run of nine goals in five games from midfield didn't seem quite so earth-shattering.

Forty years on, the shock is easy to summon. The murder of a musician who provided the soundtrack of my generation as it emerged, blinking, into the sunshine of supposed freedom carries historic weight. It was the sort of social convulsion which compels us to remember where we were when we heard of it, and felt its emotional force.

At the risk of sounding shallow, I invariably associate football with many such events of global significance. Like music, art and literature, it evokes a mood. It stimulates memories of a particular time and place. Matches and individuals, teams and tournaments, are improbably aligned to moments of far greater magnitude and importance. It remains a contradiction, a distraction that focuses the mind.

This was an age in which news percolated, rather than cascaded. The World Wide Web was almost a decade away from development. There were few updates to share immediately with curious Ipswich players, who congregated in the hotel lobby as the weather worsened and doubts grew as to whether the match would take place.

The locals were preoccupied with rumours of more immediate significance. Poland, it seemed, was on the verge of being repressed like Hungary and Czechoslovakia. Wire services suggested Soviet tanks were massing on the border, to spearhead an invasion designed to ensure the stillbirth of democracy.

The region's textile industry was in near-terminal decline. Rationing was inadequate; meat supplies would be halved over the next six months, leading to hunger marches in the city that involved 30,000 mothers and their children. Alan Brazil joined goalkeeper Paul Cooper in handing out chocolate to local fans. An enterprising local lad left the hotel with Brazil's cassette copy of The Police's debut album.

The Scottish striker, a trim and bubble-permed version of the bon viveur of breakfast radio, had scored one of Ipswich's five goals in the first leg at Portman Road. Jacek Machcinski, the Widzew manager, had publicly failed in his attempt to entice Bobby Robson into betting on the outcome of the return, which quickly became an unwanted chore.

It was minus 17 degrees Centigrade when Robson's compelling team of contrasting qualities went out to protect a comfortable lead on an unplayable pitch covered with frozen snow. As we ploughed through a distinctive pre-match meal, wild boar casserole, the kit man dislocated his shoulder, twice, ferrying the skips to the venue in an ancient van which regularly slithered into roadside ditches.

The old Stadion Widzewa, which would be demolished in early 2015, was bleak. Only one stand was partially covered; the crowd stood, exposed on wooden benches or on steep unprotected terraces. Most kept warm by necking litre bottles of vodka and baiting soldiers, who responded to a hail of snowballs by waving their machine guns at head height as if they were fly swats.

Such a comical gesture of defending communist orthodoxy carried echoes of the pantomime. International footballers, meanwhile, were doing their best impression of Bambi on Ice. Lodz, who had highlighted football's long-lost meritocracy by beating Manchester United and Juventus in previous rounds, won through a farcical goal by Marek Pieta ten minutes into the second half.

A simple pass between Steve McCall and George Burley stalled in the snow, leaving an unbalanced Terry Butcher out of position. Wark was unable to turn sufficiently quickly to cover on the treacherous surface and Russell Osman's sliding tackle could not prevent Pieta from scoring. It was a career highlight for the future president of the Polish PFA, who succumbed to cancer in 2016 at the age of 62.

The goal prompted Robson to send on Kevin Beattie, whom he described as 'the best English-born player I've ever seen'. Unlike his team-mates, who wore woollen tights and mittens, the Carlisle-born defender, who won only nine England caps in a career ended, at the age of 28, by chronically arthritic knees, strode out in a short-sleeved shirt.

He was immensely strong, deceptively athletic, fast and mobile, with a powerful left-footed shot. He had also been inured to hardship since childhood because of his father's drinking, which often resulted in him and his eight siblings going without food for days at a time. Robson's first act, in signing him as an apprentice in 1970, was to buy him a pair of shoes to replace his father's hand-me-downs.

Modern sports science would have warned Beattie off constant cortisone injections. He broke his arm in the last match of his career, a 1-0 defeat to Manchester City, in extra time of that year's FA Cup semi-final at Villa Park. That cost him a place in the 5-4 aggregate victory over AZ Alkmaar in the two-legged UEFA Cup final; it needed a persistent public campaign to overturn UEFA's original decision not to award him a medal.

He had a difficult transition from the game and was on benefits before becoming a much-loved local radio commentator, but died as a result of a heart attack in September 2018, aged 64. He was subsequently voted Ipswich's greatest player. Fans helped raised £110,000 for a bronze statue in his honour at Portman Road, erected opposite that of Sir Alf Ramsey.

That defeat in Poland was a minor inconvenience. Robson made the team bus wait, so we could file our match reports. Fuelled by Georgian champagne and port, supplied by the Cobbold brothers, owners with cut-glass accents and formidable thirsts who were known to all as Mr Pat and Mr John, we sang Beatles songs on the three-hour, 75-mile journey to Warsaw airport.

I associate another Beatles song, 'Get Back', from the *Let It Be* album, with another world-defining event, the fall of the Berlin Wall on 9 November 1989. It was a rare day without football (I had endured Wimbledon's 1-0 League Cup replay win over Middlesbrough at Plough Lane, which drew only 3,554, the previous evening), so it was possible to follow events in real time on TV.

The sudden sense of freedom was initially overpowering, but gradually replaced by the realisation it was not universal. That night I remembered the defiance and curiosity of jazz musicians I had met in a cellar bar on the eastern side of the Wall, near Checkpoint Charlie. The cheer which rang around the aircraft when the pilot announced we had left Soviet airspace on our return from the Moscow Olympics came back with abrupt clarity.

My thoughts, over the next days, settled on the experience of travelling to Albania, three years earlier, when it remained a closed nation despite the death of one of history's half-forgotten dictators, Enver Hoxha. The memory of that Beatles song being played pointedly as a political gesture seemed suddenly fresh.

The apparatus of repression Hoxha established over four decades was sustained so successfully many inhabitants were unaware of the Wall's fall for months. It was not until 11 December 1990 that the isolated authoritarian regime was overthrown. It had held out for longer than any, apart from that in the Soviet Union. Football, as so often, helped me to join the dots of history.

With only a small number of strictly vetted Catalan journalists given visas, Terry Venables agreed to the ruse of including me as an interpreter in the club's delegation to a first-round UEFA Cup tie against Flamurtari in Vlore, site of a former German and Italian submarine base on the Adriatic coast. It was the start of what would be the last of his three seasons as Barcelona manager.

Derided as 'a nobody' when he succeeded César Luis Menotti, Argentina's chain-smoking, World Cup-winning manager, the future England manager had immediately established his credentials by leading Barcelona to their first La Liga title in 11 years in 1985. Had they won the European Cup the following year, instead of being beaten on penalties by Steaua Bucharest in a sterile final in Seville, he would have been confirmed as a Catalan folk hero.

Instead, in another indication of the infighting that continues to blight the club, such an inglorious failure to fulfil an overpowering ambition proved to be the beginning of the end. Venables, who brought in Mark Hughes alongside Gary Lineker, and eventually allowed the popular Steve Archibald to leave on loan to Blackburn Rovers, was suddenly vulnerable.

He was linked, irrevocably, to Josep Lluís Núñez, a propagandist president who ran the club ruthlessly, as a personal fiefdom. The UEFA Cup was viewed as a second-tier prize; the least Venables could do to give himself a chance of survival was to win it. Unthinkably, Barcelona would lose to Dundee United, the eventual finalists, in the quarter-final.

Fissures were already starting to open when we flew into Tirana, a ghost city in which ox carts trundled down empty Stalinist boulevards. One faction had coalesced around Bernd Schuster, the maverick German midfield player who had been pushed down the pecking order by the arrival of the two British strikers. Another increasingly influential group was quietly plotting to install Johan Cruyff as head coach.

Lineker was utterly at ease in such a new and challenging culture. Media-savvy and sufficiently aware of the conventions of respect that he made a point of learning Catalan, he would score 21 goals in his first season and be celebrated as El Matador. Hughes, by contrast, was quiet and introspective. He felt the weight of the *Blaugrana*, the blue-and-garnet striped shirt.

'This is different,' he remarked sardonically, as the Barca circus rumbled into Vlore, a port that remained a stronghold of the *Sigurimi*, the Albanian secret police. We had made a four-hour coach journey from Tirana, passing parched fields studded with pillboxes and concrete bunkers built in a fit of anti-Soviet paranoia, to an Independence monument for a photoshoot.

It was chaos. Players, posing on steps leading to a stark, triumphalist statue, which towered 55 feet above scrubby parkland, were swamped by local urchins, scavenging for sweets and snacks. I gave one boy a packet of Opal Fruits (Starbursts, kids); his feral look of suspicion as he sniffed the sweet wrappers was replaced by childish glee as he savoured the flavours inside.

The match, played in oppressive heat the following afternoon, was a reciprocal culture shock. Local estimates suggested 15,000 were squeezed into a stadium with a capacity of 11,000. The official attendance was 13,000, suggesting they simply split the difference. The flat roofs of austere buildings overlooking the ground were crammed with hundreds more. Scores hung from third-floor balconies and windows.

When Vasil Ruci, a future Flamurtari manager, volleyed them into a 65th-minute lead, players in the Albanian national colours of red and black ran wildly across a narrow cinder track towards their fans, who were climbing sharp steel fences. It took until the first minute of added time for Barcelona to avoid the calamity of defeat.

Lineker held the ball up on the edge of the box before feeding Manolo, whose side-footed pass into the inside-right channel was finished emphatically by substitute Esteban. Albanian players slumped to their knees in despair; they would play heroically in the return leg at the Camp Nou, and force a goalless draw, but would be eliminated by that away goal.

The Barcelona party, ferried back to the capital for an overnight stay, wound down in the traditional manner in the hotel's basement bar, where we were joined by self-styled 'liaison officers', multi-lingual young men and women who had shadowed our every move. When I congratulated one on his impeccably accented English, he revealed he had learned through listening to the BBC World Service.

We both knew the substance of his admission: he would have required the highest level of security screening to do so. He went further, implying he knew my background by asking my views about the British newspaper industry, and smiled archly when Paul McCartney's familiar lyrics, 'get back to where you once belonged', filtered through the tinny sound system.

I often wondered what became of him as his nation descended into social chaos and economic disarray, exploited by organised crime. His cunning and cynicism probably served him well. As Albania struggled with the collapse of communism, the globalisation of football entered a new, highly commercialised phase with the World Cup in the United States.

That's when macabre melodrama collided with slapstick musical comedy. Where were you when OJ Simpson was declared a fugitive, triggering a televised car chase watched by 95 million in the US alone? I was in the stands at Chicago's Soldier Field, attempting to rationalise the hallucinogenic experience of watching the United States welcome the world through the medium of football and interpretive dance.

Friday, 17 June 1994, was a day for the ages. A former NFL icon, who ended it on suicide watch, crying continually in a cell that measured 7ft by 9ft, revealed the dark side of the American dream. A leaden-footed, lip-synching Motown legend became the unwitting star of a farcical World Cup opening ceremony, trailed as 'majestic, awe-inspired, star-studded entertainment'.

The setting, with the stadium's Doric colonnades set against a cloudless sky, was spectacular. It has a storied sporting history – Bill Shankly visited as an act of homage to Gene Tunney, who beat Jack Dempsey there in the infamous Long Count heavyweight title fight of 1927 – but the tone was set by Oprah Winfrey, broadcasting royalty, who fell off the dais in the act of introducing Diana Ross.

Newly elected president Bill Clinton assured the global audience that 'the love of soccer is now a universal language to bind us all together'. As he added: 'This game represents the unity of all peoples', the band struck up the 'Star-Spangled Banner' and four F16 jets staged a low-level flypast. Hardly understated, but at least he got his lines right.

Not so Ross, who scampered on, in front of a capacity crowd of 67,000. She ran the length of the field through giant balloons, a cascade of confetti and dancers in co-ordinated white costumes and blinding smiles, who were ritually butchering the traditions of Busby Berkley. The singer, who was doing similar damage to the anthem 'I'm Coming Out', faced football's moment of truth.

The ball was on the penalty spot. A goalkeeper crouched unconvincingly on the goal-line, his arms limp and wide. She took a stutter step, which in hindsight owed more to high heels than an ambition to emulate Antonin Panenka, and hooked the ball so far left of the goal it ran out of steam on the way to the corner flag.

That, in itself, was enough for any Bloopers DVD. The crowning glory was the stunt which went ahead, regardless, as she trilled: 'I want the world to know.' The goal frame exploded into two pieces, supposedly as a result of the power of her errant shot, and collapsed. Cue press box hysteria, which inevitably filtered through to TV's global audience through open microphones.

No one, least of all holders Germany, could follow that. The opening game against Bolivia, won by a Jürgen Klinsmann goal on the hour after a rush of blood by 'El Loco', goalkeeper Carlos Leonel Trucco, was instantly forgotten as our attention was diverted by the unfolding dramas on the Los Angeles highway system. Despite that, the launch of the tournament wasn't the dubious omen, or the allegory for American ignorance, many had assumed.

It was the most financially successful World Cup, a corporate plug-fest which broke the average attendance record of 69,000. Crowds totalled nearly 3.6 million, a figure unsurpassed despite the tournament's subsequent expansion from 52 to 64 matches. Team USA, rechristened Team Miracle by Madison Avenue marketeers, were a hot ticket; 93,869 watched a tragically fateful 2-1 win over Colombia at the Rose Bowl in Pasedena on 22 June.

The aftermath of that match, the first US victory in the finals since a Joe Gaetjens goal defeated England in 1950, projected Kipling's Twin Imposters on to a different level. Earnie Stewart, raised the son of an Air Force veteran stationed in the Netherlands, was in tears as he considered the 'once in a lifetime experience' of scoring the day's second goal.

The simultaneous tears of Francisco Maturana, Colombia's manager, were prompted by fear and foreboding. 'We have let everyone down,' he said, sweat forming rivulets from his temples to his chin. 'This is not what people expected of us. Losing is not bad. It is the way we lost that hurts. It's incomprehensible.'

His denials that he had resigned before the match were unconvincing. Midfield player Gabriel Gomez was too scared to attend, having withdrawn from the team two hours before kick-off when death threats were issued against his family in Medellin. His elder brother Hernan, Maturana's predecessor as national manager, had resigned in identical circumstances the previous year.

Released from the golden handcuffs of being obliged to follow England, who had failed to qualify, I had switched to the West Coast, shuttling between Pasadena and Stanford, another shrine to college football, to follow the story of the hosts and Brazil, who would be in a seemingly permanent state of crisis and still win the World Cup for the fourth time.

The cocktail of chaos and criminality was familiar. Romario watched, visibly amused, as reporters swapped punches with security guards in the interview zone, before dedicating his efforts to his father, who had been held for a $7million ransom the previous year. Bebeto, his striking partner, had his preparation for the tournament disrupted by the attempted kidnap of his pregnant wife and brother, who fought off armed assailants.

Little wonder manager Carlos Alberto Perreira, a former psychotherapist, looked in need of therapy himself. 'Thank God I have a good family and I am financially secure,' he said, in the bizarre setting of their training base in Los Gatos, a retirement community. 'Sometimes I say to myself: "Is it really worth it? Do I want to go on?" You have to be a kind of Robocop to do this job.'

Brazil ruined the cheesiest of storylines on 4 July by defeating the US with a Bebeto goal in the last 16 at Stanford. By that time, Colombia's captain Andrés Escobar was dead, shot six times through his back and into his lung, stomach, neck and forearm, as he sat at the wheel of his car behind El Indio nightclub in Medellin.

His murderer's subsequent trial failed to silence conspiracy theories that he had been assassinated on the orders of a drug cartel.

Escobar's own goal in the defeat to the US, the first of his career, was a typical consequence of diligence and desperation, a sinew-stretching attempt to cut out a low cross from the left by American midfield player John Harkes. He was obviously aware of an unmarked US forward behind him, centrally situated seven yards from goal.

His touch, with his right foot, diverted the ball past goalkeeper Óscar Córdoba, whose momentum was taking him towards the far post, away from the source of the cross. Knowing the fatal consequences, I still find it difficult to watch slow-motion footage of Escobar lying on his back, eyes closed and wincing, with his hands across his face.

Yet to those filing running reports for last editions, on a match that kicked off at half-past midnight, UK time, the drama was a stroke of good fortune that enriched the colour of the occasion. Stewart's goal, seven minutes into the second half, offered insurance; this was a notable upset and an early answer to those who doubted the hosts' quality.

The aftermath was harrowing. Watching TV footage of 100,000 mourners filing past Escobar's body as it lay in state on a basketball court was a uniquely uncomfortable process. Reading what was to be his valedictory first-person piece, written in Bogota's *El Tiempe* newspaper on his return to Colombia, remains unbearably poignant.

'Life doesn't end here,' he wrote. 'We have to go on. Life cannot end here. No matter how difficult, we must stand back up. We only have two options: either allow anger to paralyse us and the violence continues, or we overcome and try our best to help others. It's our choice. Let us please maintain respect. My warmest regards to everyone. It's been a most amazing and rare experience. We'll see each other again soon because life does not end here.'

But his did, suddenly and violently. I had stopped referring to any sporting setback as 'tragic' immediately after the Hillsborough disaster, which occurred on the day my second son, Aaron, was born. I couldn't bring myself to go ahead with a planned visit to Anfield, for a Champions League match against Boavista, on 9/11.

Football requires context, care and consideration.

Chapter Eleven

House of Cards

THE EYES had it. They were unyielding, and scanned the first-floor room at 10 Downing Street like those of a hawk, seeking unsuspecting prey in a cornfield. Margaret Thatcher might have applied a smile as carefully as she applied her lipstick, and moderated her tone in thanking us for our presence, but there was no disguising her terrifying certainty.

'If you have any ideas that we're not pursuing please let us know,' she said, surveying nine football writers and broadcasters with a rictus grin that was supposed to reassure. She wanted 'thugs and criminals caught' and 'the stiffest penalties' imposed. She spoke of mobilising 'ordinary, decent fans' and suggested with revealing distaste that 'football used to be our national game'.

When she confirmed her 'blood had boiled', the senior politicians and civil servants who had scurried in her wake as she swept in shuffled uneasily. Images of slaughter in the dilapidated Heysel Stadium were horrifically fresh and shaping public opinion. Headlines, from publications across Europe and the domestic political divide, had yet to become fish and chip paper.

The *Guardian*'s editorial concluded with the demand: 'Quarantine our sad, sick game'. The *Daily Mail* led the front page with a single word: 'BLOODBATH'. Jeff Powell, one of those around the mahogany table on that Friday morning, 31 May 1985, had refused to file a report of the European Cup final on the grounds it was 'a grotesque, macabre and dehumanising experience'.

His colleague, my role model, Ian Wooldridge, wrote: 'Now you and I are the scum of the world and if you do not believe that, just read the newspapers in New York and Munich, Tokyo, Melbourne, Johannesburg, and particularly Moscow. They will judge us by association and if you wish to be associated with what happened, then I don't.'

La Libre, the Belgian tabloid, urged the authorities to 'chase the English from our stadiums forever'. In Italy *Guerin Sportivo*'s front page carried a photograph of a weeping fan cradling a victim's body, over the headline 'Olocausto'. *Corriere della Sera* used the term 'Massacro'. In France, *L'Equipe* mourned: 'If this is what football has become, let it die.'

The hangers and floggers had, as their spokesman, John Carlisle, MP for Luton North, a notorious apologist for apartheid and the tobacco industry. He demanded 'penalties that would impose on hooligans the sort of physical pain that they so readily impose on other people'.

Carlisle unsuccessfully attempted to have me sacked by the *Daily Telegraph* five years later, for writing an eye-witness account of police brutality as a rebel England cricket team flew into South Africa. His paymasters had evidently taken exception to the image I had projected, of blood, shed by defenceless protestors, congealing as it flowed down a marble staircase in the arrivals hall at what was then known as Jan Smuts airport. My editor, former Conservative cabinet minister

Bill Deedes, who gave it front-page prominence, gave him short shrift.

I answered the prime ministerial summons less than 36 hours after 39 fans had perished in the Heysel disaster, as a substitute for Donald Saunders, who covered the final for the *Telegraph*, and had flown directly from Belgium to Mexico for a three-team international tournament designed to assist preparations for the following year's World Cup.

It proved to be an object lesson in the dynamics of power. Despite her icy courtesies, it quickly became clear that Thatcher ran a Tudor court, based upon fear and fluctuations of favour. The manner in which she slapped down Leon Brittan, her home secretary, when he interjected was as enlightening as the way Neil Macfarlane, the sports minister, preened when she praised his prescience in highlighting potential security issues in the build-up to the final.

The brooding figure towards the back of the room exuded authority and an air of menace. Bernard Ingham, Thatcher's press secretary, was a prototypical spin doctor who revelled in the connotations of his nickname, the Yorkshire Rasputin. He would play a pivotal role in Brittan's eventual sacking, and went behind Macfarlane's back to amplify government distaste for the football authorities.

Thatcher went around the table, asking us individually what we would do to combat hooliganism, without straying from the subtext of a *Sunday Times* editorial, written in the aftermath of the Bradford fire, less than a fortnight previously. It described football as 'a slum sport played in slum stadiums increasingly watched by slum people, who deter decent folk from turning up'.

Any attempt to put the problem into a societal and economic context was rejected. Her faith in the ability of 'decent' fans to self-police was continually expressed, without regard for the realities of a toxic environment. Intriguingly, and perhaps unsurprisingly, Cabinet papers would give the misleading impression that we agreed with her arguments.

I descended the staircase, framed by portraits of past prime ministers, and returned to the real world with a profound sense of pessimism. She had a preconceived notion that football fans were, like striking miners, the enemy within. As virtual second-class citizens, they had forfeited the right to trust and respect. They required the closest of monitoring, to the point of being caged.

The FA withdrew English clubs from Europe within 48 hours; it would be five years before a frigid version of normality would return. Football matches were subjected to alcohol bans, increased police powers and a series of ill-designed membership schemes. Official attitudes would harden and Ingham's influence would be felt in the demonisation of Liverpool fans at Hillsborough.

The attempt to dehumanise victims, and undermine their advocates, remains an obscenity. For the sake of relatives like Steve Kelly and Margaret Aspinall, the tragedy must never be tolerated as a rapidly fading scar on society. Cruelly abbreviated lives demand respect and remembrance, even as age wearies the loved ones left to mourn.

Steve, now 67, had intended to cycle from Liverpool to York Minster and Ripon Cathedral on the 31st anniversary of the disaster to light candles in memory of his brother Michael. He was unable to do so until last September because of the pandemic. The candle in Ripon was inscribed with the word 'Imagine', Michael's favourite song.

Michael Kelly was a quiet man. He loved the lyricism of John Lennon, the urban poetry of Kenny Dalglish on the ball in front of goal. Liverpool Football Club was his abiding passion. He worked nights in Bristol as a warehouseman and attended every game, home and away. He loved Anfield, the ritual of football, a couple of pints and home cooking in the family's terraced house in Old Swan.

Steve, his younger brother, was a Blue, an Everton fan. He often joked that 'the only difference between us is the colour of our shirts'. His life changed, irrevocably, when he found Michael's body in a cold church hall in Sheffield. His brother was the last of Hillsborough's 96 victims to be identified. He was 38.

There are still days when Steve can only find peace by visiting the Hillsborough memorial at Anfield, and tracing his brother's name with his forefinger. He is still occasionally seized by an illogical sense of guilt. I have never forgotten the pain in his eyes when he told me: 'There are so many people walking around, with a great weight on their shoulders.'

I sensed he was speaking about himself, and felt similarly speaking to Margaret Aspinall, who, at 69, has retired as chair of the Hillsborough Family Support Group. Her public persona as a campaigner was defiant, resourceful, engaging and optimistic. Yet that sense of duty, of unfailing, unselfish responsibility to others, masked the gravity of her loss and the nature of her sacrifice.

She was haunted that James, her 18-year-old son, could still have been alive when a police officer placed his tunic over his head as he lay on the pitch, before being carried on an advertising hoarding to the gymnasium which doubled as a mortuary. A fragment of memory forced me to look up a particularly poignant interview with her, for an adult education blog from 2013:

'No matter how old you are, when you are dying or you feel you are going to die, the person you ask for is your mum. That's what makes it more heart-wrenching, when you weren't with them, and you think, what was he thinking? Was he saying: "Where are you, Mum?", "Help me, Mum"? "You were there when I took my first breath, where are you for my last?"

'That's the hardest thing a mother can take. That does not take away from the father's feelings – it does not take away from brothers, sisters, grandmothers, grandfathers, what they feel – but I think with a mum, it's different, and it always will be.'

1989 would be Year Zero in terms of breaking football's cycle of decline, but the enduring disgrace of the relatives' subsequent fight for justice warns us against reading too much into the game's gentrification and superficial social acceptance. The 2019 acquittal of David Duckenfield, the match commander, from charges of gross negligence and manslaughter relating to his role in the disaster, was the final insult.

Some things have remained constant. Fans are mistrusted by Thatcher's children, who abandoned the pretence of even-handedness when it came to readmitting spectators to sporting and cultural events after the initial lockdown in 2020. In their class-conscious time warp, football fans remained unworthy, malevolent Neanderthals. The consequences for clubs were catastrophic.

Oliver Dowden, the latest invertebrate assigned to the ministerial cul-de-sac of the Department of Culture, Media and Sport, blithely allowed the arts, and their more genteel constituency, greater leeway. He beamed for the cameras as the Royal Ballet welcomed back audiences. If he was embarrassed that the London Palladium was crowded on successive nights, for a variety show and a promotional evening with Arsène Wenger, he did not deign to reveal it.

He was rightly called out by Rick Parry, who, for all his faults as a manipulative chairman of the EFL, hit the perfect tone in a coruscating letter that accused the government of 'victimising' the game: 'While football grounds in Rochdale, Grimsby, Mansfield & Carlisle might seem an awful long way from Glyndebourne or the Royal Ballet, they are nonetheless equally important parts of our nation's heritage.'

The response was predictably vindictive. The first four tiers of English football were pointedly excluded from the government's £300million winter survival package, announced in mid-November and delayed until the New Year by typical bureaucratic indolence. The plan was ideologically incoherent, intellectually flawed and societally bankrupt. It represented a singular failure of understanding.

Instinctive sympathy with Dowden's recycled argument that, having spent £1.2billion in the previous transfer window, Premier League clubs could afford to look after lesser brethren, would have been reinforced had his administration been consistent in ensuring British businessmen and global corporations, sheltering their cash in tax havens, had acted similarly.

Instead, taxpayers' largesse was distributed roughly along party lines. Boxing, an aspirational working-class sport, was ignored. Rugby union was assigned £135million, despite over-indulged Premiership rugby clubs having a fraction of football's community impact. In an age of shameless cronyism, it was unsurprising that horse racing received a Dido Harding dividend of £40million.

Some athletes are more comfortable than others at being involved in a transactional relationship with politicians that recasts them as court jesters. Kevin Keegan's artless enthusiasm, relentless energy and long-term prominence proved useful to governments of contrasting colours. He pioneered the development of a player's personal brand when David Beckham was a toddler. A prime ministerial photoshoot was another promotional gig alongside a modelling session, a pop song, a TV advertisement or the opening of a shopping centre.

He and Emlyn Hughes posed outside Number 10 to plant a mock kiss on Margaret Thatcher's cheek as she sent the England squad off to the 1982 World Cup, from which she had considered withdrawing them because of the prospect of playing Argentina in the aftermath of the Falklands War. Keegan played head tennis with Tony Blair at the Labour Party conference in 1995, a couple of weeks after welcoming John Major, Thatcher's successor, to St James' Park with a Newcastle United shirt.

Blair regarded his 21-second exchange of 27 consecutive headers with him as TV gold, since 'at last, I have done something to impress my children'. He improbably claimed to be a Newcastle fan who had watched Jackie Milburn play from a seat in the Gallowgate End (Milburn retired when Blair was four, and the Gallowgate was a terrace). That detonated a minefield of tribal sensitivities, but he knew how to use sport for his own ends.

Approached by Steve Cram, the Olympic medallist, I helped to set up a Sports Foundation for Blair in the North East in 2007, immediately after he had stepped down as prime minister. It operated for a decade, and trained more than 6,000 coaches for schools and clubs in ten sports, including athletics, basketball, cycling, tennis, rowing and football.

Its launch was particularly instructive, since it gave me first-hand experience of how a natural politician switches between private and public mode. Blair lit up in the presence of prominent athletes or potential allies; his voice became more mellifluous and he made eye contact in a manner that sought to make any exchange personal and memorable.

The best politicians are hyper-aware of the power of their personality. Bill Clinton's presence electrified Wimbledon's traditional audience of matrons, yummy mummies and middle-class middle managers during a four-and-a-half-hour delay in play in 2001. He caressed their cultural G spots, chuckling at the rain, praising Tim Henman and lamenting his own 'slow and inaccurate' tennis game.

Maybe it was the lingering sugar-rush of community singing led by Cliff Richard, but as the Centre Court purred at his praise for 'the greatest tournament in the world', I had the distinct impression he wouldn't struggle for mixed doubles partners.

In Blair's case, the element of superficiality was balanced by his background work. He had an understandable instinct for organisation, thought incisively and flattered strategically. He appreciated the influence of his reputation and strived to use it positively. He also ploughed £700,000 of his own money into the project, an act which generated unwarranted cynicism.

Being involved in the political process leaves plenty of dirt beneath the fingernails. My best tutor in the ways of Westminster was Richard Caborn, the finest sports minister in recent memory. We worked closely on the establishment of the English Institute of Sport, which has subsequently been seen as a watershed moment in the improvement of our Olympic fortunes.

He taught me the practicalities of his role, explaining that 'as a minister you know the Civil Service will try to kick your ideas into the long grass. The trick is to prioritise four or five policies, and tell them you will make their lives hell if they get in the way.' He protected our backs and shared our frustrations, especially with the ignorance and arrogance of the football lobby.

We pushed the principle of a centralised centre of excellence, in which football would share expertise and intellectual capital on a mutually beneficial basis, nearly a decade before St George's Park was opened with a predictably narrower brief. Caborn took his lumps, most notably his failure to persuade others to build football into the original design of the Olympic Stadium, but was a force for good in difficult circumstances.

Few politicians have the authenticity of allegiance demonstrated by Blair's successor Gordon Brown, whose insistence that 'football is part of every workplace, every street, and every family' reflects a philosophy forged as a Raith Rovers supporter. He began watching them at the age of seven, and helped save the club from bankruptcy in 2004.

Brown can still recite the team he saw in his first Raith game, a local derby against East Fife on New Year's Day 1958: 'Drummond, Polland, Mochan, Young, McNaught, Leigh, McEwan, Kelly, Copland, Williamson, Urquhart.' His touchstones, the sale of boyhood hero Jim Baxter to Rangers, leading Bayern Munich at half-time at the Olympiastadion in the UEFA Cup in 1995 and beating Rangers in the Ramsden Cup final in 2014, are those of a genuine fan.

David Cameron, his successor, failed the sniff test. It is all very well to grandstand before the cameras at a G8 summit, celebrating Chelsea winning the Champions League in a penalty shoot-out against Bayern Munich in the presence of German Chancellor Angela Merkel, but managing to confuse Aston Villa, his supposed team, with West Ham offered minimal wriggle room.

He claimed 'brain fade' since both play in claret and blue, but also fell victim to the politician's curse of a half-forgotten quote, in his case delivered on his entry to the House of Commons in 2001. According to Hansard, which is not in the habit of embroidering members' statements, he reflected that, though many MPs 'are either lawyers or football fans, I have to confess I am neither'.

That such artifice was used as a political weapon against him underlines football's movement into the mainstream. It has become achingly fashionable, almost obligatory, for public figures to profess and parade their affiliations. Yet, for certain politicians in what is becoming a post-truth society, footballers remain convenient distractions or habitual scapegoats.

Matt Hancock, health minister throughout the pandemic, chose the lowest common denominator in the early stages of the crisis by encouraging perceptions of footballers' greed. By insisting they should take pay cuts without referencing others similarly placed in music, the arts, industry, finance or, most pertinently, politics, his thinly veiled contempt proved discordant and untimely.

When it suited a broader political aim, and guilt trips had served their purpose, the professional game was urged to return as a symbol of normality. Dominic Raab, the foreign secretary, went as far as to suggest the resumption of the Premier League would 'lift the spirits of the nation'. The sense of expedience was transparent, and spectacularly missed the point.

Football can lift the mood, personally and collectively, but to inflate its spiritual significance at a time of national crisis is crass and shows a basic lack of understanding. Its joy lies in the simplicity of its reference points, and the privacy of its most satisfying pleasures. It is democratic, in that it can be enjoyed on a park pitch, or in the temples of the professional game.

It offers escapism when the world is crowding in, identity in the midst of anonymity. It is, to use a phrase coined by Arrigo Sacchi, and popularised by Jürgen Klopp, 'the most important of the least important things in life'. As the hapless Boris Johnson was to discover, it also happens to offer the sort of platform that can shake the House of Cards to its very foundations.

Chapter Twelve

Sing Your Own Song

THE FRAIL old man, wrapped in an overcoat and wearing a black fur hat to combat the winter cold, was borne into Soccer City on the back of an extended golf cart. Flanked by six bodyguards, and given additional protection by a seventh who literally covered his back, he smiled widely and waved hesitantly as the high-pitched wail of countless vuvuzelas gave way to an insistent chant.

'Madiba ... Madiba ... Madiba ...'

An historic circle was complete. Nelson Mandela, father of modern, multi-racial South Africa, was making a cameo appearance at his country's coming-of-age party, the 2010 World Cup final. He had made his first formal speech as a free man in the stadium on his release from prison in February 1990. This would be his final major public appearance before his death, and memorial service at the same venue, in December 2013.

The Zulu word, *isipiwo*, destiny, was in vogue. Madiba, to give him the respect afforded by his traditional Xhosa clan name, had successfully used sport as a cornerstone of his nation-building. It was no panacea for enduring inequalities, poverty, political graft and savage rates of crime, but it proved to be a powerful source of collective pride and a compelling symbol of common humanity. Following that process, over two decades, was one of the great privileges of my trade.

As a young lawyer and activist, Mandela enjoyed boxing, but considered sport to be inconsequential to the cause. It took incarceration on Robben Island, and the initial three-year struggle for inmates to be allowed to play football, for him to appreciate the potency of its human chemistry. That the prison authorities compounded his punishment by building a wall in front of his isolation unit, preventing him from watching any matches, merely added to the game's significance.

The Makana Football Association, named after a Xhosa warrior who drowned attempting to escape from his British captors on the island in 1820, ran in several guises from 1966 until the prison's closure in 1991. A nine-club league, with each club fielding three teams in separate divisions, bonded political factions, taught the importance of administrative detail and allowed subtle resistance to their oppressors.

Thirty-minute matches were played on irregular pitches each Saturday. Makeshift goals were created from the flotsam of Table Bay, driftwood and discarded fishing nets. Old car tyres were pummelled into studs, worn on the soles of women's shoes with the heels removed. Inmates were brutalised, broke rocks and barely survived on thin porridge in a regime designed to dehumanise, but had a cherished freedom of athletic expression.

Just as Republican prisoners smuggled hurling and Gaelic football results into the H blocks at Long Kesh internment camp during the troubles in Northern Ireland as a defiant gesture towards normality, slithers of football news from the outside world, distributed surreptitiously by Ahmed Kathrada, another ANC leader serving a life sentence in isolation on B Block on Robben Island, raised spirits and stimulated debate.

Kathy, as he was affectionately known, became a huge Leeds United fan after a cousin secured a subscription to *Shoot!* magazine. He viewed Billy Bremner, one of its columnists, not as a provocative midfield player and captain, but as a leader with revolutionary zeal. He was doubly devastated when Leeds fans rioted following the 2-0 defeat by Bayern Munich in the 1975 European Cup final.

'The news burst upon the prisoners like a bombshell,' he wrote in a heavily censored letter to his cousin. 'We have always thought the English were so polite and even-tempered. Have they changed so much, or have we been wrong all this time in our opinion?' As the years coalesced, and the trickle of external information continued, Mandela realised the effectiveness of the international sports boycott in affecting the psyche of the white ruling class.

My first experience of apartheid, the ill-fated rebel England cricket tour led by Mike Gatting in January 1990, instantly convinced me that normal conventions of journalistic neutrality were not an option. I had been primed by Sam Ramsamy, who organised the anti-apartheid movement from London, and would go on to become South Africa's IOC member.

His introduction to leading ANC activists led to clandestine daily briefings in Johannesburg, conducted from the back seat of a BMW with blacked-out windows. We were assured of our safety during demonstrations because 'the comrades know who you are'. Official resistance was harnessed by human rights lawyer Krish Naidoo, secretary of the non-racial National Sports Congress, who had visited Mandela in prison two months previously.

'We are selling this tour to black people as a symbol of apartheid,' he explained, sitting in a small office dominated by a poster detailing Martin Luther King's 'I have a dream' speech. 'It is all about money. What value is there in cricketers saying they would like to see this system for themselves? If I take them to Soweto and they look at children sleeping on the floor, what is the point of the exercise? Are they going to leave their fees, their 500,000 Rand, for blankets?'

Coaching programmes were collapsing due to the tour's polarising effect. Good people like Zenzele Mabokwe were being compromised. He worked in the Elkah section of Soweto with boys who answered to such forenames as Peace, Justice and Hope. 'We have given these boys a glimpse of a different, better life,' he reflected. 'If we abandon them now, we will be left with bitter, frustrated young men.'

His mood was as bleak as the setting, a dusty expanse littered with broken glass and faeces that served as a football pitch. My mood was hardening. If the blood shed by unarmed protestors on the rebel squad's arrival in Johannesburg was haunting, the first match of their tour, played in the Boer War siege town of Kimberley, was an affront to the notion of human dignity.

Razor wire, protecting the wicket against sabotage, was only removed when Dr Ali Bacher, the tour organiser, argued successfully in the local courts that the match should be allowed to go ahead. He at least offered water to around 2,000 protestors, corralled behind three barricades in temperatures approaching 100 degrees. The mayor, C.J. De Jager, gave each tourist a diamond.

As he pontificated about cricket being 'a game traditionally played by gentlemen', the riot police, over which he had nominal control, were being outflanked. Having prioritised the quelling of associated disturbances in the nearby township of Galashewe, they could not prevent protestors marching on the ground from the settlement at Florianville.

The youths were loud but peaceful, as they paraded outside the wire mesh fences at the de Beers country club, which had been ringed with four layers of barbed wire. During the lunch interval, which seemed a surreal genuflection to colonial convention in the circumstances, I watched a spectator take his son to the edge of the plateau, on which the pitch stood, to survey the scene.

He gestured towards the crowd, which had grown to around 3,000, and bent down to address the wide-eyed boy, who could have been no more than eight. 'Baboons,' he exclaimed. 'Baboons. They're baboons ...'

At that moment, as helicopters hovered overhead, the prospect of apartheid being dismantled and a peaceful transition to decency and normality being completed seemed inconceivable. The sickness in that man's soul, and the doomed innocence of the child, distilled a nation's torment and its unsustainable burden.

Play resumed, with Gatting scoring 75 after coming to the wicket nine minutes into the afternoon session, as police dogs, initially tethered in the shade of acacia trees, were set on the protestors, who scattered as they were peppered by rubber bullets.

Bacher, an essentially decent man who had made a huge political misjudgement, confided: 'I think I've made the biggest mistake of my life.'

Gatting, asked to dwell on the unreality of the experience, beggared belief. 'A few people were singing and dancing,' he said. 'That was it. There was nothing else. We were more concerned about the cricket than anything else.' It was crass leadership, irrespective of the incredible insensitivity of his comments. His subsequent lionisation, as MCC president, can only be seen as a systemic miscalculation.

His players were dealing with worried families in the UK, where television images of the disturbances were damning. The touring party was subjected to passive resistance at their hotel, where waiters refused to serve their meals and maids avoided making up their rooms. Darker elements of the apartheid regime had evidently not been idle: I, and several colleagues, returned to the same hotel to find that our belongings had been disturbed in our absence.

In what we were told was a classic ploy by BOSS, the secret service, our luggage had been dragged into the centre of the room. A piece of clothing, removed from a drawer, was ostentatiously placed over the suitcase handle. They wanted us to know we were being watched: we already knew our first editions were being instantly transmitted back to South Africa.

Football still dominated the back pages in the black press. 'Screamer' Tshabala, a manager whose legend was assured when he fainted in his technical area after a late 40-yard winner by Aubrey 'Sense of Knowledge' Lekwane, was busy reinventing himself as 'the Shoeshine Man' at Mamelodi Sundowns. I assumed he was not being literal when he promised his team would 'burn up the grass'.

Beeld, the leading Afrikaans newspaper, was rather more engaged. I was one of five English writers whose portraits occupied the top half of a broadsheet front page on the morning of the second match in Bloemfontein. Translation of the accompanying opinion column was unnecessary when assorted spectators spat at us; a subsequent scuffle in the press box between rival sets of journalists made a perfect day complete.

The tour was a national embarrassment and a political liability since negotiations for Mandela's release from prison, promoted by the reforming regime of President F.W. De Klerk, were at an advanced stage. It collapsed after a desultory 'Test match' with Gatting, who suggested on arrival that he 'didn't know much about apartheid', admitting: 'I understand a lot more about South Africa now.'

The activists who had outsmarted him were on the right side of history and politically rewarded. Naidoo became principal legal counsel to the ANC, and a trusted presidential adviser. My daily contact during the so-called nuisance campaign, Mthobki Tyamzashe, set government sports policy in the post-apartheid era. He helped organise the Rugby World Cup in 1995, and was a pivotal figure in the unification of South African football.

'Isolation brought home that we could do something through sport,' he reflected when I returned in 1994 to cover the first post-apartheid rugby tour, by Will Carling's England. 'The Gatting fiasco really turned things around. At the time those of us in opposition were just a disgruntled group. That tour bound us together. It made us understand that, together, we could win.'

Mandela's statecraft dominated the following year's World Cup. He and Archbishop Desmond Tutu were standard-bearers of the Masakhane campaign, named after an Nguni word which, loosely translated, means 'working for one another'. I met him at a function for his Children's Fund, and was struck by the contrast between his serenity, which is to be expected of someone treated as a living saint, and his watchfulness in reading the room and those around him.

The force of his example was being felt. I visited Lock Kabane at an adult education centre in Soweto. Ten white policemen had just joined his township rugby club, and were helping with funding. 'I could never before offer the police my heart,' he admitted. 'It was dark with suspicion. I feared them, resented them. They were my enemy. But they came to me and said: "We have changed." That I could not ignore.'

The symbolism of Madiba, in a Springboks jersey and cap, handing over the Rugby World Cup to Francois Pienaar at Ellis Park, the high altar of Afrikaanerdom, was compelling. It was a unifying triumph, celebrated by township crowds who watched on televisions powered by car batteries, but football remained the people's game.

When Chester Williams, a black man excelling in a quintessentially white sport, had been recalled for the quarter-final, the story merited only 27 words in the *Sowetan*, the socially aware tabloid newspaper that took the pulse of its community. The broader significance of the shy, self-effacing winger's selection was deemed secondary to football's daily diet of drama.

Headlines that day were shared between Ephraim 'Shakes' Mashaba, an emerging coach who would go on to have two spells as national team manager, and the fallout from the abandonment of a league game in the township of Sebokeng between Orlando Pirates and Vaal Professionals, whose fans registered their displeasure at some controversial refereeing decisions by staging a gun battle with security guards.

South African supporters still tend to ignore the Marquess of Queensberry rules when roused, but the tinderbox reputation of the Soweto derby, between the Pirates and the Kaiser Chiefs, has been tempered in recent years. Five matches in the fixture have been abandoned, but the days in which visiting referees, such as England's venerable Norman Burtenshaw, were obliged to flee for their lives from vengeful crowds have gone.

I had little option but to become a Pirates fan during my only experience of the fixture, a pilgrimage to Orlando Stadium tacked on to the end of the Nedbank Challenge golf tournament in Sun City. The quality of the football in a 1-1 draw with the Chiefs was as marginal as that of the

Pirates sweatshirt I wore, which subsequently fell apart in the wash.

Its skull and crossbones motif, shared, incidentally, with St Pauli in Germany, was everywhere. The crowd was loud and unsegregated. Although no official attendance was released, it looked, and felt, like about 50,000, 10,000 more than official capacity. Face-painted Chiefs fans were a riot of yellow, topped off with clown glasses, wigs and *mararapas*, decorated miners' helmets.

Vicarage Road, it wasn't. The Den staged tea parties by comparison.

The local version of English football's staple diet, a burger made from indeterminate meat, garnished by stewed onion, was mopani worm, a giant caterpillar which, if it survives, emerges as Gonimbrasia belina, a species of emperor moth. No problem, I reasoned, remembering my survival of a snack of boiled silkworm purchased in a cardboard cone from a street vendor during the Seoul Olympics.

Big mistake. The taste? Think soil, sprinkled with sulphuric acid. If that tempts you out of some warped sense of culinary masochism, think again. My intestinal tract contracts at the memory. Suffice to say I was delighted to discover that Ronald McDonald and his mates had decided to subject the 2010 World Cup to calorific carpet-bombing.

The drawstrings of history were tightened during Africa's first finals, when the nation acknowledged its debt to heroes of the resistance, and simultaneously attempted to rationalise spending $3billion on a football tournament when many of its citizens were still without electricity, modern housing, efficient hospitals and acceptable levels of education. Danny Jordaan, the principal organiser, insists it has a valid legacy:

'There was never money taken away from the delivery of essential services,' he stressed to Reuters, in an interview that coincided with the tenth anniversary of the final. 'We changed the negative perception of the country. There was the sentiment that Africa did not have the capacity and that it couldn't be trusted. We were under so much pressure to deal with the world's negativity, but after the World Cup, we saw a lot of that Afro-pessimism end.'

Realistically, in such a socially sensitive role, he could say little else. The fact remains that World Cups, on every continent, attract white elephants to the corporate watering hole. Cape Town's Green Point Stadium, futuristic setting for the worst World Cup match I have had the misfortune to attend, England's goalless draw against Algeria, is losing £6m a year.

The Moses Mabhida Stadium in Durban, billed as 'a defining landmark to match the Eiffel Tower, Sydney's Opera House or The London Eye', has never made a profit. Its annual deficit, which averages around £4m, would be worse without its greatest attraction, a bungee-jumping platform on the 106-metre arch from which visitors leap towards the pitch.

The national team, Bafana Bafana, failed to progress from the group stage, but had the consolation of a victory over the remnants of the rabble that represented France, the holders. England were put out of their misery by Germany in Bloemfontein, where Frank Lampard's flagrantly over-the-line 'goal' offered a meagre fig leaf to cover Fabio Capello's richly deserved embarrassment.

Even such an enduring controversy seemed to miss the point of the tournament. The deeper meaning of that World Cup lay in the backstory of South Africa's struggle towards multi-racial democracy. Contemporary local heroes, such as the controversially excluded Benni McCarthy, Everton's Steven Pienaar and the Chiefs' Siphiwe Tshabalala, were dwarfed by such political pioneers as Sedick Isaacs, Lizo Sitoto and Tony Suze.

FIFA's kleptocrats loved the symbolism of the involvement of the founding fathers of the Makana Football Association, which had been celebrated in an outstanding book and film, *More Than Just a Game*. Sepp Blatter and Jack Warner, his corrupt vice-president, preened during their photoshoots with them on Robben Island.

The three former prisoners were figures of substance, who accepted their responsibility for testifying to historic injustice. Isaacs, a private man, shaped by the professional disciplines of being a mathematician, educationalist and epidemiologist, posed in Mandela's cell and recalled: 'When you got here, you were no longer a person. You were a thing.'

'Football saved many of us,' said Sitoto, who spent 13 years in exile from 1978 after serving 15 years on the island. 'When you were outside playing, you felt free.' Sitoto passed away in 2012, as did Isaacs. The footballing freedom fighters were fading away, like other generations, from other wars.

Ahmed Kathrada, the avid *Shoot!* magazine reader jailed alongside Mandela as one of the Rivona Eight, died, aged 87, in March 2017, following brain surgery. It was left to Suze, Prisoner 501/63, who died seven months later, aged 75, to fashion their epitaph: 'Unless you sing your own song, the hymn sheet will be buried away. Your history will disappear, no matter how noble it is.'

Chapter Thirteen

Fragile

SPORT IS lived in the moment, but some images are indelible. Their power is invariably generated by a combination of setting and circumstance. They stir the deepest and occasionally the most disturbing emotions. In the case of the beggar performing for scraps outside Stade Municipal in Bamako, Mali's capital, they prompted a profound sense of guilt.

He was little more than a child, 'douze ans' as he told a group of French mechanics from the Peugeot team, with which I was embedded during the Paris–Dakar rally. His name was Oumar. He scrabbled around in the red dirt on all fours; polio had weakened his pelvis so catastrophically it could not support his spine, and he was unable to stand upright.

The disease had made him a social outcast. The World Health Organisation announced its eradication in Africa in August 2020, but back then many destitute polio survivors were physically and mentally abused. Some were shut away in institutions. Oumar existed on the streets. He had a solitary possession, a spongy, scavenged football. It was cradled in a calloused palm before he made a calculated leap of faith that the foreign visitors would not abuse his trust.

He pushed it a couple of feet towards the mechanics and gestured to his head. There followed the most bizarre game of head tennis between them. Oumar's eyes were laser beams; they locked into those of the strangers. A crowd gathered, but I found it difficult to watch since the spectacle demeaned and dehumanised him. He looked like a dog playing catch. I felt complicit.

When it was over, the mechanics emptied their pockets of loose change and energy bars, and promised to meet him early the following morning, when the rally cars would be released from the stadium to resume an 8,000-mile journey from Versailles to the pink lake at Dakar in Senegal, via Algeria, Niger, Mali and Mauritania. They acted in good faith, but it was a promise they were unable to keep.

Extraordinarily, the Peugeot 405 driven by world champion Ari Vatanen, who had built a two-hour lead over 17 days, spent largely in the Saraha desert, was stolen overnight. At 7.15am, Jean Todt, leader of an 80-strong team, took a telephone call in the lobby of the Sofitel, a relic of Stalinist architecture from an era of Soviet influence.

His caller, who spoke in African-accented French, introduced what sounded like a European man, who demanded a ransom of 25 million Central African Francs, around £100,000, for the car's safe return. A meeting place was arranged, but when Todt appeared with as much money as he could muster, the thieves, fearing a trap, failed to show.

By this time, as dawn broke, Bamako echoed to the screech of police sirens. Vatanen, besieged by TV crews, was understandably aghast. 'Tell me we're in a movie,' he implored. The car, hardly inconspicuous since it was a garish yellow, was found some two hours later on open ground on the outskirts of town, next to a junkyard.

The Finnish driver arrived at the start line with minutes to spare, only to be told he faced disqualification because rules dictated that all cars had to be available for scrutiny half an hour beforehand. He drove under protest, passing 120 cars on a manic sprint through the dust to another football stadium, the Chinese-built Stade Olympique in Nouakchott, Mauritania, where, the following day, he was thrown out of the rally.

The intrigue did not end there. It was initially assumed, but never proved, that the car had been stolen as part of a vendetta between Todt and Jean-Marie Balestre, an autocratic former member of the French SS who ran motorsport's global governing body, FISA. It was several years before Vatanen admitted he had learned it was the work of mercenaries, former French Foreign Legionnaires.

I had got to know him during the early stages of the rally, when we camped in the desert. The big skies and sense of isolation suited his philosophical nature. He reminded me of Ayrton Senna: his spiritual sensitivity, shaped by tragedy and supressed vulnerability, was at odds with the competitiveness that allowed him to win the Paris–Dakar four times.

He was not expected to survive a crash at 120mph in Argentina in 1985, in which he fractured vertebrae in his back and neck, crushed his rib cage, punctured his lung and had his right knee compressed so badly it was almost flat. His blood pressure plummeted. He was delirious. His skin turned blue and then grey. 'I was,' he admits, 'living from second to second.'

Todt described his hospital ward as 'couloir de la mort' – death row.

Physically, he faced 18 months' painful rehabilitation. Mentally, he struggled to live with his demons. He became deeply depressed, seized by an illogical obsession that he had contracted AIDS through blood transfusions, infecting his family. He drew incremental strength from his faith and his gradual acceptance of fate before he 'emerged from my nightmare'.

In later years, when his defiance of convention led to him accepting me as his co-driver on the RAC rally, he would often reflect that 'the beauty of life is its fragility'. He had come to terms with its cruelty, using his father, who died instantly in a head-on car accident when he was aged eight, as a point of reference. The irony that his father was driving to a funeral that had, it transpired, been held the previous day, was instructive.

Vatanen 'learned a lot about humanity' in Africa and campaigned for social causes as wide as climate change and Down's syndrome awareness in his subsequent ten-year political career as a member of the European Parliament. He understood the contradictions of his life because he rationalised its insignificance.

He returned to the Dakar rally, despite understanding the logic of criticism led by *L'Osservatore Romano*, the mouthpiece of the Vatican, which condemned it as 'a vulgar display of power and wealth in places where men continue to die of hunger and thirst'. I struggled with my conscience, too, because the human cost was too onerous.

The death of three competitors that year was in keeping with the macabre reputation of the race, which had cost 17 lives in the previous nine years. Three more deaths, caused by passengers leaping from the Dakar to Bamako train after it was engulfed by fire, were attributed by local police to a rally team cooking breakfast next to the track.

Three further fatalities were haunting. Baye Sibi, a ten-year-old girl, was killed in the Malian town of Kita when struck by a rally car as she attempted to cross the road in a cloud of dust thrown up by the preceding competitor. A mother and daughter died in Mauritania on the rally's penultimate day when they were knocked down by a film crew's vehicle.

Thierry Sabine, the event's founder, had been killed in a helicopter crash, travelling to a football match in Mali two years previously. The *Economist* suggested annual expenditure on the rally was in the region of $100million. The costs, human and financial, could not logically be justified given the poverty of its setting. Shaped by Gallic machismo, and transmitted to a global television audience of 600 million, it had the air of imperial indulgence.

Vatanen, a compassionate man who supported a school for African children suffering from birth defects, tried hard to negotiate the moral maze. 'We need to do unreasonable things in life,' he insisted. 'If we only do reasonable things, humanity will start to go backwards. We need to do unreasonable things, to push the limits. We have to exceed ourselves.'

Sport reflects the imperfect world in which it is staged. In many aspects, it is a by-product of colonialism, whether that involves the arcane Victorian rituals of cricket being transplanted on the Indian subcontinent or the spread of football throughout Africa by French settlers. Mali is a case in point; football, a national obsession, was introduced in what was then French Soudan early in the 20th century.

The first organised leagues, open to Africans, were established in the 1930s. The most prominent club in the initial wave, Jeanne d'Arc du Soudan, was formed by the missionary Révérend Père Bouvier just before the Second World War. It was a mixed-race team also known as Bamako Métis, after the French term for 'mixed-blood' – which played exclusively against white colonial sides.

According to the Soccerway research site, Malian players were playing professionally in 54 nations in 2020. A bloodline can be traced, across half a century, from Salif Keita, the first Malian to be voted African Footballer of the Year, in 1970, to the Wolves forward Adama Traore, who followed colonial convention last October by ignoring his Malian parentage and opting to play for Spain, his birthplace.

No nation defines itself through football with greater zeal than Brazil, where – despite the rival claims of Thomas Donohoe, a Scottish expatriate who staged a six-a-side match in the Rio suburb of Bangu in 1894 – Charles Miller is generally regarded as its founding father. Son of a Scottish railroad engineer and a Brazilian mother, he was born in Sao Paulo in 1874, and sent to England to be educated at the age of ten.

He spent a decade in Southampton before returning with two footballs and a book containing the 13 rules of the game. A good enough centre-forward to have already played for St Mary's Church of England Young Men's Association, forerunner of Southampton FC, he organised what is widely considered to be the first official match in Brazil, between teams of British workers representing Sao Paulo Railway and the Gas Company, on 14 April 1895.

The rest, as they say, is history.

It seems somehow appropriate that Brazilian football is habitually careless with its greatest assets. Garrincha, a genius, drank himself into an early grave. The Maracana fell into such disrepair that a stand collapsed during a final between Botafogo and Flamengo in 1992, killing three fans and injuring 50 others. When I made a personal pilgrimage three years later, capacity had been reduced from 130,000 to 40,000. It had the air of a looted palace.

It was fully restored before the 2014 World Cup, which was billed as a return to football's spiritual home. In seeking to celebrate *futebol*, the fusion of racial harmony and artistic expression captured by the classic book of the same name by Alex Bellos, symbolism was overplayed to the point of cliché. You couldn't move on Copacabana without tripping over TV and radio reporters describing the culture of beach football in Rio as if it was a ritual enacted by a lost tribe.

Away from the beaches, in the badlands of the Amazon basin, the familiarity of football is used as shorthand to illustrate the rate of deforestation. More than 24,000 square miles, the equivalent of 8.4 million football pitches according to the Royal Statistical Society, have been cleared over the past decade. It was there that the game spoke most surprisingly to me.

I was competing in a four-man British team in the Camel Trophy, a 1,100-mile rally along disused jungle tracks that took us from the municipality of Alta Floresta, where its founder, Ariosto da Riva, fought a 12-year running battle with prospectors who poisoned local rivers with mercury, to Manaus, Amazonia's largest city.

The $300million folly of the Arena da Amazônia was built in Manaus, and rapidly abandoned a generation later. I saw football in its most primitive state, in violent, anarchic goldfield settlements like Castello dos Sonhos, where barefooted children played with a hand-fashioned rubber ball in the main street on which the bodies of two men had been dumped overnight.

They had made the fatal mistake of attempting to rob a truck driver, who shot them with the wooden-handled Colt 45 he kept in his cab for such eventualities. Life was cheap in the frontier town, into which 4,000 people had flooded within a month of gold being found nearby. The driver's daily rate for logging activities was five grams of gold a day, paid in advance.

The settlement's owner demanded 15 grams from each prospector, mainly young men with tired eyes and mud-stained faces, for the use of rudimentary wooden shacks. In the equally basic bar, where miners drank vodka from the bottle and watched football from the Rio and Sao Paulo leagues on a grainy television, they approved of the simplicity of vigilante justice.

Amazon Route 163, the only supply route, resembled a First World War trench and stank of decay. Cloying, caramel-coloured mud was up to three feet deep in places. Yet when the sun touched the jungle canopy, and parrots flew noisily through gently ascending mist after torrential rain, it had a stark beauty.

Such an event would be inconceivable today, when the reality of climate change is inescapable. With rainfall levels reduced by 40 per cent, scientists warn that the rain forest is reaching a tipping point, where it will evolve into a savannah-like mix of woodland and grassland. A 60 per cent increase in fires in the Amazon in 2020, compared to the previous year, testifies to the accelerating rate of destruction wrought by loggers and ranchers.

Nothing prepares you for the extent of man-made damage to virgin rain forest. Cresting a hill, to see a denuded valley, in which goats gnaw at the scorched earth around blackened tree stumps, is a reminder of the unsustainable price of supposed progress, enforced by illegal land-grabbers and excused by avaricious politicians. I summon the image and feel an urge to apologise to my children, and their children.

Something as transient as football should feel insignificant in such circumstances, yet I lost count of the number of pitches I saw in indigenous villages, through which we passed on the way into Manaus. Away from what passes as civilisation,

Brazil's biggest derbies are a collective experience. Since there is no electricity, gasoline-powered generators fire up a communal television set and the village sits down to watch.

The derbies reflect the nuances of a nation of 200 million people. Flamengo against Fluminense captures the colour and clamour of Rio. The rivalry between Palmeiras and Corinthians, clubs with Italian and English influences, reflects the combustible nature of life in Sao Paulo. The so-called Grenal, between Grêmio and Internacional in the southern city of Porto Alegre, is closer in spirit to the psychodrama of Argentinian football.

Back in Rio, I met a sad old man for whom only one derby mattered, Charlton Athletic against Millwall. Ronnie Biggs, the Great Train Robber, was scratching a living selling a tired story to curious tourists. $15 bought entry to a barbeque at his apartment, where assorted tat, t-shirts and coffee mugs bore his name and his face, creased by what he probably imagined was an inscrutable smile.

He was inordinately proud that he was once visited by Stanley Matthews, and claimed to have seen goalkeeper Sam Bartram play at the Valley in the twilight of his career. He spoke fondly of former players like Billy Kiernan, a long-serving left-winger, and Eddie Firmani, who had three spells at the club before becoming manager. His homesickness was tangible.

His son Michael, a musician to whom he owed his freedom due to a legal twist of fate, was a peripheral presence. He accompanied his father to England when he gave himself up to the British authorities, and spent five and a half years, between June 2007 and January 2013, as a self-styled football consultant, bringing young Brazilian players over to the UK and Europe for trials.

Biggs died at the Carlton Court Care Home in Barnet on 18 December 2013, aged 84. He was cremated on 3 January the following year, after being given a guard of honour by Hells Angels. A Charlton Athletic scarf was draped over his coffin. It was tempting to believe football had been a constant in his life, but to be brutally honest, I didn't believe a word he said.

Chapter Fourteen

In the Arena

*'It is not the critic who counts; not the man who
points out how the strong man stumbles, or where
the doer of deeds could have done them better.
The credit belongs to the man who is actually
in the arena, whose face is marred by dust and
sweat and blood; who strives valiantly; who errs,
who comes short again and again, because there
is no effort without error and shortcoming; but
who does actually strive to do the deeds; who
knows great enthusiasms, the great devotions;
who spends himself in a worthy cause; who at
the best knows in the end the triumph of high
achievement, and who at the worst, if he fails, at
least fails while daring greatly, so that his place
shall never be with those cold and timid souls
who neither know victory nor defeat.'*

ON LEAVING the US presidency, Theodore Roosevelt spent
a year hunting in Central Africa. He then toured Egypt, and
visited Berlin, Naples and Oxford before giving the speech of
his life at the Sorbonne in Paris on the afternoon of 23 April

1910. He entitled it 'Citizenship in a Republic' and dwelled on his family history, the lessons of war, human rights and the debasement of society by cynicism. Along the way, he defined an eternal sporting truth.

The section of his speech, which came to be known as 'The Man in the Arena', prompted wild applause from an audience of 3,000, which, according to his biographer Edmund Morris, included 'ministers in court dress, and army and navy officers in full uniform'. Down the years, I've seen Roosevelt's words reproduced in the offices of countless coaches, in corporate boardrooms, dingy gyms and locker rooms suffused by the smell of stale sweat.

The passage was quoted in Richard Nixon's resignation speech, and given by Nelson Mandela to Francois Pienaar, the Springboks captain at the 1995 Rugby World Cup. It was even partially reproduced in a three-line tattoo on the left forearm of Miley Cyrus, the professional wild child who, in her latest incarnation, identifies as a pansexual, pescatarian popstar.

The sentiment Roosevelt expressed is powerful and perpetually relevant, since it confers the power of unqualified respect on the athlete. It puts privileged observers of great deeds, hollow victories and crushing failures in their place. It balances excess, because it refocuses on the human qualities required to flourish in an occasionally inhuman environment.

We take the remorseless physicality of rowers, the reckless durability of rugby players, the obsessive perfectionism of professional golfers and the casual courage of jump jockeys for granted. The binary nature of life for those in the arena – win or lose, earn or starve, kill or be killed – discourages concentration on anything but the outcome.

Innocence dies hard, but it has its limits. Mine was reached at 3.40am on Tuesday, 27 September 1988, when telephones began to ring in the Press Village at the Seoul Olympics. The biggest sports story of the 20th century, Ben Johnson's positive drugs test following the dirtiest race in history, the 100 metres final on the previous Saturday afternoon, had broken.

It is an exaggeration to say I was in prime condition, having just returned from a birthday party for the *Daily Mail*'s Ian Wooldridge in the entertainment district of Itaewon. It was a rare night off, and the magnitude of the scandal was literally sobering. We were on Monday evening's first edition deadline in London; as presses paused, I was obliged to ad-lib a 1,500-word commentary on the implications.

Working on instinct and adrenaline in such a situation is the closest my trade gets to an out-of-body experience. It is a strange, almost mystical process that involves succumbing to the moment. You have no idea where the thoughts, which translate into words and sentences, are coming from, or whether they will form a cogent argument. Blind trust and blind terror decide your fate.

Ken Mays, the *Daily Telegraph*'s formidable athletics correspondent, had just gone to sleep. He ran naked around our communal flat in a blind panic when roused, but filed for second edition after being thrown into a shower. Elsewhere in the complex, friends became lifelong enemies; certain colleagues were allowed to sleep, undisturbed, by those who wanted the story for themselves.

Though no punches were thrown to the best of my knowledge, the victims' fury at their betrayal was plain and easy to appreciate. I did not see my bed for 48 hours, and have never since trusted an athlete's profession of virtue or suggestion of persecution, regardless of their nationality. In case you were wondering, a Team GB vest does not confer moral credibility.

Track and field, once emblematic of purity, has been marginalised by understandable doubts about the validity of performance. Those doubts, too, cloud cycling. They are spoken of in whispers in many sports, including football. They scour the spirit and invade the brain. I have consoled Olympic rowers and swimmers as, taunted by the assumption they had been denied a gold medal by chemically enhanced cheats, they shed bitter tears.

I lacked their talent and capacity for punishment, but wanted to experience their life in the arena. It has provided some of my most enriching experiences, but has not been without cost. The outcome of my involvement, in a stillborn attempt to break the round-the-world sailing record in a revolutionary catamaran named *Team Philips*, is a source of enduring regret.

The project captured the idealism and vaulting ambition of the Millennium celebrations. It was built over two years, using locally recruited staff, at Totnes in Devon, where 1,200,000 people visited an interactive Challenge and Adventure centre. A crowd of 60,000 saw us lower the carbon-fibre boat into the River Dart on 4 March 2000, ten days before she was officially named by the Queen in a ceremony at Tower Bridge.

I had already competed in a round-the-world race with Pete Goss, the skipper, and Andy Hindley, his right-hand man. We were part of a six-man crew, saddled with a huge sense of expectation. The catamaran, in the words of designer Adrian Thompson, 'was more like a fish than a Formula One car' and looked like a nautical version of the *Starship Enterprise*. It was larger than the Centre Court at Wimbledon and had twin masts the height of ten double-decker buses.

Our fatigue was monitored by a globally renowned sleep expert, Claudio Stampi of Harvard University, who advised NASA astronauts. Our food was freeze-dried and carbo-loaded.

Our fitness programmes were designed by Bernie Shrosbree, who worked with racing drivers like Jenson Button. Only fate was out of our control.

I was at the helm on a two-man watch with Andy just after dawn on 29 March in relatively calm seas off the Isles of Scilly. We were travelling at a gentle 17 knots. A loud bang signalled that a 45-foot bow section of the port hull had sheared and was breaking off. Helicopter footage of the subsequent rescue attempt was carried live on TV, and photographs featured on many of the following day's front pages.

Extensive repairs were made after a review of computer modelling by the design team, but in October, on a second sea trial in the Atlantic, with the aim of reaching New York, the windsurf-style masts began swaying alarmingly due to problems with the innovative bearings which supported them. I was faced with a definitive dilemma.

I had a young family to think about, and suspicions that the repairs would be rushed, to meet the deadline of a race that began from Barcelona at the stroke of midnight on 31 December, to rationalise. I knew also that, because of my role as columnist on the *Mail on Sunday*, the hardest decision of my life would be the most public.

I announced my resignation through the newspaper, and explained my reasons in an understandably tense face-to-face meeting with the crew. I had challenged a sacred convention of loyalty. I had no problem with personal risk, but felt that a line was in danger of being crossed unnecessarily. Since my departure created a stir, Pete had every right to respond in kind.

An article under his name began: 'It's not every day that you wake up to find your project on a platter with your head in its mouth, all coated in a rich and emotive glaze laced with words such as cursed, madness, obsession and risk to life. As with most things in life it's all about perception. Mine happens to differ with Mike's.

'It is always hard to face up to one's personal truths. Many drift through life without doing so and the truism that "it takes a big man to say no" is one that has always had my deepest respect. In a sense Mike and I are both right and have the courage to stand by our convictions. In my case, this is not with blind regard for the consequences.'

Team Philips was abandoned when it began to break up in a freak storm in the mid-Atlantic in December. Pete and the crew leaped to safety, on to a German freighter alerted by the Mayday call, and were taken to Halifax, Nova Scotia. Part of the accommodation pod was detected six months later, floating off the southern coast of Ireland.

The most significant discovery, a section of one of the hulls, was found adrift, south-west of Iceland in June 2002, and taken to the Vestmann Islands. I visited the volcanic outcrop with sailmaker Graham Goff; the wreckage featured the names of hundreds of supporters, who had helped with fundraising, and had the feel of a broken gravestone.

It was eventually retrieved, and became the centrepiece of an exhibition at the National Maritime Museum. Though time healed to a degree, my friendship with Pete, someone for whom I have implicit respect, has never been the same. In a strange way, it helped me to realise that athletes across the sporting spectrum are components of calculable value in a global business model.

Many questionable things are done in their name, sometimes without their knowledge, but just as often with their active co-operation. When confronted by evidence of the ills that surround them, the temptation is to excuse, rather than reproach. How often do we blindly repeat the mantra 'great game, shit industry'?

Boxing is compelling, partly because of its contradictions. It features the worst aspects of human nature, as demonstrated by exploitative promoters and verminous camp followers, but is validated by the authenticity of the athlete. A fighter's career, even as a multiple champion, is a collage of suspicion, sacrifice, pain and punishment. Many come from damaging backgrounds, which instil a sense of desperation. Imperfections in character are common, without necessarily being definitive.

Most are treated like pieces of meat. Tony Tucker was a joint venture company, Tucker Inc., when he fought Mike Tyson to unite the heavyweight titles in 1987. A 10-1 underdog as holder of the inferior IBF belt, he managed to survive the full 12 rounds, despite covertly boxing with a broken right hand, damaged in training. When he left the ring, battered and bruised, his problems multiplied.

Cedric Kushner, his former promoter, immediately claimed 18 per cent of his $1.9million purse. Investors Josephine Abercrombie and Jeff Levine also took 18 per cent. Their silent partners, Dennis Rappaport and Alan Kornberg, were owed 13 per cent. Trainer Emmanuel Stewart was paid 6 per cent. Grotesquely, Bob Tucker, his father and trainer, had a 12 per cent share in him.

Bob Tucker was a rambling, incoherent figure when British writers visited his hotel room in the build-up to the fight at the Las Vegas Hilton. He interrupted his unstructured accusations of financial villainy several times to visit the toilet, from which he re-emerged blinking and sniffing. We exchanged knowing glances; it duly transpired that Tony, who had spoken self-deprecatingly of himself as 'the invisible champion', shared his father's cocaine habit.

Worse was to come. Bob had secretly sold 150 per cent of his stake in his son to other investors, who were disinclined to wait for their money. The US tax authorities relieved Tony of what remained of his purse. He had, in effect, been beaten up for nothing; his strength of character, in avoiding penury, overcoming his drug habit and making a sufficiently successful comeback to lose another title fight, against Lennox Lewis more than six years later, was extraordinary.

The colour of the circus, created by cartoonish malevolence, desperately concealed vulnerability and street wisdom, attracts the best of my trade. As the great Ed Schuyler Jr, who covered his first title fight for Associated Press in 1963, said: 'If you can't write about boxing, you should be selling shoes. It's a writer's sport. Because the material is so rich, the stories write themselves.'

I wasn't fit to carry the spit bucket for writers and reporters of the quality of Hugh McIlvanney, James Lawton, Ken Jones, Paul Hayward, Donald McRae, Kevin Mitchell, Colin Hart and Steve Bunce, but bluffed my way around the ring from the mid-Eighties. With Tyson's psychodrama and sagas involving Marvin Hagler, Sugar Ray Leonard, Roberto Duran and Thomas Hearns, blandness was impossible.

The madness of the environment was occasionally contagious. Such subterfuge would be impossible today, given the shackles applied to those on the online chain gang, but, covering one particular Tyson title fight, I was among several writers who filed copy in the name of a magisterial colleague, who went missing in the build-up.

He was eventually found, after a two-day search, in a bar on the edge of the desert, dancing the samba with a lady of a certain vintage who evidently could not believe her luck. The precise details of what went on in Vegas stayed in

It begins with a ball. Me, aged 20 months, with my first football.

Hidden heroes. Royal Marines football team, 1945/46 season. Olly Goss, my father-in-law, is seated to the left of the manager, whose cane signals his authority.

Look at their faces. Just look at them. Barry Endean has just scored Watford's winning goal against Liverpool in the 1970 FA Cup quarter-final, when I was ball boy. See what it means to fans of all ages.

Watford's win forced Bill Shankly to break up his first great Liverpool team. He was so in love with the game he played Subbuteo in his living room. That love was not reciprocated.

Saturday Night's Alright for Celebrating. Elton John, Graham Taylor and the Watford team that had just clinched runners-up spot in the First Division, five years after being promoted from the Fourth.

Funeral for a Friend. Two mourners pay their respects to Graham Taylor, who galvanised a club and a community, without being treated with appropriate respect by the country.

Pinch me. High class ringers in this press team in Switzerland. Two future England managers, Terry Venables and Howard Wilkinson, line up alongside a childhood hero, Bobby Charlton, who scored the winner with a trademark thunderbolt.

Brian Clough in his pomp, insisting on posing with the European Cup, retained by Nottingham Forest the previous evening in Madrid, and the hack pack. I'm centre shot, alongside Billy Wright, England captain in three World Cups.

The Greatest. Muhammad Ali stopped the traffic by walking out of the Hilton hotel and holding court in the middle of Park Lane. I'm not sure he was entirely impressed by my line of questioning.

Mike Tyson after a sparring session at Johnny Tocco's gym in Las Vegas. He provided compelling copy, though he was so soft-voiced we had to lean forward to confirm the quotes.

Politics, power plays and paranoia. The Opening Ceremony of the Moscow Olympics, my first, set the tone for an ideologically-driven demonstration of state supremacy. Idealism limped in a distant last.

Eyes of an owl, instincts of a shark. Margaret Thatcher confirming her prejudices in the immediate aftermath of the Hillsborough disaster. Her credo, that football fans deserved to be treated as second class citizens, endures.

Morning suits, a vintage Roller and champagne: the only way to cover the Melbourne Cup, the horse race that brings Australia to a standstill. My journalistic hero, the Daily Mail's Ian Wooldridge, is flanked by Allan Forrest of the Financial Times and Alan Hubbard of the Observer.

Another form of homage to Woolers, waiting to follow in his sled tracks down the fearsome Cresta Run. The boot temporarily protecting me from potential oblivion belonged to Adolf von Ribbentrop, grandson of Hitler's Foreign Minister.

What we couldn't see in the press box, high up in the Azteca Stadium. The left hand of God, employed by a flawed genius.

When football really was a matter of life and death. I avoid using the term tragedy in sport, but this own goal against the US in the 1994 World Cup, which indirectly led to the murder of Colombia's Andrés Escobar, fully merits the description.

Vegas. Suffice to say he was on parade, suited and booted, on fight night.

The time difference, in Nevada's neon-lit purgatory, took a sledgehammer to time clocks. Writing became a largely nocturnal activity; we tended to convene at around 4am, after filing to London, in the Flame, a bar populated by off-duty croupiers, cocktail waitresses and the deans of US boxing journalism, Pat Putnam, of *Sports Illustrated*, Dave Anderson, of the *New York Times*, Mike Katz, of the *New York Daily News*, George Kimball, from the *Boston Herald*, and Schuyler.

Putnam, who made his name by breaking the story of Muhammad Ali changing his name from Cassius Clay, was a master of the one-liner, with a sense of mischief that extended beyond his death, following stomach surgery, in November 2005. I became aware of his legend in 1987, when he enlivened a press conference at Caesar's Palace prior to Leonard's fight against Hagler.

Promoters insisted there should be no questions relating to Sugar Ray's recent eye surgery, but as the principals settled on the podium, Putnam yelled from the back of the room: 'Ray. How many fingers am I holding up?' Even Leonard laughed. Wiseguys tend not to be tolerated, but he was given due deference as a writer who had been compared favourably to A.J. Liebling, the *New Yorker* columnist who coined the term 'the Sweet Science' to summarise boxing's 'heroic transactions'.

Putnam was already assured of respect as a Marine veteran, left with one lung and chronic back problems following 17 months as a prisoner of war in Korea. He spoke regularly of two tours of duty, during which he was awarded four Purple Hearts and a Navy Cross. As late as 2008, three years after his death, he was being hailed as 'rawhide-tough' in a fulsome tribute in the *Philadelphia Daily News*.

The piece attracted the attention of the POW Network, set up by Mary and Chuck Schantag, a Vietnam veteran permanently disabled when he set off grenades on a Vietcong officer's belt during hand-to-hand combat during the Tet Offensive in January 1968. Using Freedom of Information requests to investigate Putnam's claims, they discovered he did not exist in Marine Corps archives or in any medals database.

His wartime exploits were a fantasy. The exposure led to him being denied a place in the International Boxing Hall of Fame, a travesty given his empathy with fighters developed during 40 years devoted to detailing their rituals and raw courage. The sport's traditionally tenuous relationship with the truth made the moralising even harder to take.

Boundaries blur easily in boxing. Mike Marley has spent the last 25 years as an attorney. His law practice in New York specialises in defending those accused of 'drunk driving, homicide and manslaughter, drug and gun charges, robbery, grand larceny and sex crimes'. Having founded the International Cassius Clay Fan Club at the age of 12, he was boxing correspondent of the *New York Post* when we first met.

He crossed the floor to work for Don King Productions, for whom he handled Tyson's public relations, and then managed a small stable of fighters, including world champions Shannon Briggs and Terry Norris. That sort of CV is the equivalent of juggling nitro-glycerine while suspended on a high wire strung across the Brooklyn Bridge.

In 2020, King and Tyson re-emerged as boxing's undead. King, the former Cleveland numbers racketeer responsible for the death of two men, had lived in relative obscurity in Florida for a decade, after acquiring a $150million fortune as a promoter, before, at the age of 89, he proved he had lost none of his capacity for lucrative disruption.

The vehicle for his attempt to destabilise the heavyweight division was a postponed fight between Trevor Bryan, holder of a confected 'interim' WBA title, and Christopher Lovejoy, a 36-year-old who had previously fought only one opponent with a winning record but was somehow being touted as a potential challenger to Anthony Joshua.

'I'm bringing some life back into the business again for the love of the people,' King told the Boxing Junkie website. 'I'm giving the people what they want. The country is divided. I want to show that working together works.' Some of us were more inclined to remember the less charitable observation by Larry Holmes: 'King's an equal opportunity dirtbag. He screws everybody.'

Tyson, who once sued King for $100million (he accepted an out-of-court settlement of $14million), returned to the ring in November 2020 for an over-hyped, pay-per-view exhibition against Roy Jones Jr. He lived down to promotional expectations by promising to 'disable' the former four-weight world champion who had been earning a crust as an actor, rapper and commentator.

They had a combined age of 105 and, without judges, scuffled to a ceremonial draw through eight two-minute rounds. Snoop Dogg, whose commentary was understandably distinctive, since he had smoked marijuana throughout a preceding concert performance, compared them to two uncles brawling in the backyard. Tyson donated his $1million purse to charity, and described himself as a humanitarian.

'In a perfect world, I'm a missionary,' he said, with apparent earnestness. I've heard of muscular Christianity, but that takes the biscuit.

I feel fortunate to have covered Tyson at his peak in the late-Eighties, when his hand speed and reflexes were phenomenal, and his complex, intimidating personality made him a global bogeyman. Compressed against the wall at Johnny Tocco's gym in Vegas, in a room barely big enough for a full-sized ring, we would watch him back up sparring partners and pray they didn't duck. His shrill gasps of exertion were haunting.

Tyson terrified Michael Spinks into a 91-second submission in Atlantic City, having done likewise to the British press corps when we were given an audience in his penthouse suite in the Trump Plaza before the fight. He was refusing to speak to the US media at the time, but welcomed us since he had studied grainy newsreels of British boxing and imagined London was shrouded in perpetual pea-soup fog.

Our mood was as bleak as the setting, a faded resort dependent on the fleecing of busloads of pensioners from New York, who arrived with bags of nickels and dimes for the slot machines. Persistent news stories that Tyson had assaulted his then wife, actress Robin Givens, needed to be checked out. It was a kamikaze mission for which only Colin Hart, the *Sun*'s universally respected boxing writer, had the required intestinal fortitude to volunteer.

We took out the usual insurance, filling our notebooks before Colin did the necessary, in a tone of sweet reason. Tyson stiffened in response, spat 'sit there', rose from a white leather armchair and drew back a glass partition before stalking into the private areas of the suite. He returned, less than a minute later, with Givens, who giggled nervously and asked after life in the old country.

Tyson placed his fist gently against her temple. 'Guys,' he said, miming a punch, 'if this [his fist] hits that [her temple], that would explode.' That sufficed as a denial; we made our excuses and left. Little wonder Frank Bruno repeatedly crossed himself on the ring walk before their rematch in 1996; Tyson needed only eight minutes to batter him into a retirement complicated by mental health issues.

Boxing's reputation as the Hurt Business is well founded. It is the only sport where a reporter's notebook is likely to be stained by spit, sweat, phlegm or blood. Like many, I rationalise my attraction to its thrilling intensity by comparing its disciplines favourably to the more stylised violence of UFC. It's not a conscience-free choice, since I was at ringside in an era of savage domestic rivalries which featured two tragic fights that forced the sport to confront its duty of care.

Nigel Benn, beaten by Michael Watson and Chris Eubank, knocked Gerald McClellan out with calamitous consequences in the tenth round at the London Arena in February 1995. Rumours began to circulate that the American had been taken to hospital as we awaited the post-fight press conference. He had collapsed with a blood clot on the brain; it left him blind, virtually deaf and with permanent short-term memory loss.

The following day's front pages contained vivid images of his distress. A sense of revulsion, and calls from the General Medical Council for boxing to be banned, revived a debate that acquired understandable urgency on a nightmare night in September 1991, when Watson slumped on to the chest of Jimmy Tibbs, his trainer, in the ring at White Hart Lane.

A desperate right uppercut at the end of the 11th round by Chris Eubank, who had been on the canvas himself 20 seconds previously, caused cataclysmic brain damage, which subsequently required six operations. Though initially alert, Watson was unable to defend himself after being sent out for the final round. Referee Roy Francis screamed at Tibbs: 'He's gone, Jim, and you know he's gone.'

Lying on the floor in his corner, with his head propped against a doctor's briefcase, Watson's life began to ebb away.

I was not as close to the drama as my colleague Steve Bunce, who gripped the ring rope against which the back of Watson's head had been propelled with such devastating force, but had never before sensed such blood lust and malice in the crowd.

It was just before 11pm. Everyone was on their feet, in a state of fevered excitement. Police struggled to restore order as fights broke out in the stands. There was no resuscitation equipment in the ring. The first hospital to which he was taken was similarly ill-equipped. Peter Hamlyn, the neuro-surgeon who operated on him at St Bart's hospital, regards his recovery as 'a miracle'.

Sport has a capacity to shed light and warmth, even in the darkest, coldest moments. Bunce, who helped Watson fashion his autobiography, *The Biggest Fight*, and Hamlyn, who insists 'Michael has done more for me spiritually than I've done for him physically', have forged enduring friendships with the stricken boxer.

There were valid doubts that Watson would be able to talk, or walk again when he emerged from a 40-day coma, but, in a deeply affecting triumph of the human spirit, he completed the London Marathon over six days in 2003. Eubank and Hamlyn were alongside him as he crossed the finishing line in the Mall. Subsequently awarded an MBE for his services to disabled sport, he remains an inspirational character.

His legacy is secure; fighters have been saved because of safety improvements imposed following his ordeal. His story was told brilliantly by Bunce, whose garish Hawaiian shirts and machine-gun delivery of bullets of boxing folklore mask a compassionate, empathetic nature. I learned much from his ability to humanise his friend's struggle, from mastering a simple bowl of rice and peas to re-evaluating his life as a committed Christian.

Watson contributed to the Forgiveness Project, a secular organisation that shares the testimony of both victims and perpetrators of violent crime, and other life-changing traumas. The aim is to 'bear witness to the resilience of the human spirit and act as a powerful antidote to narratives of hate and dehumanisation, presenting alternatives to cycles of conflict, violence, crime and injustice.'

He dwelled on the strength he gained, praying for Eubank: 'I knew he was suffering. If you've got a heart – and he has – you can never be the same after something like this happens. I didn't feel any anger towards him because it could have happened either way. You have to let bygones be bygones. I knew if I had animosity about what Chris had done to me, I'd be breaking myself down mentally as well as physically. How could I then move on?'

Life in the arena is raw, and its lessons are revealing, especially when they are delivered on the planet's biggest stage.

Chapter Fifteen

Lost at Sea

Friday 30 April 1993. 06.30 4°15S 15°05W

Words somehow seem irrelevant. It's happened. This race
has cost someone's life. We've just had an extraordinary team
briefing on deck to tell us Bill Vincent was lost overboard at
17.30 yesterday. The shock was immediate and profound. All
those silent, private nightmares had come true. We knew the
risks, but the timing of Bill's loss is hardest to take. We'd done
the Southern Ocean, taken our punishment. We'd survived
what everyone thought would be the most hazardous part of
the race.

Perhaps it is too easy to talk complacently of derring-do.
Perhaps it is too easy to fail to appreciate the scale of something
like this. Like Bill, none of us were wearing our life jackets at
the time he went over the side. It had been a mellow kind of day.
The light was beginning to fade. The wind was warm, the sea
the richest blue. There's so much to marvel at out here, despite
the ocean's capacity for malevolence. We've always said it can
take us whenever it wants, and now it has.

I feel an awful sense of guilt, having exulted in the fact that
Bill's yacht, *Heath Insured*, lost a lot of miles to us last night.

How were we to know that his crew were mounting a search for him? His loss hits us all, deeply. We identify with what has proved to be a fatal attraction. It has been our unifying force. All you could hear, during our minute's silence on deck, was the soft slopping of waves against the hull. All you could feel was a gentle rocking movement. All you could see was people struggling with the darkest emotions. I wasn't the only one to weep silently.

Saturday 1 May 1993. 11.00 1°23S 17°31W

Emotions remain raw; memories remain vivid. It has been a strange 24 hours or so. The race has continued in a vacuum of disbelief. We're close to crossing the Equator, into the Northern Hemisphere, and there are so many unanswered questions. The search for Bill was called off at 10.30am yesterday. Medical advice dictated further efforts were futile. Adrian, the skipper, gathered his crew around him in the cockpit and conducted a simple service. We can only guess at the sheer, gut-wrenching trauma of it all.

The problem is that Bill's death is not necessarily the end of the story. Adrian prefaced the inevitable inquiry by collecting statements from each crew member. It appears Sam Brewster, Carole Randall and Adrian Rayson were the last to see him alive. It seems he never broke the surface again after going down. He was evidently not a strong swimmer. It would have taken only an instinctive breath, underwater, to fill his lungs and ensure he kept descending.

He could have panicked, but something doesn't add up. It took me a while on the foredeck with Pete (Goss, my skipper) to ask the terrible question. Suicide? Bill was a quixotic character. Was impending normality, going back to being a carpenter at the university in Bath, too much? Pete thought not: 'People who want to do that would do it at night,' he reasoned. But the fact we both gave such an awful prospect some thought is revealing. It's a sombre time.

'The sea is a cold, cold grave,' said Pete. What is truly terrible is that Bill's family have no body to mourn. An aching void cannot be filled.

The *Independent*, 29 May 1993

THE CREW MEMBER lost overboard during a round-the-world yacht race took his life by making a 'deliberate and perfectly executed dive', an inquiry was told yesterday. At a Department of Transport hearing in Southampton, Adrian Rayson, a crew member, said: 'He did not jump, nor did he fall. The dive appeared to be a premeditated act.'

William Vincent, 47, a carpenter from Bath, appeared depressed before diving overboard 450 miles off the West African coast during the British Steel Challenge, an eight-month amateur race in which 10 yachts circumnavigated the world. He had been one of 13 crew members on *Heath Insured*, which sailed into Southampton on Thursday, the last yacht to finish the race.

Samantha Brewster, 24, of Woodbridge, Suffolk, said she saw Mr Vincent out of the corner of her eye when he went to dive off. 'I turned round to look at him. He had his left foot on top of the pushpit and was stepping up. I yelled "Bill". At the same time he dived over the stern and swam away,' she said.

He looked back at the yacht, but he appeared to make no effort to attract the crew's attention, Mr Rayson told the inquiry. Adrian Donovan, 35, the captain, said at the hearing attended by Mr Vincent's wife Pauline, a teacher, that he heard Miss Brewster scream that a man had gone overboard. He was on deck in seconds, but although buoys were used to mark the spot, the crew lost sight of Mr Vincent in the swell.

Lookouts were posted and a search continued through the night but he was not found and, eventually, the crew held a short service in the cockpit before resuming course. Mr Vincent, who had two teenage sons, had appeared preoccupied since leaving Cape Town on 17 April on the last leg of the 28,000-mile race, Mr Rayson, of Henley, Oxfordshire, said.

'Since leaving Cape Town Bill Vincent had seemed prepossessed with a personal problem and appeared listless and depressed.' But in the two days before he went overboard on the evening of 29 April, he seemed happier. 'I did not have a hint of his apparent desperate state of mind. His diving overboard was a tremendous shock,' Mr Rayson said.

Michael McDonnell, the marine superintendent holding the inquiry, said the crew had made every effort to try to rescue Mr Vincent. He made a formal finding that Mr Vincent was lost at sea, believed drowned.

* * *

A mental image forms as I read the personal journal, retrieved from my kit bag for the first time in more than a quarter of a century. It is a vision of a colourful figure with a Southern Ocean beard so luxurious his wife and sons didn't recognise him when he disembarked in Hobart, the second of our three ports of call, and headed to the bar. Bill Vincent was not short on company since we all had war stories to share.

We relished defying the sailing establishment, which decreed that amateurs racing around the world the wrong way, against prevailing winds and tides, was madness. Each of us carried two motivational passages, literal articles of faith provided by race organiser Chay Blyth, who could neither sail nor navigate in 1970 when he set himself the task of completing the so-called 'impossible voyage' of a solo circumnavigation, east to west.

The first quoted German philosopher Johann Wolfgang von Goethe: 'Whatever you can do or dream, begin it now. Boldness has genius, power and magic in it. Begin it now.' The anonymous author of a piece entitled 'Press On' continued the theme: 'Nothing in the world can take the place of persistence. Talent will not; nothing is more common than unsuccessful men with talent. Genius will not; unrewarded genius is almost a proverb. Education will not; the world is full of educated derelicts. Persistence and determination alone are omnipotent.'

The public response to our Everyman (and woman) adventure was unrestrained. During the course of the race around 25,000 letters were addressed to me at the *Daily Telegraph*, whose innovative sports editor David Welch gave me licence to train and compete over two years. They were from all ages and both sexes; one was even from Bobby Charlton, who identified with the scale of our ambition. This was our Moonshot, an other-worldly, life-affirming experience that could be shared by strangers.

Nature was almost hallucinogenic. It looked as if an unseen inferno was raging behind the headland as our yacht, *Hofbrau*, made the final approach to Cape Horn; the colours of the sunset deepened from peach and orange to crimson and the deepest purple. We were skirting the last stretch of land at the end of the world; the cold air was thick with the sweet incense of rotting vegetation. This was where, in 1521, Magellan's crew feared they were sailing through the gates of Hell.

Ahead lay thousands of miles when we were beyond rescue, other than by our own, or by a rare passing container ship. Pete

Goss gathered us in the cockpit. He had our complete trust and respect; we were about to be confronted by his notion of his duty of care, underpinned by the clinical logic of his background in the special services.

'This is likely to get a little rough,' he announced. 'If anyone goes overboard in bad conditions I will not endanger the lives of the rest of the crew by turning the boat around to try to get you.' When he had only his own safety to contemplate, four years later, he turned back into the teeth of storm-force winds to rescue Raphael Dinelli, a fellow competitor in the Vendee Globe, a non-stop solo round-the-world race that requires remarkable fortitude.

Dinelli's boat had capsized in surging seas, when the mast snapped and porthole windows exploded. He had lashed himself to the stump of the broken keel on the upturned hull in freezing temperatures and was essentially waiting to die. He felt angry at the waste of his life, and the pain he was in the process of inflicting on his wife and child.

An Australian Air Force P3 Orion aircraft dropped him a life raft ten minutes before his boat sank. He was alone for a further ten hours until it returned, flashing landing lights to signal his position to Pete. He negotiated 30-foot waves, scooped the stricken sailor up on the deck and was struck by the gratitude in the eyes peeping through a slit in the survival suit. The French nation's gratitude was ceremonial; Pete was subsequently awarded the Légion d'Honneur by President Chirac.

The sea can seduce, but its savagery must never be forgotten.

Our first major iceberg, an estimated 800 yards long and 400 yards deep, was spotted, some seven miles away, at 3.15 on a Saturday morning. It had a violet hue as day began to break; I was one of three crew members assigned to the bow to watch for growlers, huge blocks of recently shed ice that lurked beneath the surface, capable of causing catastrophic damage.

As we sailed closer, the main berg was translucent. Its edges were angular and its surface starkly layered. The beginning of a cave-like hole on its face, and the spray clouds eroding its far side, signalled the inevitability of protracted destruction. The colour of the sea as it surged intermittently over the base of the visible ice, a cerulean blue caused by refracted light, was the most beautiful I had seen.

The beast, our first Southern Ocean storm, lay in wait, two days later. Winds built from 30 to 74 knots over five hours from 6am, and we were in emergency mode. Huge seas, with sequences of up to five metallic grey waves measuring up from 20 to 50 feet, swept the deck. Fate decreed where you landed; it invariably involved the full length of your lifeline.

When a 42-tonne steel yacht falls off a plateaued wave, the havoc wrought below decks has to be seen to be believed. The force prised the galley table from its foundations and forced up floorboards. Lightbulbs and fire extinguishers exploded. Stores smashed through wooden restraining boards and floated in a film of filthy water.

Despite being strapped in, off-watch crew members were thrown through their lee-cloths and out of their bunks. Ribs were broken, shoulders dislocated. On deck, in an emergency two-man watch, looking through the platinum light of an unpolluted moon at waves beginning to break above the mast, the precious nature of life was unspoken, but unavoidable.

The ordeal might have been physical, but the compensation was spiritual. Awe proved to be a much more powerful emotion than fear. The sea was not a random collection of water molecules; it had an aura, definable mood swings. It was a living entity that reinforced our ultimate insignificance. When the race was over (we finished third), a sense of dislocation lingered.

I had found what I had been looking for on other assignments, indulging childhood fantasies while driving racing cars around Silverstone, rallying around the Arctic, and sleeping on a Cambridge undergraduate's floor before going out on a dawn training run in the build-up to the University Boat Race.

An appreciation of the need to belong.

I can still see the crack in *Hofbrau*'s mast, opening to the rhythms of the sea with the safety of Tasmania three days away. I can still hear the sardonic laughter of my crew mates, as we cursed the defect in our characters that led us to become involved in a project that delivered deprivation and desolation. We took our inspiration from a fast-fading photocopy of *The Seafarer*, a literary relic of Anglo-Saxon England whose anonymous author spoke to us down the centuries.

I can sing a true song about myself,
Tell of my travels, how in days of tribulation
I often endured a time of hardship …
He who loves most prosperously on land does not understand
How I, careworn and cut off from my kinsmen,
Have as an exile endured a winter on the icy sea…

For the first time, football had failed to set the rhythms of my life; I was absent for the majority of the inaugural Premier League season. Though the football results were transmitted to the boat each Saturday evening, triggering reflexive club tribalism among the crew, they were only a fleeting fascination. It didn't seem that important. Professionally, this presented a problem.

Indifference to Manchester United's first title win for 26 years didn't really go with familiar newspaper territory of football-driven opinion. Eric Cantona, signed soon after the round-the-world race began, might have beguiled other columnists with his best impression of Jean-Paul Sartre, but, stridently ignorant of his impact, I had no inclination to follow his metaphorical trawler.

Mentally, I was still lost at sea. Less than a week after the other nine boats in the race fleet had headed back out into the Solent, for the instinctive but deeply moving gesture of escorting Bill's yacht on the final miles of its tragic journey, England lost a critical World Cup qualifier in Norway. The tabloid crucifixion of Graham Taylor seemed senseless, an obscenity.

An assignment in the Falkland Islands, using the government airbridge, which involved flying from RAF Brize Norton in Oxfordshire to Mount Pleasant, with a stopover in Ascension Island for refuelling and crew change, offered the promise of depressurisation. My host, Patrick Watts, a radio DJ who sent clandestine messages during the conflict after initially being forced to broadcast news of the invasion at pistol point, understood my need for solitude.

Nominally, the aim was to play what was billed as the world's most remote golf course. It had only ten greens, but 18 holes, and measured 4,700 yards with a par of 67. Several of the bunkers were created from craters caused by shelling from British field guns during the undeclared ten-week war. One of the holes was named in honour of Nick Taylor, a Royal Naval Harrier pilot shot down nearby.

Lieutenant Taylor's body, still in its ejector seat, was recovered 80 metres from the site of the crash by residents of Goose Green and buried under Argentine supervision with full military honours. The grave, behind a white picket fence, is lovingly tended and an annual memorial service is staged on 4 May, the anniversary of his death.

There was something cleansing about the perspective of being alone in such a setting. I was about to return to a world which took Bill Shankly's sardonic maxim about life, death and football too seriously for its own good. The air, still chilled towards the end of a Southern Hemisphere winter, was intoxicating. The silence was symphonic.

That sense of serenity lasted as long as the first major sporting story on my return, Ian Botham's final appearance in first-class cricket against the Australians at Durham. The *Telegraph* offered me the rare honour of the entire back page for an occasion that generated wall-to-wall veneration in the rest of the national press.

The booming headline over my report – 'Botham exits all paunch, no punch' – captured the self-indulgent sourness of my mood. Others struck the right note, highlighting the warmth of his valedictory address, in which he compared himself to a battered Ford Escort. The result of the tour match was meaningless, and rendered inevitable by rain that curtailed play until 2.30pm, but I wanted him to wage Holy War.

I still cringe when I read the intro: 'Ian Botham's cabaret career began early yesterday when, with a theatrical bow and a pantomime performance, he bade farewell to first-class cricket. He looked more like a publican than a peerless all-rounder during the death throes of Durham's draw with Australia. The brief standing ovation, as he led the team off, smacked of duty rather than devotion.'

Having annihilated a national icon, I blathered on into kitten-drowning territory: 'It was a burial without tears, a strangely sterile climax to a vivid story. In truth, it was the sort of occasion that could only be enjoyed by those who derive perverse pleasure from such reminders of mortality as a bloated Brigitte Bardot or a haunted, hunted Greta Garbo.

'Botham has always been closer to Captain Hook than Peter Pan, having sheaves of press cuttings to prove he is neither innocent, nor immortal. For all the effectiveness of his final 11 overs in the game, he could have just as easily slipped behind a striped curtain, and treated the attendant school parties to an impromptu Punch and Judy Show ...'

Talk about failing to read the room. Fortunately, my mentor Ian Wooldridge recognised the warning signs, and administered the most elegant of bollockings, washed down by a rip tide of gin and tonic: 'That yacht race could make you,' he said. 'But it could just as easily break you.' His truth was typically inescapable. I knew I needed something, or someone, in which to believe.

Enter Bobby Charlton.

I used his letter to me, following the race, to secure an interview with him on the pretext of United's impending defence of the Premier League title. They would become only the fourth club to win the Double that season, when the legend of Sir Alex Ferguson began to be embellished. It was due reward for loyalty and far-sightedness.

Sir Alex has never forgotten the support he received from the club legend during a campaign of vilification that led to 'Fergie Out' glove puppets being sold to United fans before what it is popularly assumed to be the turning point of his career, an FA Cup third-round win at Nottingham Forest on a fateful Sunday afternoon in January 1989.

He held court after the match in a large-windowed corridor between the dressing rooms and the official entrance and seemed embarrassed when reminded of the post-match bear hug, in which he swallowed Mark Robins, the scorer of the only goal: 'Ach, that was just relief,' he said. 'Those last 15 minutes are when you age. It was eyes shut and praying. That's when you need the luck. Today we got the breaks. That's the difference.'

Beyond the obvious evidence of how insidious pressure can be in football management, even when exerted on such a strong character, I was taken by the significance of something that was easy to overlook, the gold signet ring Ferguson wore on his left hand. It had a square face, on which was inscribed a Red Devil, the insignia that appeared on the club badge from the Seventies.

The sense of identity suggested by the ring formed the theme for my conversation with Charlton, who came across as being shy and sensitive, rather than aloof, as some had warned. He needed little invitation to praise the manager's professional rigour, moral courage and emotional intelligence, but gave such personal qualities an additional dimension by connecting them to the club's tragedies and traditions.

The Munich disaster, of which he became the only living survivor when Harry Gregg passed away in February 2020, was an obvious reference point. Charlton spoke of a daily communion with ghosts conjured in the mind's eye. His recollections of 'the poor boys' were simple yet deeply affecting. They have greater relevance today, since he is yet another voice fading into history.

Here was a childhood hero, hinting at the humanity that is so often overlooked by the process of fame and universal adulation. The overwhelming impression was that he saw success across the generations, from Busby to Ferguson, as a duty – necessary homage to those friends and team-mates whose lives were cut short.

Ferguson persuaded him to address the first-team squad on the 50th anniversary of the crash in 2008: 'Tell them about

Munich, Bobby, tell them about the makings of this place,' he implored. 'Tell them what was passed to them so many years ago, before they were born, and what they should represent every time they go out on the field. Tell them what it means to play for this club.'

Young players like Wayne Rooney and Cristiano Ronaldo listened in awestruck silence. Within four months, they would win the Champions League, the monetised version of the European Cup, in Moscow's Luzhniki Stadium, tightening the bonds of collective understanding. Ferguson, the father figure, had seen another generation come of age.

Meeting Charlton marked the first time I had considered, in any great depth, the principle of a football club as a family, an imperfect, emotionally driven unit that requires commitment to a common philosophy. There would be inevitable disappointments, disputes and disruptions that could only be dealt with honestly and, occasionally, harshly.

Football as an allegory for life? Much to my surprise, I found I could get on board with that.

Chapter Sixteen

The Art of the Impossible

WHEN BOBBY Charlton needed to mourn after Munich, and to heal, physically and mentally, he found sanctuary in 114 Beatrice Street, on a row of terraced colliery houses in the pit village of Ashington in Northumberland. It was only there in the family home, 'a little boy lost', according to his mother Cissie, that he rediscovered the will to play football.

His father, a miner at Linton Colliery, a six-mile bike ride away in Morpeth, was known as Boxer Bob. Legend has it that he won the money for Cissie's wedding ring fighting in a fairground booth. He had little affinity with football despite the fame of his sons; coal dust would claim his life, through the cloying agonies of pneumoconiosis.

Cissie, who nursed him to the end, was coaching a local junior football team at the age of 73. Her four brothers were pros; a cousin, Newcastle United's 'Wor Jackie' Milburn, was a definitive local hero. Beatrice Street produced three Footballers of the Year in six seasons; the Charlton brothers, Bobby and Jackie, were preceded by Burnley's Jimmy Adamson, who won the award in 1962. Is such a phenomenon due to nature or nurture? The debate between the relative merits of genetic inheritance, environmental influence and life experience dates back to the fifth century BC, when Hippocrates, universally regarded as the father of medicine, promoted the importance of 'genetic predisposition'.

Bobby Robson was brought up in similar circumstances to the Charlton brothers, at 28 George Street in the pit village of Langley Park, 35 miles south of Ashington. The two-bedroomed terraced house had only an outside toilet. The fourth of five sons, his moral compass was set by his parents, Christian teetotallers who applied their faith simply and powerfully.

His pride in his father Philip was touchingly unrestrained. He toiled 180 feet underground for 51 years, hewing coal in claustrophobic seams as narrow as 20 inches in height. As England manager, his son never passed up an opportunity to remind us that he missed only one shift in his working life. 'That's graft, that is,' he would say, introducing him with due reverence.

Philip took his sons to watch Newcastle United, but when football intervened in the form of a professional contract at Fulham, after Bobby had left school at 15 with the intention of following him down the pit, he insisted he train part-time for his first season and continue his apprenticeship as an electrician on the Festival of Britain site on the South Bank of the Thames.

It was difficult to believe the slight, gentle figure, with thick glasses and a flat cloth cap, was a disciplinarian. Bobby inherited his work ethic and his belief in the common man, even if he did see fit to protect him in later life. A friend would be routinely assigned to take Philip for a cup of tea whenever Bobby had to conduct England press conferences, which tended to degenerate quickly.

Morally and materially, Bobby was from a different era. When he won his first England cap in 1957, scoring twice in a 4-0 win over France before being dropped immediately in favour of Bobby Charlton, he did not own a car, walked to training, and earned only the maximum weekly wage, £20.

He was never envious, but never quite came to terms with the wealth of contemporary players. On one infamous occasion, when Kieron Dyer asked Newcastle's team bus to turn around because he had left a £65,000 pair of diamond earrings in the shower at the Hawthorns, he could not hide his bewilderment. Asked to recall it years later, he needed only a wry, two-word summary: 'Fucking hell ...'

Times change. Coal-mining communities that produced generations of footballers have been forcibly repurposed; today's players tend to reflect a more fractured, transient culture. Pits are museum pieces; hi-tech start-ups on soulless business estates have yet to fill the social void. The values pit villages encouraged, resilience, compassion, and inter-dependence, are being lost.

Football, once the expression of those communities, is increasingly selfish, superficial and judgemental. Robson remains the most impressive England manager I worked with, but the nature of managing the national team has been transformed, despite its intermittent irrelevance. Gareth Southgate, trapped in a vacuum throughout the first phase of the pandemic, emerged in late summer, 2020, to find agendas had evolved.

Despite the shift in emphasis to an increasingly self-serving club game, he was still expected to produce a winning team, and knew through the experience of playing for six England managers that he would be second-guessed by football illiterates. Being thrown into a world of corporate messaging, mental health campaigns and bio-secure bubbles was less predictable.

The manufactured controversy triggered by Phil Foden and Mason Greenwood breaking quarantine in Iceland went beyond the usual prurience and empty moralising. The treatment meted out to Greenwood, in particular, was pernicious. As the newest kid on the block, a young black player making his senior England debut in a breakthrough season, he was fresh meat for predictable predators.

The *Sun* news reporter who dialled in drooling drivel about the 'Man United ace' enjoying a 'heated romp' after he 'scoffed jelly babies' with an 'Icelandic beauty' during 'a night of shame' followed up with a confected tale about Greenwood 'inhaling hippy crack' with 'a female pal' that was so old it deserved a place in the British Museum.

Closer, in spirit, to the leering impotence of Sid James than the linguistic majesty of Shakespeare, the stories were derivative, and deadly dull. They were also dangerous, since they incited curtain-twitchers, closet racists and cyber-warriors to pile on a young man who had made the mistakes young men make when they feel insulated by celebrity.

Southgate left the pair out of the England squad during the next international break, in October, but even someone of his natural empathy and even-handedness was affected by the toxicity of the fallout: 'All management roles are difficult, but this is a job like no other in terms of the things you have to deal with. You're in a position where you're answerable pretty directly to government. You're in a situation where you're dealing with the royal family. You happen to be a spokesman for the nation.'

Managing England involves mastering the art of the impossible. Only two of the 19 men who have attempted to do so, Walter Winterbottom and Alf Ramsey, had more matches in charge than Robson, who lost only 18 of his 95 games. The caring characteristics and strength of spirit he brought to the job reflected his heritage.

One of his most attractive attributes, beyond the perseverance that sustained him through five separate instances of cancer, was his capacity to be true to himself. In the early phase of his England management, I was in a small group covering Euro 84, who chanced upon him on the Champs-Élysées. He was a wide-eyed tourist, explaining that, although he had visited Paris many times in his career, he had never before emerged from the football bubble.

Over the next couple of hours, we joined him in ascending the Eiffel Tower and the Arc de Triomphe, Napoleon's homage to the victories of his Grande Armée. His sense of wonder as he looked down at the sweeping avenues and elegant squares of the city was palpable. It was a long way, spiritually and geographically, from the Durham coalfields that made him.

Though notably tolerant and tender towards troubled players like Paul Gascoigne, he was no one's soft touch. The mythology of Italia 90 tends to underplay its chaotic inception. Labelled 'a prat' and 'a plonker' in the build-up, things became poisonous when a club chairman with links to the FA hierarchy leaked news of his intention to join PSV Eindhoven after the World Cup.

One of my enduring images of him is his appearance in the FA Chamber, the day before his squad travelled to Sardinia, venue for the initial group stage. 'I have woken up this morning to a world I cannot believe in,' he said, in an acidic but profoundly sad reference to headlines that condemned him as a feckless traitor for merely following a prudent career path after FA chairman Bert Millichip suggested his contract would not be renewed.

His eyes, caught in the glare of TV arc lights, were ablaze with rage and wounded pride. Graham Kelly, the embodiment of bureaucratic mediocrity as FA secretary, yelped: 'We're not having a shambles in front of the moving cameras,' and was pointedly ignored by photographers who scuffled to capture a cameo of anger, acceptance or weakness.

'You're something special, sunshine,' Robson hissed at one, who leant over the table towards him and thrust his lens in his face in an insolent invitation for the manager to react.

Battle lines had been drawn. An air of mutual enmity consumed final preparations. A 1-1 draw in the last official warm-up match in Tunisia led to derivative, openly mocking headlines like 'For Allah's sake, go'. Allegations that a liaison officer, Isabella Ciaravola, had become romantically involved with England players provoked unprecedented hostility.

FA officials, caught in the crossfire between angry players, sullen hosts and news reporters who scented blood, were somehow persuaded by an advertising executive that it would be a good idea for England to score a symbolic own goal in a charity match against a Sardinian select team in the provincial capital of Oristano, six days before the tournament started. Steve McMahon duly obliged before any opponent had touched the ball, and England went on to win 10-2.

Gianfranco Zola, who had just won the Scudetto with Napoli, returned to his home island to play for the first hour, but, instead of being beguiled by England's supposed gesture of solidarity, locals regarded it as an inappropriate act of condescension.

The fact that 200 armed police and an encircling helicopter were deemed necessary to monitor the crass exhibitionism of a dozen or so England supporters, sitting on the concrete steps of the only stand, hardly helped.

Team-mates playfully chanted 'Scab, Scab' at mild-mannered Everton full-back Gary Stevens when he returned to the bus after being seen speaking to a journalist. Peter Beardsley, who scored a largely meaningless hat-trick, snapped: 'I'm saying nothing. You've all been slaughtering me.' Even the genial Terry Butcher was pushed over the edge by the Sunday tabloids: 'My mum and dad read that rubbish. Why should I have anything to do with you?'

The artillery barrage continued, unabated, with calls for the team to be sent home as 'a disgrace to the nation', but within a month, they were hailed as national treasures. Since this would be the last World Cup finals in which England appeared before the internet era, those of us in Italy, caught up in the daily dramas, were inevitably isolated from the wider impact of the team's progress to the last four.

Over time, such an emblematic defeat as that suffered in the penalty shoot-out against Germany becomes like cracked ice, so that memory is refracted through slithers that act as a personal prism. Small details loom large. Butcher, for instance, vividly recalls the German team bus drawing alongside theirs outside the stadium after the game. He could see and hear them 'singing and shouting'. It is a sound that lives on in the darker recesses of his imagination.

Visiting the team hotel in Asti, the morning after elimination, I was struck by the staff's consternation that the fax machine had jammed due to the number of messages of support received. Robson held court in the garden; he spoke so sensitively about Gascoigne needing 'to tread carefully because the world is at his feet' – it was as if he had a premonition that the player's iconic tears would become increasingly bitter.

Unlike many, the England job didn't define him, or scar him indelibly. It couldn't dilute his generosity of spirit, or destroy his dignity. The pain lingered, especially when he recalled the hysterical response to him starting the third phase of a storied managerial career in the Netherlands, but it was tempered by the loyalty he expressed towards colleagues like Don Howe, his former team-mate and assistant:

'It was quite ridiculous, outrageous and obscene what happened to me, but there it is,' he said, in an affectionate film, shot years later. 'Couldn't stop it. Nothing I could do about it. I had to explain to the players what had happened and Don said: "You don't have to explain anything. Players understand. They're going to be transferred before, during and after this World Cup. You're doing the same."

'He was very sensible about it and very intelligent. He was very supportive of me. He stood with me. That's why he's been a close associate of mine, and I've loved the fella. I mean loved him. He's been a great, great guy for me, Don Howe. We played together. We finished together.'

Bobby Robson has a physical legacy, his cancer foundation, but also left an intellectual inheritance, through the knowledge he shared with young coaches. Sven-Göran Eriksson's affinity with him goes beyond their common experience of the England job, to the study visit he made to Ipswich Town under him when in his first managerial role, at Degerfors in the second-tier Superettan.

Eriksson's reminiscence of 'a great man and a great, great manager who died too early' mixed warmth and sadness. Like many contemporaries, he was intrigued by Robson's 'unique' ability to relate to players several generations removed from his own. He was in philosophical mood when we spoke, having sheltered from the pandemic at his lakeside home in Sweden. 'Human life is more important than football, but at least now they play,' he said, wistfully.

The thought occurred that, at 72, he had accepted that he was in his dotage. It was dispelled with a twinkly chuckle and the observation: 'That's a terrible word, retire. If someone serious asks I would still try to sit on the bench, and try to be more clever than the other guy, on the other bench.' Within 24 hours, he was being linked to his fifth national team job, with Jamaica.

Nothing came of it, but he is nothing if not adventurous. At the end of his five-year, 67-match sojourn with England he resembled Harold Lloyd, the silent movie star, in the stunt scene in which a house collapsed on and miraculously around him. He glanced over his shoulder at the surrounding chaos, appreciated the extent of his good fortune and headed for the hills.

Nothing subsequently, in an increasingly surreal journey from Manchester City to Mexico, Thailand, the Ivory Coast, China and the Philippines via Notts County and Leicester City, came close to offering the tantalising mixture of celebrity and credibility that becoming England's first foreign manager delivered.

'On the night Kevin Keegan resigned I had a call asking: "Can you leave Lazio?"' he recalled. 'We had just won the Scudetto. I replied: "You're joking. It's impossible. I am not English." But two or three days later, the FA called and asked seriously. I thought about it for two minutes. You can't say no to England. If I did, I would have regretted it for the rest of my life.

'I am very proud of what I did with England. That was my biggest job, for sure. It was bigger than I thought. It's beautiful because it unites 60 million people in a beautiful dream. Italy is a great football country, but it doesn't get behind its national team in the same way.'

He can be forgiven an old soldier's reverie, but the inevitable conflict between club and country became a conflagration where Sir Alex Ferguson was concerned, especially when Wayne Rooney was questionably taken to the 2006 World Cup. Eriksson fought his corner with surprising intensity, but the territory has long since been neutralised. All that remains is respect and recognition:

'What Sir Alex did, over 25 years or so at Manchester United, is impossible for anyone to repeat. His style is not my style, and there were times he could have killed me, but I always admired him. It was nothing personal. He had a huge passion for his club. For him, Manchester United was everything. He defended the colours. He would say: "Don't disturb us."

'As a manager you should be yourself as much as possible. Don't try to be the new Mourinho, or the new Ferguson. You have to have your own personality, your own philosophy, your own way of doing business. The danger, for a young manager, is that he changes because he is criticised, on the pitch or in the dressing room. Follow your heart. Keep to your faith.'

Regrets? Sven had a few, but, then again, too few to mention. His easy-going nature didn't prevent him from admitting that successive failures in penalty shoot-outs in the 2004 European Championship and the 2006 World Cup 'made me feel like shit'. Losing to Portugal in Gelsenkirchen was 'mentally very difficult, the worst defeat of my life' because he genuinely believed the tournament was England's, for the taking.

His claim that he was unaware of the club-driven cliques subsequently cited as a limiting factor by Frank Lampard, Rio Ferdinand and Steven Gerrard, is puzzling, since, in its most charitable light, it represents a startling failure of sensitivity to his squad's mood, which dissipated in the paparazzi-clogged streets of Baden-Baden. As for the endless debates about the balance of his midfield, he appears as bored as the rest of us with idle conjecture.

How should he be remembered? His successor Steve McLaren was a significant downgrade, and Fabio Capello was infinitely more cynical. England, or more to the point the self-styled technocrats of the FA's high command, rarely received full value from Sven. They were seduced by a previous incarnation, the incisive technical and tactical coach who had a golden spell with four clubs in Serie A when it was at its zenith.

Doubt his pedigree, though, and the names he quotes speak for themselves. He cites Diego Maradona's impact at Napoli as supporting evidence for his conviction that he was a greater talent than Lionel Messi, a cross-generational genius. Roberto Falcao was 'my coach on the pitch' for Roma, a role fulfilled at Sampdoria by Roberto Mancini, 'who knew football. He acted like a coach, a kit man, a bus driver. He controlled everything.'

Closer to home, dwelling on the era in which he fell in love with English football, he highlights the formative mentality of Liverpool's Boot Room, which was nurtured by Bob Paisley and sustained by Joe Fagan and Ronnie Moran. He believes Bobby Charlton was 'a great, great player, not just because of his talent, but because of his way of being'.

It's sad, then, that in the eye of the British public, he remains a cartoonish figure, stacking the dishwasher in the midst of his latest tryst. It is the fate of England managers to be remembered for deceptive trivialities. Glenn Hoddle may deny he discarded Paul Gascogine from his 1998 World Cup squad, with traumatic consequences, to the soundtrack of Kenny G, but he is as inextricably linked to 'the weasel-toned saxophonist' of New York Times legend as he is to faith healer Eileen Drewery.

In football folklore, nothing became Kevin Keegan more than the manner of his departure, resigning in the toilet after the last match at the old Wembley. Terry Venables might have been a coach of generational quality and pan-European impact, yet his alter ego, the crooner backed by the Billy Amstel Jazz Band warbling 'What Do You Want to Make Those Eyes at Me For?' will forever be at the microphone.

Eriksson, typically, frames his frustration with a gentle chuckle: 'In Italy they will kill you because of what happens on the pitch. In England they make a big story of your private life. It happened to me, and I could see Rooney having the same future as Beckham, after the 98 World Cup. That's why, before I left, I told the press: "Don't kill him, kill me." They treated him OK, and he went on to have an incredible career.

'The game has changed on the pitch due to the high-intensity runs, but off it has changed a lot. When we won the UEFA Cup with Gothenburg in 1982, the press existed with us. They were on our bus, in the same hotel. We trusted them. Now, with social media, it is so different. Controlling that makes it very, very difficult for a manager.'

Mantraps, steel-springed snares in which the victim's leg is trapped by sharp spikes, have been illegal in England since 1827. The modern equivalent, a secretly filmed sting set up by a national newspaper, effectively ended Sam Allardyce's England career after 67 days. The feeding frenzy, created by footage of him discussing investment opportunities in football with an undercover journalist posing as an Asian businessman, consumed him.

It was ultimately immaterial that police, investigating football corruption, cleared him of having done anything illegal. He was legitimised, legally, but still stigmatised, socially. Despite subsequently managing Crystal Palace, Everton and

West Bromwich Albion, three of a record eight Premier League clubs with which he has been associated, the image of him, unshaven and surrounded by the media outside his Bolton home at the height of the hysteria, endures.

When I suggested he was under siege, he exclaimed: 'I was, I was,' before settling into a more measured explanation of what happens when a dream job becomes the stuff of nightmares. 'It's something you don't want to experience, for sure, ever,' he said. 'It doesn't matter whether the story is true or not; you are guilty. Showing I wasn't guilty was very difficult, a long hard road.

'Without going into it too deeply, the lack of support or a bit of faith from the FA particularly at the beginning really made it worse. Had there been a cooling-off period, waiting to see what the real evidence was, it would have been clear that I didn't break any rules. But, in the public eye I was portrayed as an absolute fraudster, almost. The papers picked up on that. The politicians jumped on the back of it. Yet when my case was proven, where were they?'

His professional record, of being only the 31st manager in English football to oversee more than 1,000 competitive matches, was compromised. His solitary match in charge of the national team, a 1-0 win over ten-man Slovakia in Trnava, secured by a 95th-minute goal by Adam Lallana, remains a statistical oddity.

'Well, there's always going to be a "what if",' he acknowledged. 'It'll be at the back of my mind for the rest of my life. I've had the England job, even though it was only for 67 days. Everybody warned me about the job, that it was a poisoned chalice, and I felt the full force of that. I will never forget the hurt, and the disgraceful action of a lot of people.

'Watching the World Cup in Russia was pretty difficult, even though I'm an England supporter. But on a positive note, you overcome adversity. You move forward and look back on your career. Your family picks you up. They say: "Look, just look at what you've done. How many people have done what you've done? You should be proud of what you've achieved."

'Criticism has a bigger effect on the family than me, because this skin is now tough. I call it my rhino skin or my elephant skin because that's what is needed when you are in the front line, not only for the criticism, but also for the praise that comes your way if you are successful. Everything has changed massively, through social media.

'It's easy to sometimes worry about yourself, your players and what is going on at the football club, but if I didn't have a great family, I don't know how far I would have gone. They've been behind me all the time, been through all the trials and tribulations. A few years ago my wife said: "I just can't do it anymore" because of all the bickering she would hear in the stand.

'She couldn't enjoy a game, even if we were winning, because she would be picking up on the few who still criticised. She found it intolerable, and decided to stay at home. It's something you have to learn to manage. It's the same at school; you have to see the teacher and explain you have a high-profile position and that your son or daughter might be picked on.'

The Big Sam persona, captured by images of Allardyce lounging back in the dugout, chewing gum with a relish Desperate Dan reserved for a Cow Pie, is another illusion. Throughout our conversation, I noticed he kept intertwining his fingers as if squeezing out unpleasant memories. As a senior member of the League Managers Association, he was a prominent supporter of their contribution to the 2020 Heads

Up campaign, in which speaking about mental health was seen as a strength, rather than a weakness:

'As a nation we are struggling with mental health issues. It would be silly to ignore that managers, under this enormous pressure, are beginning to suffer from anxiety or possibly depression. Can they identify it, see it for what it is, and get some help? The LMA have been brilliant in appointing specialists in the area, who can be seen privately.

'A manager's job has always been lonely, but it's becoming lonelier than ever. Reaching out confidentially to someone is very, very important. In the early days it would be to another manager, to talk about problems. For me, it would be Sir Alex Ferguson. You can meet up through the LMA, but the younger guys don't seem to have as much time to come together, as we did years ago.

'Football is a great game, but it is a difficult industry to work in. It's about being able to cope, because the upside, the adrenaline rush, is so great. I've lost count of the times my wife has said: "Will you please leave it alone now?" and you can't. That upside always outweighs the difficulties there are in the game.'

But do you find out who your friends are?

'Absolutely. And there's not many. You can count them on one hand. If you think you've got more than that, you're kidding yourself.'

Chapter Seventeen

Funeral for a Friend

WE SAID farewell to much more than a football man on that fusty February day in 2017. We heard of the husband, who married Rita, the girl who did his make-up when, aged 13, he played Lord Grizzle in the school play, *Tom Thumb the Great*. We realised just how much he meant, in so many ways, to so many different people.

A frisson of recognition passed through the congregation when Joanne, his eldest daughter, spoke of his mantra, 'family first, except on matchdays'. Football management is the enemy of domesticity; its demands are relentless, unyielding, and extremely difficult to place into proper perspective. Graham Taylor knew its capacity for cruelty, but in the final reckoning the caricature was laid to rest.

The game was omnipresent, and not merely in the form of celebrated figures paying their respects, like Sir Alex Ferguson and Arsène Wenger. The service lasted a neatly symbolic 90 minutes. The supporters, who stood in the rain on top of the multi-storey car park overlooking the church, needed only to look to their right, and above the roofs of terraced streets, to glimpse the football ground, and the club he transformed. Karen Taylor, his other daughter stood in the 300-year-old pulpit and urged us to look beyond the accountancy of his passing, the dates that registered his birth and death, aged 72, from a heart attack. Numbers are blind to the quirks and qualities that made him such a generous, engaging and challenging figure. They are mute since they cannot match the eloquence of his story.

We are told football is a results business, but ultimately, isn't that also a randomly constructed half-truth? Scorelines are merely impressions, whispers of events. Matches acquire their lustre and longevity through the intimacy of the memories they inspire and the depth of the personalities they involve. The statistical shorthand of scorers and attendances found in sequence over the latest league table is incidental.

Graham lived the cliché by setting his stall out early in his relationships. One of our first conversations revolved around his father Tommy, who joined the *Scunthorpe Evening Telegraph* in 1946, initially writing under the nom de plume 'Poacher'. He was its chief football writer until his retirement in 1983; Graham was inordinately proud of his father's reputation as a champion of his community.

He had the art of detecting a companion's heartbeat. He quickly learned that our respective parents did not own a car between them; Mum drove a tractor for the land army and Dad trusted his bike. He used to laugh when I blamed him, light-heartedly, for being unable to bear to watch the DVD of the 1984 FA Cup final, which Watford lost 2-0 to Everton.

He admitted he couldn't bring himself to watch it, either.

I've still got the three-hour tape, containing pre- and post-match coverage. It's gathering dust, and will never be converted into a CD. I don't need it to remind me of the individuals and images I associate with the occasion. They preclude me from forgetting and, in the case of a bubble-permed exhibitionist of a referee named Roger Milford, who cost Wilf Rostron a chance to captain Watford at Wembley by unjustly sending him off in a routine league fixture, forgiving.

In a sense, that was a time of transition. I envied my brothers and childhood friends their fun and face paint when I popped into the estate pub for a pre-match pint. The Highwayman was under such siege it resembled the American embassy compound in Saigon on the day the final helicopters were evacuating civilians to safety. Trust me, that place contained a few blood brothers of the Vietcong.

I was suited and booted, with a gold-and-red tie hinting allegiance, and primed to cover my first final for the *Daily Telegraph*. Mum, who had never watched live football, travelled with us on a Metropolitan line train that reverberated with giddy, extravagantly expressed optimism. Her day was made by sitting next to comedian Freddie Starr, adjacent to the Royal Box at Wembley, where Elton John shed definitive tears at the old hymn, 'Abide with Me'.

That moment is captured in a favourite black-and-white photograph, taken for the *Sunday People* by David Cattani. Elton has pushed back a wicker chair and is standing in the front row, drawing his left hand across his left eye. Consoled by his new wife, Renate Blauel, he is looking slyly but longingly, out of a watery right eye, at a television cameraman focusing on his churning emotions.

Five seats along, Neil Kinnock, the Labour leader, is oblivious to the fuss. Five rows back, in a cream summer suit, Bobby Robson is standing beside a peak-capped Wembley steward. He is the only recognisable football figure in the picture. Those around him, mainly elderly, bespectacled and balding men, accompanied by ladies in hats that were probably recycled in Sunday church services and village fetes, reflect the end of an epoch.

Almost in spite of myself, I thought of that image when John Motson spoke on Elton's behalf at Graham Taylor's funeral. The incident seemed to summarise the pop star's realisation of what the game meant to him as an emotionally repressed child brought up in Mock Tudor suburbia. Wembley had personal connotations: his uncle, Roy Dwight, famously scored for Nottingham Forest in the 1959 FA Cup final, broke his leg before half-time and played only twice again.

We all have our friendly ghosts through football.

Elton's address, delivered distinctively in his absence, was unsparing and focused on a lecture from Taylor 'that shook me to the core'. It concerned his increasingly dissolute lifestyle: 'He told me how foolish I was and how I was letting myself, and more importantly the club, down. As you can imagine, those words rang so true and I will never forget them. To love somebody you must be prepared to be honest and open. And Graham was the most honest and open man I've ever met.'

Watford's defeat at Wembley that afternoon signalled the beginning of the end of a spiritual journey, personally and professionally. I grew away from the club as my horizons broadened, though I was at Villa Park as an era ended in 1987, when injuries forced Taylor to select a wine waiter, Gary Plumley, in goal for an FA Cup semi-final against Tottenham.

Watford lost 4-1 and, in an unconscionable act of self-satisfaction from a set of supporters who once craved such occasions, couldn't sell their ticket allocation. Due to a quirk in the circuitry of my brain, I hear Elton singing 'love lies bleeding in my hands' as I type those words. It is the earworm from Hell.

History has a habit of repeating itself. Taylor joined Aston Villa on their relegation to the Second Division, and within three seasons had established them as runners-up to Liverpool in the First Division. England beckoned invitingly after Italia 90, and the world duly fell in. There were too many wishing him to fail and like his immediate predecessor, Bobby Robson, he flew too close to the *Sun*.

No other newspaper finds such inspiration in vindictiveness, or plumbs such depths when sport finds itself, often tangentially, on the news agenda. As a journalist's son, Taylor understood the quick-wittedness of the infamous Swedes 2 Turnips 1 back-page headline, following England's defeat by the hosts at Euro 92. It did not stop him turning down a characteristically cloth-eared invitation to the retirement party of the sub-editor who dreamed it up.

His bitterness, initially expressed privately, was reserved for the then editor, Kelvin MacKenzie, the most malignant presence in British journalism in my career. According to MacKenzie, superimposing Taylor's head on a turnip and projecting it at the top of the front page, was 'a bit of fun'. Hardly Hogarthian satire, even at the most basic level, it invited humiliation, which lingered and mutated over many years. Even Taylor's wheelchair-bound mother-in-law was drawn into the hysteria.

It took 15 years for him to acknowledge the consequences. He was derided by drunks, who threw beer over him after a game at Brentford. He was spat at by strangers at Sheffield United, and sworn at indiscriminately in the street. His wife and daughters were ridiculed. As he said: 'If somebody puts a turnip on your head it gives an impression to people of a certain intellect that they can treat you like anything.'

Our relationship had cooled, an inconsequential element of the fallout from his departure as England manager and, specifically, the notorious press conference he staged at the Novotel in Rotterdam, the day before the 2-0 defeat to Holland effectively confirmed the failure to qualify for the 1994 World Cup.

The scene is portrayed, graphically, in *An Impossible Job*, a fly-on-the-wall documentary that depicted him as a conflicted, comical inadequate. He had chosen to change a winning team, and responded to questions with manic, misplaced positivity. By making a call to arms to the wrong people, and in confronting Rob Shepherd, a writer for the short-lived *Today* newspaper, he merely made himself look silly:

'What's the problem with everybody? What's the matter with everybody? Particularly English people. Come on, come on. Rise yourself. Get on with it. Look for your win. Oh, Rob, I can't continue giving ... Listen, Rob. I cannot have faces like yours around about me. I'll tell you this now. If you were one of my players, with a face like that, I'd fucking kick you out. You would never have a chance, son. Get yourself up, man. Put a smile on your face. We're here for business. Come on.'

The laughter, initially nervous, became frantic as the exchanges acquired a surreal edge. I was sitting close to a group of Dutch journalists, who went from slack-jawed disbelief to feverish hilarity in seconds. They, and I, knew what we had to write. A tipping point had been reached, and Taylor had fallen into the abyss occupied by so many of his predecessors.

I wrote that the job was too big for him, knowing he, and most likely his family, would regard it as an 'Et tu, Brute' moment. The injustice of the following evening, in which Ronald Koeman should have been sent off before scoring, added to the poignancy of his plight. The film, an ill-conceived attempt at openness, captured him raging risibly at a bewildered linesman. He was subsequently cheapened by such catchphrases as 'Do I not like that' and 'Can we not knock it?'

The loyalty he engendered among his Watford players was underscored by Luther Blissett: 'I will never forgive some of the journos for what they did to him. It went well beyond professional criticism. It was deeply personal. It was awful, nasty, vindictive. It caused a great deal of damage to a good man who had my greatest respect.'

It felt fitting that there was not a single reference to Taylor's time as England manager in his funeral service, which ended in a spontaneous round of applause as his coffin was borne out of the church. The intensity of the pressure on football managers has increased in the three years since, to the point where many feel candour is counter-productive. Perhaps the football world will be a more measured, compassionate place, post-pandemic.

Perhaps.

Few observers are inclined to count the human cost of the profession, registered by a vignette of which I was unaware until I read Graham's posthumous autobiography, crafted by Lionel Birnie. He admitted he was so consumed by latent tension and disappointment he felt emotionally exhausted watching the 1994 World Cup on television.

After each match he would retreat into the back garden of his home in Little Aston in South Staffordshire and gently kick a ball around for ten minutes or so in the darkness. It was a comforting, child-like response that signalled an enduring love and a hurt that took him two decades to finally acknowledge:

'It hurts. And that is what really, really annoys me about other people: they have no recognition of how much it hurts you. They think you don't care, and those people that know it hurts you, they put the knife into you so it hurts you even more. I wanted so much to be successful. I wanted us to win the World Cup.'

Ironically, he would have fitted in well as a journalist, his fall-back option had he not made a career in professional football. He understood its esoteric delights, having been struck by the sweet smell of printers' ink when taken back to the *Scunthorpe Evening Telegraph* offices as a child, by his father. He wrote his own newspaper columns later in life, and adapted to the rough and tumble of the press box.

He was a thoughtful companion, doing his bit for his commentary team by collecting the half-time teas. His interventions were tactically acute, and there was an elegiac quality to his broader observations on the creeping elitism and financially driven cynicism of the modern game. The only time I saw him careworn in later life was when he was carrying out his duties as chairman at Watford, under an appallingly ignorant and consistently duplicitous owner, Lawrence Bassini.

It turned me against the club which nurtured my love for the game. I found what I was looking for in the earthy realism of Millwall, despite increasing doubts about conventional allegiances. This confession is unlikely to win many friends, but I find myself habitually placing greater store by personal association.

To give an example, I root for any club for which my son Aaron happens to be working as a scout. Occasionally our professions converge; while researching a previous book as a guest of Barcelona, he asked me to assess a player on loan at Cultural Leonesa that he was pushing for Norwich City to sign. I was suitably impressed by Emi Buendia's performance against Barca B; Norwich duly paid £1.3m for the Argentine, whose value has since soared beyond £30m.

We all see the game through a personal prism. Death is an integral part of the mythology of football, and, for me, there is a symbolic accessibility about Taylor's statue, cast in bronze, outside Watford's ground. It depicts him in his first spell at the club, leaning forward on the old wooden bench that was set back from the touchline. It is almost as if he is inviting visitors to sit next to him since there is room either side.

I don't mind admitting I did so the last time I was at Vicarage Road. I promise it was not just a convenient prop for the documentary we were filming there. I still feel his presence at the place where my football education effectively began. Paradoxically, his decency and benevolence was best summed up by a largely overlooked sequence in that fateful documentary.

John Barnes, who had been the subject of virulent tabloid criticism, was being jeered persistently by the Wembley crowd. The match was still going on as Taylor turned, leaned back from the bench, and addressed a group of abusive fans, sitting nearby. 'Eh,' he exclaimed. 'You're talking about another human being …'

Graham Taylor's spirit infused the poem read out by his duaghter Karen at his funeral. He slowed down enough to consider what is true and real, and always tried to understand the way other people feel.

Chapter Eighteen

Who Cares for the Carers?

TONY ROBINSON is the best coach you've never heard of.

He was too pure, too distinctive, for professional football. His honesty was relentless and his refusal to compromise standards for short-term reputational gain was a liability. Obsessively detailed, occasionally playful, he demanded as much from himself as he did from the boys who played for him. He never betrayed their trust and recognised each one as an individual.

He had his foibles: he gave them nicknames, because he had difficulty retaining family names. My son, Aaron, was known as Jesper, after Jesper Blomqvist, the Swedish winger who played for Manchester United at the time. Robinson coached him for three years as part of a youth team that excelled in Milton Keynes, and across the Eastern region, before being fed into the mincing machine of the academy system.

I recently found a ball signed by the Under-12 version of that team, after an unbeaten 2000/01 season, at the back of a cupboard in my son's old room. Age had given the deflated, once-white Mitre Mondo a creamy pallor. All 18 players in the squad had made their mark in black felt-tipped pen. Still shy of revealing slyly practised autographs, most applied their nicknames in capital letters, or in artless joined-up script.

Hands, logically enough, was the goalkeeper. Tiger was also useful in that department, but preferred to play outfield. PC, Chopper, Rocky and Titch were centre-backs. Choc Ice was a feisty left-back. Nike, Top Cat, Strat and Sprite were mates from the same estate. Deadly, Sparky, Magic, Bullet, Zico, Jesper and Jammers attacked in waves.

In terms of natural talent, at least four of them should have progressed beyond scholarships, to the professional game. Yet they were worn down, spat out by the system. In the main they were betrayed by myopic, self-obsessed coaches and clubs who, in the early years of the academy system, had little conception of the complexity of youth development.

Some were deemed too small, the excuse of the unimaginative tutor. Others fell out of love with the game. Several were misunderstood because of difficult backgrounds. Many were victimised because they knew their own minds. My son spent four seasons at Northampton Town's academy. With the exception of one outstanding age group coach, Stuart Hardy, the standard of coaching was poor and the atmosphere politically fraught.

I had a benchmark because of my work, and kept my own counsel. I had seen too many boys ruined by the reflected ambition of overbearing parents. Too many coaches embodied the mediocrity of archaic county associations. The complex process of easing boys through the hormonal minefield of adolescence, in a highly competitive, naturally pressurised situation, seemed beyond them.

Aaron realised the limitations of the environment, took his coaching badges from the age of 16 and used his degree in sports coaching science to enter professional football as part of a new generation of recruitment specialists, scouts who combine old-school instincts and perception with analytical insight. He worked for Aidy Boothroyd and Chris Wilder, impressed Stuart Webber, a prototypical sporting director, at Wolves, and progressed with him to Norwich, before taking a senior role at Middlesbrough midway through the 2019/20 season.

Like many parents, I encouraged my children to seek freedom of expression through sport. Fun was paramount. My eldest son, Nicholas, was a successful schoolboy rower. My other son, William, a talented goalkeeper, and my daughter Lydia, a fast winger recruited into the MK Dons' academy, flirted with football before concentrating on music.

Robinson, a tall, softly spoken and even-tempered man, incorporated a father's care and compassion into his coaching. Antonee, his youngest son, was a familiar figure as a toddler, meandering along the touchline with a ball at his feet and a smile etched permanently on his face. Fate had several surprises in store, some more pleasant than others.

Antonee spent most of his childhood in Liverpool, his mother's birthplace. Tony set up an IT business there, after moving the family from Milton Keynes. He had taken out US citizenship after travelling to White Plains, in Westchester County, New York, at the age of 13, to be with his Jamaican mother. He spent nine years in the US, and played soccer for Duke University before returning to the UK.

The Robinsons lived three minutes from Finch Farm, Everton's training ground. Everton offered Antonee an academy place at the age of 11, when they heard Blackburn Rovers were ready to give him a two-year contract. He was small and would not mature physically until he was 16, but impressed as a fast, athletic and intelligent left-back, whose refusal to be intimidated by bigger boys augured well.

He had been shielded from the worst excesses of youth football at grassroots level, though on one occasion he returned from a Saturday morning game wearing only a coat. Tony's initial instinct was that he had been mugged; it transpired that his wife Kelley was so disgusted by the coach's continual insistence that all players pass to his son, that she called Antonee off the pitch, undressed him in the car and threw his kit out of the window.

His father remained at arm's length during his initiation in the professional game; his mother took him to the majority of matches, and would consciously stand where he would struggle to see her. Neither became involved in parental politics, which reflected the fault lines of an institution dominated by a clique of long-serving coaches.

Coaching attracts dreamers and schemers. More altruistic members of the profession are inspired by the teachings and traditions of such mentors as the late Dick Bate, a renowned coach educator at the FA. 'I'm a coach because of the game,' he once said. 'How it is played, how it evolves, and how it is taught just fascinates me. It captures my imagination more than anything in life.'

These are the men who understand their responsibility to the child. They recognise their duty to make reasoned choices, after careful consideration, because their decisions can be life-changing. Other less scrupulous individuals have proliferated in the era of the Elite Player Performance Plan, which has enhanced employment prospects in what amount to football factory farms. The principal talent of such men lies in building and protecting a powerbase.

Tony Robinson likens Finch Farm to 'Rome under Caesar' but reveres Alan Irvine and Joe Royle for their role in nurturing his son. In late January 2020, he accompanied Antonee on an early-morning flight to Italy, where the former mascot, a 22-year-old full US international who had been excelling in the Championship with Wigan, was due to sign for AC Milan for £10million.

Antonee underwent a medical and was ferried with his father to Casa Milan, grandiose headquarters that hum an aria to the 120-year history of a fabled club. They were greeted in the boardroom by Paolo Maldini, arguably the greatest left-back of all. At 52, he still looked as if he could play 90 minutes before showering and walking straight into a photoshoot for *Italian Vogue*.

As technical director, he had been alerted to Antonee's potential by scouts, who had seen him play for the US Under-23s in a tournament in Spain the previous November. 'I have watched hundreds of hours of tapes,' he announced. 'The one thing I have noticed in every single game is that he never gives up, no matter how well he is playing. I can make this guy world class.'

Dreams can come true. Until they become nightmares.

News filtered through that Antonee had failed the medical because Milan's doctors had detected an irregular heartbeat. Further tests were required, but there was insufficient time for the transfer to go through before the winter window closed. Maldini, devastated on his behalf, offered to disguise the real reason for the collapse of the deal by blaming his club for failing to agree a fee.

'Antonee is like Spartacus,' said Tony, reflecting on a moment of almost unimaginable hurt and concern. 'He will just not be broken.' They were hugely impressed by Maldini's humility and thanked him for his additional offer of refuge in Italy, but returned home to wait for the result of additional tests. Tony told his son: 'Your life comes first.'

Football entered lockdown, postponing surgery designed to correct the abnormality, which, mercifully, was not the result of a congenital defect. Once it became clear it was a consequence of his body's sensitivity to the caffeine shots he had taken before matches, to increase energy levels, Antonee abandoned the pretence that he was injured.

During the delay to his corrective surgery, which had been rescheduled from March to June, his heart corrected itself. He was outstanding in a Wigan team relegated from the Championship only due to a 12-point deduction for financial irregularities, and, following renewed interest from several Premier League clubs, signed for Fulham for £2million in the summer.

His father, meanwhile, was dealing with another hidden element of the global pandemic. He had been working holistically with rejects from the academy system; 19 boys, given another chance in the US college system due to links he forged in his playing days, returned home unable to continue their education. While academic life was on hold, he attempted to place them in local semi-professional football.

Having paid £500 to register as an intermediary, despite admitting, 'I didn't really know what I was doing', he is formally qualified to explore other avenues. One such project involves a joint venture with Alaves, the La Liga club from the Basque region, and its basketball arm, Saski Baskonia. An English version of their international academy, which offers sporting and educational opportunities, is a long-term goal.

The US initiative is an extension of his influence at the intersection of sport and social work. Robinson recognised raw talent in Merseyside and Manchester, a region 'completely saturated with football', and initially agreed to coach a disparate group of boys, prematurely dismissed as difficult cases. By the end of their third season, they had won the best youth league in Liverpool; scouts descended and took seven players back into the academy system.

'It was such an eye-opener. They were brilliant footballers, but no one in the system could discipline them. I had got to the stage where it had to be about more than winning for me. I had to do something with my life. The word quickly got out. In the end, we had groups of Under-15s, 16s and 18s touring the North-West, playing the top academies. When we lost, it was usually down to fitness.

'I never saw myself as a football coach. First and foremost, I saw myself as a teacher, offering guidance to the individual. Football is the easy bit. Academies just want the finished article. A lot of coaches are clueless when it comes to dealing with kids from the estates. They don't want to deal with problems. Whatever they say, they're not interested in polishing raw diamonds.

'They're only interested in the elite. They've raped grassroots football, where half of the kids aren't even fit. I work in the middle sector, with the disillusioned ones. They're enticed into the system, given the dream, and it breaks them when they're told: "No thanks, kid." Professional clubs are messing up kids' heads at younger and younger ages.

'I see them, crushed. I'm dealing with young people who are depressed. In many cases, agents have already seduced them, and their parents. The kid thinks he is a big shot. The moment he is released everyone drops him. No one gives a monkey's. No one bothers to help. No one is there for him. Well, you know what? Every kid matters.'

The emotional strain is magnified and reflected towards those who seek to help. Just as the lost boys barely warrant a second thought, those left to pick up the pieces are expected to absorb punishment. This was a key element in my falling out of love with football; it was too rapacious, too casual in dismissing the damage it created.

Imagine yourself in Pete Lowe's position. You are a highly successful youth coach, who has followed your conscience and moved into player welfare. The transition might have been seamless because you have a compassionate nature, but the associated trauma is very real. How would you deal with a father, asking for help after discovering his son by chance preparing to take his own life in the garage at the family home?

The young man was 19. Summarily rejected after eight years at a Premier League academy, he had renewed his dream of a football career by earning a college scholarship in the United States before his alcoholic mother, estranged from his father, begged him to return to the UK. When he did so out of a sense of filial duty at the expense of his second chance, he discovered she had terminal cancer. He nursed her diligently before despair set in.

Lowe suggested we meet at a golf club on the outskirts of Manchester just before lockdown. We sat on high-backed, velour-covered chairs, nursing cups of coffee in a quiet corner of a large locker room, which offered a degree of privacy. He spoke quietly and exhaled deeply as he considered the pain with which he was confronted:

'It was one of those plea-for-help phone calls: "I don't know what to do. How do I deal with this? This is what has happened." The dad was a lovely man. He didn't articulate whether his son had intended to commit suicide, but to me that's irrelevant anyway. In that situation you learn not to ask questions you want to ask. It is not appropriate.

'How did I feel when I got that call? I really should say to you that I was shocked that the game should have allowed this to happen, but in all honesty I can't. I'm sullied by the game, because of my experiences within it. I wasn't shocked because something like this has been a disaster waiting to happen for many years.

'The boy had lost his football career. I'd first seen him at the club a couple of years before. There weren't as many clouds around his face. There was some sunlight coming through. Now he knew football was ending for him. He knew there was no professional contract. He'd had his dream taken. He now carries a negative package with him that is very hard to get rid of, perhaps even impossible.'

Lowe works outside the system, for PlayersNET, a typically undervalued organisation that has been undermined by the politics of football funding. He arranged for the boy to see a counsellor, who had herself been driven to attempt suicide because of post-natal depression, and put the father in touch with a charity that builds networks between similarly affected families.

'That boy has had tremendous adversity to manage,' he reasoned. 'To my knowledge, no one from the PFA has contacted him. I find that inconceivable, to be quite honest. The boy is meant to be a PFA member for life. I ask an open-ended question: if that person was a well-known individual within the game, and he tried to do that to himself, what would be the reaction?

'It wouldn't be the indifference a young person gets. It's as simple as that. We will pick up the papers one day, turn on the television or the radio, or flick through social media on our phone, and open the story of a cataclysm, of a young player killing himself. There is nothing more certain than that.'

There was a terrible prescience to his words. On the evening of Sunday, 25 October 2020, news emerged that Jeremy Wisten, a defender given six months' notice of his release by Manchester City's academy in December 2018, had been found dead the previous day at the family home in Wythenshawe. He had just turned 18 and had taken his own life.

The familiarity of his story was horribly acute since I had previously visited his school in the course of my research into youth football. A relatively late developer, born in Malawi and spotted in local football at the age of 13, he was among the City prospects who attended St Bede's College, an independent Roman Catholic educational institution in Whalley Range on the south side of Manchester.

His progress as a promising defender in City's Elite Development squad was stalled and ultimately ended by a long-term knee injury. He retreated to his bedroom and wept when he was released, and withdrew into himself. He no longer had the bond of football with his friends at the academy and felt stigmatised by his misfortune.

He had a series of unsuccessful trials, lost heart and succumbed to depression. His parents, Manila and Grace, mourned 'a very happy boy who was taken away too soon'. They praised the club's pastoral programme, but called for football to be more vigilant in offering mental health advice to young players and their families.

Manila, his father, stressed in an initial statement: 'Boys or girls whose contracts come to an end or are released by all clubs need some care beyond that time. There is often a focus on this at the professional level in sport but maybe not so much at the lower level. I think this would help cases like that of our son. We want to prevent a family going through the same experience as us.'

Later, speaking to the *Sunday Times* about his son, he added: 'He had these lows and thoughts going around his head.

Like "What if I never got injured? What if I had been treated better? What if I had found another club? Maybe I could still be playing football.'"

England international Raheem Sterling led those paying their respects. Mason Greenwood dedicated his first Champions League goal for Manchester United to Jeremy, a regular opponent in youth football. Cole Palmer revealed a t-shirt, commemorating his friend, immediately after scoring City's winner in the FA Youth Cup final. Former team-mates contributed to his funeral costs through GoFundMe accounts, set up by those grieving for 'a beautiful soul'.

City responded by 'formalising' their after-care systems, organising well-being screening with sports psychologists for every player aged 12 and above. The club also pledged to telephone released players on a monthly basis for six months. Though admirably intentioned, it highlighted a principal fault in football's approach to talent development.

It is not a precise, bloodless process. Too many important decisions are taken reactively instead of proactively. Too many avenues of assistance are closed off because of systemic self-defensiveness. Too many men like Pete Lowe and Tony Robinson are treated with suspicion, and occasional resentment, instead of being embraced for their notion of care.

Robinson contacted me immediately, on hearing of the tragedy: 'I deal with lads like this every day. How many more are out there, treading in this quicksand? Something must have gone horribly wrong because Jeremy should have had a queue of takers. I can only imagine the pain his family is going through.'

Lowe was also quick to call. He was consumed by an illogical sense of guilt that his campaign for a more cohesive after-care programme for young players rejected by the professional game had somehow failed Jeremy Wisten. His mood begged the question of who cares for the carer, the individual obliged to deal with angst and anguish on a daily basis in a football environment?

I knew him well enough to ask an unfair question. Had he ever reached the edge of the abyss?

'I made my mind up that I was going to tell the truth when anyone asked me a question like that. Throughout the years I was in the game I found staff, irrespective of their roles, dealing with issues that were bigger than the job, more than the game. It was being a mentor, a guide, a teacher, an unofficial parent. It was being a listener, watching kids laugh and cry in the same conversation.

'It was listening to kids giving you the most profound, deep-lying stories that shook you to the core. That can't fail to have an effect on you. I'm at home two years ago, in a quiet corner of the house, trying to do some work. I'm not able to write, not able to think. I have this huge mental block. If there is one thing I am good at it's thinking. I don't know why. I'm known as a problem-solver.

'I find my hands are shaking. I have never drunk, but it is almost like I'm suffering delirium trauma from drink. My heart rate is flying and I have sweat pouring down my brow. I'd forgotten what I was writing at the table. I was sitting in what I call my quiet chair. The sun always shone through into that room. That's why I love it. There was life in that room because of the sunlight.

'I just sat there and cracked up. There was nobody in the house. I found myself speaking to Scottie, the cat. I'm very fit physically, but actually thought I was having a heart attack. It took me an hour to calm down. I didn't say anything to my wife. I made an appointment to see my doctor, who just happened to work for the football club. When I walked into his consulting room, he took one look at me and knew what it was. He said he'd been waiting for me to come and see him.

'All this comes from me being a solution-finder. You go home not having solved some of those problems, with all the crap on your mind. Your wife wants a husband. Your children want a father. You don't speak about your issues. You get up the next morning. You go to the training ground at seven o'clock. You pick up more problems immediately after breakfast. You've still got to solve the issues from the day before.

'What eventually happens is that you become really good at solving other people's problems but not your own, because you ignore your own. You know, deep down, that it is best to distance yourself, because you are in a personally damaging situation, but you cannot because you have to help a person who is even more damaged.

'The machine inside you takes over. You just do it. The human being takes over. That's why I am happy to talk about having that breakdown two years ago. I talked to Tony Adams about it. I've never forgotten him saying he needed to share. Giving out, and giving back, was a means of handling his sobriety.'

Did Lowe reach the point where he hated the game?

'Yes, and I can identify the moment for you. A member of staff, who was a fantastic carer, knocked on my door and said: "We've got a problem downstairs with a young player. Any chance of you speaking to him?" I went down into the changing room and found a child absolutely erupting. He's not crying. He's convulsing from the pit of his stomach. There's an issue.

'You must show humility. I waited for what felt like an eternity for that boy to speak to me. It probably took ten minutes for him to be able to do so. He's 14, a Year Nine at school, in a very emotional state. Trust me. I don't care how hard you think you are, that gets to you. In your mind, that's your child in front of you, and all you want to do is put your arm around him.

'You can't do that for obvious reasons. You must stay in control of your emotions in the most difficult moments. He'd asked to see me. I knew his name, and his age group, but didn't know him that well. I gave him my word that what he told me wouldn't go beyond the safeguarding officer. His mum and dad didn't know what had been going on. He was living with Mum but wanted me to speak to both of them. I did so that night.

'He was being bullied by a coach, because he wasn't good enough to provide the coach with the results that gave him kudos. These people work in default. I call them dark destroyers. Their callousness is the biggest thing I have struggled with down the years. It's the slow drip from the tap that wears the stone away. It splits you in two.'

Why endure, then?

'It's the kid who walks in and says: "Pete, have you got five minutes?" He thinks he isn't good enough and is still there two hours later. Football propagates fear. You get players on the edge of really taking off, potentially making the big stage, and then they complain about an injury. You look a bit deeper, speak to the physio, and find out the injury is relatively minor.

'You discover that the real issue is the fear of walking down the tunnel. They describe it as like being in a coffin, seeing eyes peering in at them. It's the moment they've waited for all their football life, and yet they can't face it. You can't prepare players for that. It is spontaneous. Performance is destroyed by the most meagre things.

'Your job as a coach is to know those players inside out. What are their mum and dad's names? Do they have a cat and a dog? Do they have brothers and sisters? Have they got a girlfriend? Who are their mates in the changing room? Where do they go at weekends? You sit in a changing room and watch faces. The eyes are moving. Behind those eyes is the real picture.

'I had one lad come in with his hair falling out through stress. The landlady alerted me that she had found hair on his pillow. People think young players learn to cope as they get older. Bullshit. If you're going to your digs at night thinking your coach doesn't like you, the depth of that feeling is so intense.

'I had some young parents, in their late twenties, come to see me. Their 11-year-old son, a reserve goalkeeper, was hauled off in a tournament after conceding two goals in 15 minutes. He was harangued by the coach in the dressing room afterwards in front of everyone. No wonder the lad was in floods of tears, and didn't want to go back.

'The goalkeeping coach hated what was going on, but didn't want to break the chain of command. That's the weakness of the system. I could advise about attempting to build bridges, but the parents had to deal with a boy who didn't want to play the game he loves more than anything on the planet. How can football do that to its young?

'It is a two-sided coin. On one side, it says: "I hate this game." On the other, it says: "I love this game." You flip the coin. It's not about power, but being in a position of influence. You can get a changing room to follow you, as a coach. You can get boys understanding how they can become leaders. Have you accepted your responsibilities? Are you happy with what you've done today?

'You see the joy on their faces as they start to develop, and maybe come through a crap time. You are not human if you are not carried along by that. They are big moments for you. It's almost a parental experience. You've helped a kid. That is your trophy. Without question, the worst thing is young people reaching the end of the road in football without having had their problems noticed.

'I can only do so much. All any of us can do is be a catalyst for change. We have to care.'

Without good men like Pete Lowe and Tony Robinson, the game is lost. Their value is hidden, incalculable. Lowe retreated to his bedroom and wept when he learned that the young man he had helped through a suicidal episode had returned to the United States, following the death of his mother, to take up another scholarship offer in a college coaching programme.

Robinson consoled himself with his involvement in a similarly redemptive episode. Charlie Scott, released by Manchester United at the age of 20 in 2018 after 14 years with the club, was an overweight labourer on a building site in Stoke when their paths crossed. Scott, a close friend of Marcus Rashford, had endured suicidal episodes after a series of unsuccessful trials, but the coach sensed tough love was appropriate.

'The first thing I said to him was "son, look at the state of you. I'm going to tell you a seemingly obvious secret." He was so out of shape, but he actually listened. Football is rarely honest with these kids. Only he could rebuild his life. He worked so hard, began to believe in himself again and his talent re-emerged.'

Comebacks are rarely climactic, instantly conclusive affairs, but Robinson's satisfaction in Scott's initial achievement, a contract with Happy Valley in the Hong Kong Super League, was felt profoundly. 'Charlie will make his way back,' he insisted. 'He has found something within himself as a person.

'What do I get out of it as a coach? President Obama said something in a pre-election rally in Florida that has stayed with me. He said: "We are not trying to create a perfect world. We are just trying to create a better one." So much needs to be done, to help those who are let down by the game, but I am just trying to do what I can do.'

Fate is not always kind. Robinson broke down at the funeral of one of his original players from my son's team in Milton Keynes in the spring of 2013. Sprite, Jamie Steers, was a young father who found life too hard to handle. The casket in which he was borne into the service was covered with his favourite number eight shirt from Robinson's team, in Brazil's traditional colour, yellow with green trim.

'It was too much for me,' he recalled. 'No one saw it coming because Jamie was the life and soul of the party, but I couldn't help thinking: "If only I had stayed in touch with him." I looked at the rest of the team. They had grown up into nice young men and were talking about coming back together for a benefit game.'

Debbie, Jamie's mother, insisted on Tony having the shirt, despite his reluctance, because her son wore it all the time as a child. 'That,' she told him, 'was how much you meant to him.'

Chapter Nineteen

Soul Food

THE PLAYERS' tunnel at the Den is football's equivalent of the hypogeum, the subterranean passageway where gladiators waited to enter the Coliseum. It is narrow and claustrophobic. You can smell the fear, sense the tension and see young men blink involuntarily when they hear the malevolent murmur of an invisible crowd.

David Forde was in his element. He would stand, last in line of the starting eleven, and scan the faces of opponents emerging from the left-hand dressing room. Anyone unable to resist the temptation to half turn, and make eye contact, was lost. He would intone, in a mixture of booming basso profondo and an incongruously soft Western Ireland accent: 'C'mon, Millwall. They're ours.'

I would try to position myself directly behind him, in front of the substitutes, since this was an essential element of my education. I learned that fear and anxiety were omnipresent in professional football, yet often hidden beneath protective layers of bravado and studied nonchalance. Forde was a classic contradiction, abrasive and assertive, but sensitive and reflective in more private moments.

A professional career had seemed beyond him when he returned to his native Galway, guilt-ridden after having been sent off for fighting with a team-mate at Barry Town in the League of Wales. He worked as a labourer, laying bricks alongside his father, and stacked supermarket shelves. Yet, through force of will and strength of character, he would play past his 39th birthday, make 489 senior appearances and win 24 caps for the Republic of Ireland.

He was one of a group of senior players I christened the Guvnors during a season embedded at Millwall for a book with the self-explanatory title, *Family*. They referred to themselves as the Secret Seven after successfully sneaking out of the team hotel on a pre-season tour for illicit sessions on the Guinness. They set and enforced unyielding personal and professional standards.

Their Everyman ethos was captured by captain Paul Robinson as he paused at the doorway of their dressing room at Wembley. 'We're playing for the people who hate their jobs, who'd love our lives,' he said. 'Let's give them something special.' He duly scored the goal that secured the team's signature achievement, promotion to the Championship in a 1-0 play-off win over Swindon Town. I abandoned objectivity, ran on to the pitch and threw myself into Forde's arms.

A decade on, in the summer of 2020, the Guvnors retained close links. Robinson coached Millwall's Under-23 squad. Neil Harris managed Cardiff City after a four-year spell in charge at the Den that, mercifully, failed to compromise his status as a club legend. Alan Dunne coached Bromley in the National League, and Gary Alexander managed Glebe at Step Five in the National League system.

Tony Craig, at 35, was starting a two-year playing contract at his fifth club, Crawley Town. Andy Frampton, initially

Harris's assistant manager, had left football to run the family firm. That left Forde, operating as a counsellor and performance coach after a journey from 'self-sabotage to fulfilment' in which he embraced vulnerability as a strength, and trust as an ally.

In the latter stages of his playing career, he had secretly started to practise Japa, an ancient meditative technique that involved reciting a mantra under his breath or in his mind. Football, he reasoned, had made him 'emotionally illiterate'; to build a second life he had to rid himself of a fear of judgement.

He spent time with a Bolivian Shaman, studied Buddhist culture in the Himalayas and visited Native American reservations to learn from the tribal traditions of the Apache, Hopi and Navajo. He drew a sharp distinction between the parochial pride and common cause of Gaelic sport and the corrosive selfishness and institutionalised immaturity of the game that made his reputation.

'As a player I had deep sensitivity, but struggled to understand myself, and to do that I had to understand the healing elements within me,' he acknowledged. 'I didn't really know who I was, and what I was doing. I had to go deep down to change. I had to break myself down and build myself back up again. That comes with negative connotations in a conventional world like football.

'Football is about the individual, but also the collective. It operates on an internal and external level. I could not be myself, and wasn't doing myself justice. I had to deal with a lack of self-belief. I had to stop listening to the inner critic, who seeks to undermine everything. I had to learn how to control the flow that comes from a bigger place, that psychological transcendence.

'The best work you can do is internal. It's not tangible. It's hard to test it psychometrically. When I entered the professional ranks it was never about the money. I loved winning, and loved competing, but overstepped the boundaries. It was never personal, but I was highly aggressive and shocked a few people.

'I looked at the cause, rather than the effect, and realised I lacked emotional and mental maturity. It was always about me trying to be the best, but I was going for the destination and totally forgetting about the importance of the journey. I missed so much because I was not emotionally present in the here and now. It came down to a basic principle. I had to return to love.'

Such unashamed spiritual sensitivity evokes suspicion and occasional derision in hidebound, hierarchical dressing rooms, yet Marvin Sordell struggled so badly with his sense of self he became suicidal. He retired at the age of 28 in 2019 after a ten-year playing career that encompassed the top four tiers of the professional game. A year later, he featured prominently in the FA's Heads Up mental health campaign alongside Prince William.

A total of 464 players, more than ten per cent of the membership of the Professional Footballers' Association, accessed counselling services provided by the Sporting Chance charity in the initial phase of the pandemic. A secondary survey of 262 players by the PFA during lockdown found that just under a quarter admitted to depression and thoughts of self-harm.

Sordell was so emotionally stunted that he reported for training the morning after his unsuccessful suicide attempt, at the age of 22, and didn't tell a soul about the depth of his depression for four more years. He ultimately found self-expression through poetry, public speaking and film making; his moral courage, in articulating the depth of his despair, is compelling.

I asked him to explain what it felt like to be so desperate that taking his own life had a desolate logic: 'It's more a lack of feeling. When I was at that point I was completely numb to everything, the highs, lows and everything in between. I was at rock bottom and just felt completely withdrawn from any emotion.

'I didn't feel the joy I'd once had playing games and scoring goals. I didn't feel a thing. A lot of people in football have been surprised by my honesty, but once you live and feel depression it's not something that ever goes. You manage to understand it and learn to live with it, but you don't just click your fingers and it's gone.

'Anybody that suffers with mental health problems will tell you they are great actors. They understand how to manage social situations, by withdrawing from them mentally or just not being there physically. When I wasn't great, I arrived for training as late as possible. As soon as it had finished, I'd be gone. While I was there I didn't say a word, hoping they wouldn't notice me.

'A lot of people thought I had some sort of attitude problem. They thought I was a bit arrogant because I wasn't speaking to people and didn't really want to have conversations. My identity was locked into football for so long. Now, having spoken about things, people understand why I may have acted differently, but I see similar signs in tons of players I have come across over the years.

'It's a hugely masculine game. Look at the heroes of the past, big tough players who played through pain. Terry Butcher playing for England with blood all over his shirt and his head bandaged up. People think: "That's a real man. That's the type of player I want playing for my club, my team, my country." They see football as going to war.

'There are numerous things that prevent players from being themselves. When you are in the public eye in the Premier League, you are an object, not even a person. You're aware that many people can put a block on things, fans, other players, staff higher up in the club. Most of the time it is better to play the political game, and just do what you need to do to survive. It's tough.

'Football began as a hobby for probably 99 per cent of players, but when you are so emotionally tied to it and invested in it, where do you escape? It changes the moment you step through that door as an apprentice. You're like, "Whoa. This is my job. I have to do things properly, by the book. I can't just go out and have fun every day."

'Players' families have to be rock solid. If you don't have that support network it can be so difficult. Even if you've got it, it can be hard. A bad performance can affect the family for the whole weekend. Plans might be cancelled because you are annoyed. When you are down and disappointed, they try to pick you up, but the only thing that can pick you up is a good performance.

'They will understand that, when they watch you on a Saturday. They are desperate for you to do well, so you will feel good about yourself. Looking back now, it must have been so hard for my wife. She couldn't help me. She couldn't drag me out of it. She was just watching me wither away.'

Forde identifies with such bleakness of being: 'We are becoming more aware of mental health, but players still become institutionalised at their clubs. There needs to be a holistic approach to helping them. I improved ten-fold once I found a sense of balance. Football's first revolution involved physiology. The next one will centre on psychology.

'Football is full of fear. Even a player who survives a cull can suffer from survivor's guilt. Everyone starts with dreams and visions. It's only now, when I see hundreds of kids trying to imagine what it would be like to become a professional footballer, that I realise that getting there is truly amazing. It is a world in which you have to be ruthless, but there are levels of security.

'For me it was about keeping my family safe and secure, giving my wife and children the opportunity for the best life. Football was my identity. If anyone threatened that, the ego stepped in. Gradually, I realised it didn't define me. Doing things differently can be so cathartic. It gave me such drive and purpose.'

Pippa Grange worked with the England team at the 2018 World Cup as part of her former remit as the FA's Head of People and Team Development. An applied psychologist, she defines herself as a culture coach. A key element of her role involves enhancing the quality of relationships within a team and understanding the way in which power, rather than managerial authority, is applied.

This is no esoteric indulgence since it was largely developed over two decades in the harsh, alpha male environment of Australian Rules football and rugby league, where she 'had to be prepared to piss people off'. Authenticity and compassion are essential since cynicism and ruthlessness merely intensify insecurity.

Football is not the only sport in which communication is deceptively double-edged: 'When you walk into British Cycling one of the first things you see is a sign on the wall that reads: "Logic, not Emotion". The overt message is "learn to control your mind when you are performing". The subtext is: "Don't bring your emotional shit here. You are here to perform." That can't work because you can't close off entire segments of your emotion.

'When we talk about the balance between physiology and psychology, it's not an either/or situation. Our frontiers have broadened around science. That's brilliant and necessary. We don't have to drop that commitment. It is more of a meeting between two elements of the human being to allow for the whole performer.

'You don't have to dumb down. We can't ignore expressions of emotion like anger, tantrums, naughty boy stuff. This is not a choice between wearing a tie-die t-shirt and playing a flute underneath a tree, or being a fantastic athlete like Raheem Sterling. We still don't understand what we mean by the athlete as a whole person. It basically means answering the question: "How can I show up at work as me?"

'As a footballer you spend your life performing and not just on the pitch. You never take the mask off. But it is not just specific to sport. We have forgotten to be human in all sorts of ways. The dynamics of power at clubs make people question whether it is genuinely OK to be who they are. If you can't show as you, it's exhausting. It takes layers off you.

'My experience over 20 years is that when you pull players to one side in that environment it's all there. They are not belligerently triumphant. When you scratch beneath the surface, everyone's story recognises the danger to the soul. Almost every player has that separate compartment. It's there. It's just no one expresses that.

'They don't want to be seen as a soft boy. They don't show anybody their underbelly. We are still talking about mental health in black-and-white terms. You are seen as capable and happy, or saddened and broken. You're OK being OK, or you're on your knees and need help. It's complex. You can't simplify this stuff.

'It's a day-to-day continuum. Wellness is very variable. It's not one or the other. I have known players, facing 18 months out after a serious knee operation, be vibrant. Then, when the clinical situation hits them, they are in a pit of despair. It is almost as if we expect a big sob story before we can accept they are not doing OK.

'The professional arena is tough. When reality hurts, people cover it up. We need to be human-centric, to keep the person front and centre. We need to ask: "Where are we all at today? Where do we want to get to?"'

The problem is getting people to listen to the answer. The modern player, already assailed by vindictive, instant judgement from strangers, is no different from any other citizen struggling to retain emotional stability throughout the insidious fluctuations of the pandemic. His fear for his livelihood, and the welfare of his family, is no less acute for the attention his trade generates.

Football clubs like Millwall are outreach centres for the University of Life. Unlike those in more traditional jobs, a player's performance review is not an intermittent, stage-managed experience, smothered by the cotton wool of HR protocols. It is a daily process, in which verdicts are delivered harshly and occasionally threateningly.

It was estimated that 1,400 professional footballers were still looking for work at the start of the 2020/21 season. Their industry is not unique in being under existential threat, but the perception of financial comfort masks reality for the majority. Mortgages still have to be paid, irrespective of economic uncertainty or supposed social status.

Grange sees the broader perspective: 'A fear pandemic has occurred alongside the Covid-19 pandemic. The last six to eight months have exaggerated in the extreme football's ecosystem. Footballers live with uncertainty and insecurity, but now it is right in their face. Big decisions are on the table. Add that to the social pressures, and it strips away any semblance of confidence. You are a bit brittle.

'When you are uncertain, what can you hold on to? Top footballers don't face financial worries, but financial health is only one part of their welfare. Soul health, or spiritual health, can be the difference between feeling empty or fulfilled. That emptiness, that base feeling of depression, is a condition of the soul. It leaves you feeling nothing, staring into the void.

'This is where the soul of football is so valuable, so right. It means something. It gives you the opportunity to hang on to something. Old school resilience in highly masculine, hyper-performing environments typically involves a demand to tough it out. That's not being resilient. That's not being tough. There is a difference between them.

'Toughness is a block of concrete, hard, solid and insurmountable. Resilience is a sheet of very flexible steel. It has give in it. It has bend and movement. Resilience ensures you can fail, fall and feel terrible, while retaining the possibility of springing back. You still have the mentality, a way of seeing the world, and the tools that will enable you to take the next step. It is a broader life perspective of challenge and recovery. Toughness is one-dimensional. You have it or you don't.'

Sordell's resilience has been tested to its limits since he retired from what he termed 'a beautiful game with an ugly persona'. The development of his film company, Oneighty Productions, was stalled by the initial lockdown in the spring of 2020. A documentary series he presented and co-produced for Yahoo! was in abeyance going into autumn.

He found himself struggling with imposter syndrome, questioned the selfishness of pursuing renewed ambitions and even considered returning to football. The field he had chosen for his secondary career was as cynical and venal as the first. Ideas were stolen; liberties were taken. He confessed: 'It's honestly draining.'

He admits to feeling overwhelmed, occasionally lost, but continues to progress. He set up Transition FC, an online platform 'which essentially looks to give footballers the tools I have found to be an absolute necessity, to build their bridge from playing to retirement.' He co-founded Swoop, an influencer marketing agency that uses social media to connect brands with the football community.

His advice to young players deserves to be heard, and heeded:

'A footballer must have a relentless belief in himself, and his ability to get where he wants to go. But the young player has also to understand that education is his friend. He needs to have a back-up plan. A handful of players might be able to sit at home and do whatever they want after their careers, but the overwhelming majority of us will need to work.

'Education equips you for later life. It doesn't matter if the subjects you have taken are large or small. It doesn't depend on the type of degree you earn. It might just come down to having an outright understanding of the world, who we are, and what we are doing here. It might involve an awareness of the history of many different things. Just having a broader personality can only be helpful.'

Forde worked with Crystal Palace's academy for a year, delivers seminars for UEFA and is involved with the European Mentoring and Coaching Council. As a former goalkeeper, he is used to personal exposure and the pressure of perfectionism. As an educator, he is conscious he has much to learn, and a lot to impart:

'What am I now? A life coach? A performance coach? If I can help someone, does it matter what my title is? Don't over-complicate things when troubles arise. Have the courage and strength to work through your fears. Don't allow yourself to be a victim. If I look back at my career, it was phenomenal, playing for so long, but at times I felt like a little boy in a man's game.

'I was on a rescue mission. Imagine what I could have done had I eradicated my fears earlier. Then we'd be dealing with a different entity. When you discover yourself you step into a place of freedom and liberation. Tap into what is within you. That release of energy is what we mean when we talk about potential. Sometimes you are your own biggest obstacle.'

My search for reaffirmation was becoming more focused. There were chinks of light, such signs of enlightened thinking as Brighton's initiative in becoming the first club to assimilate a wellness element into their performance programme. It needed more people in positions of influence, like Dan Ashworth, their technical director, to apply the human touch.

Pippa Grange made a call to arms: 'We can't reach a new horizon if we expect the same actors to come up with a different perspective. We need different types of people, a different method of thinking, to move forward with any conviction. It demands perspective. Acknowledging sport's rich human element will allow a change in attitude.

'It's the small things that matter: love, continuity, soul. The sense of shared joy when football matters to player and fan alike. That's not just silverware, the glory and sparkle. It's a broader sense of meaning, the peace that comes with greater attachment to the essence of the game.

'Football's story is a story of humanity. That's what the new frontier represents. It is about understanding its role in modern culture. It needs coaches coming in and making sure we don't deny that humanity. It is a story of love, developed for some of us when we went to our first match with our grandad 50 years ago. That's why it matters to us. It is the story of us, at our best and worst.'

Chapter Twenty

Rebirth

HISTORY HAS a habit of announcing itself with a nod and a wink. On 5 September 2020, 135 years to the day after Bury FC played its first game, a goalless draw in a friendly at Little Lever, Bury AFC played its first home game, a 1-1 draw with Nostell Miners Welfare at the Neuven Stadium, some two miles from the site of the original fixture.

The symmetry of the occasion might have prompted a neutral's wry smile, but beneath the surface passions seethed. A year after being expelled from the Football League, Bury FC was, at best, in a vegetative state. Despite the increasingly incoherent ramblings of Steve Dale, a widely reviled and ridiculed owner, only the apparent formality of liquidation remained.

Gigg Lane, the club's ground since 1885, had the air of an untended grave on that blustery morning in early autumn. Piles of dead leaves and polystyrene burger boxes were compressed against shuttered stairways. A series of shrines to doomed devotion, featuring scarves and flags, bobble hats and banners, were fraying at the edges.

It reminded me of those roadside memorials at the scene of fatal accidents. I pass one most mornings on a dangerous bend; the flowers have long since withered, leaving a wooden cross at the base of a tree. Droplets of rain had seeped into a plastic folder tied to a blue railing close to the players' entrance. The first few words had smudged, but the printed message was unequivocal.

'Bury Football Club, 1885–2019,' it read. 'Hung out to dry and discarded by an uncaring EFL who continued to give our current owner just what he craved and who now bleat they had no choice. YES YOU DID! Your so-called integrity is a sham just like your unfit for purpose organisation. You are as bad as the insects that ruined our once famous club. Shame on you all.'

A white replica shirt, given a green tinge by mould, acted as a tribute to a long-retired player, Alan Tinsley. Beneath the badge, a thin-tipped black pen had recorded his career details: 'Apps – 94. Goals – 15. 1970–75.' A supplementary inscription – '4 Generations. 1 love. 1 Club. 1 Passion.' – hinted that it had been hung by his family.

Further along the railings, a once-red shirt, bleached by the sun, proclaimed 'never give up'. Another plaintive message, hand-painted on a faded pillowcase, hung on a blue metal gate, read: 'Save our Shakers. Dale must depart.' They were tokens of frustration and idealism, which had mutated into anger and suspicion as a community had turned in on itself.

Football was edging, hesitantly, towards a new season without knowing what renewed reality would look like. With local infection rates doubling, the second wave of the Covid-19 pandemic was on the horizon. Football should not, logically, have mattered in the wider context of a fretful society, but the rancour and division it stimulated assumed inordinate importance.

I was unprepared for the toxicity of the situation. The creation of a phoenix club, and the seemingly forlorn hope that something could be salvaged from the wreckage of its predecessor, had pitched fan against fan. Relationships had fractured. Dissent and mistrust had corroded a closely knit community.

As a member of the heritage committee established by Bury AFC, James Bentley had the responsibility of recording the rebirth of football in the small Lancashire town. He and his father had agreed to sponsor the unnamed AFC player who would wear the number nine shirt. Yet the wounds were too raw, the slights too recent, for him to attend a match.

'It's like a messy divorce,' he said with a sigh. 'Friends who have known each other for years have chosen divergent paths. They now struggle to get on. I walked past somebody, a Bury fan who used to sit in the same area of the ground as me, when I went through the town centre on the way here. He made sure I was in earshot when he called AFC "rats". I cheered as loud as him when Bury were promoted in 2019. We had what seemed such a strong emotional bond. Now it has come to that.

'I am sure we are working through stages of grief. We're all grieving for our club, and people grieve in different ways. Some people are pragmatic, and think there's no way the club is coming back from this. I happen to agree with that view. Others don't. They don't see the club as being dead. It's not been liquidated, so you're stamping on the club's legacy by supporting AFC.

'The change in attitude was instant the moment AFC was created. I'm not saying which point of view is right or wrong. Both sides have been stiffed by people who couldn't care less. It upsets me because you see AFC Wimbledon posting pictures of their new stadium online. That's what can be achieved when fans are united by a single vision.'

Questions hung in the air. Must tribal loyalty overwhelm logic and decency? How can the loss of something so central to so many lives be rationalised convincingly? Should supporting a football club demand suspension of disbelief? Are fans doomed to be the cannon fodder of modern football, the poor bloody infantry sent out to fight for the brand? Why do we not seek out their stories with greater zeal?

I have rarely heard a supporter speak with greater clarity and with such modulated emotion about a passion that is perversely simple, and fiendishly complicated, than Bentley that Saturday lunchtime. He was, by turns, ardent and agitated, wistful and world-weary. It was as if, because of the setting, he felt the gossamer touch of history on his shoulder.

We were sitting on Platform 2 in Bury Bolton Street station. A black locomotive, number 80097, announced its departure for Rawtenstall, in the heart of the Rossendale Valley, with a shrill whistle, a cloud of steam and the oddly disconcerting ejection of a stream of boiling water on to the track. This was the station from which the Bury players left for Crystal Palace and the 1903 FA Cup final. They defeated Derby County 6-0 before a crowd of 63,102 and returned as heroes.

This was where Private Thomas Watts, James's great-grandfather, departed to serve in the First World War. A junior cotton plater in a local mill, he was barely 16 when he became one of the first to enlist in the Lancashire Fusiliers. Wounded in September 1917, he was registered as missing in May 1918 and returned to Bury in January 1919, having been a prisoner of war in Germany.

He married five years later, and in later life took his grandson Graham to watch Bury from an early age. Graham, in turn, passed on his passion to his son, James. Such family trees form a protective forest around clubs, large and small, but in Bury's case no one thought to build a firebreak against the ruthlessness of strangers.

The sense of loss was stark.

James, a man in early middle age, channelled the child who first watched Bury in 1988, aged eight: 'I remember my dad going to a mythical place called "the football" when I wasn't old enough to go. My first game was against Wolverhampton Wanderers. It kicked off at 11 o'clock on a Saturday morning and Bury won 3-1. I don't remember a great deal about it, other than being sat on a crush barrier and being told not to go wandering, but it quickly became the thing that my dad and I did and wouldn't be without.

'It was never about the quality of football, although we have had some good teams that have played some good football. Martin Dobson got the team playing great. Ryan Lowe did the same in our last season. I've also seen an awful lot of dross in the 31 years I spent watching Bury, but it was still something I looked forward to every week.

'You have got your routine down to a tee. You know what will happen and when it will happen. I'd go to my mum and dad's for something to eat Saturday lunchtime. As soon as the *Football Focus* titles started rolling, my dad would say: "Are you phoning a taxi, then?" I'd order one for quarter past one. At 1.16, my dad is looking at his watch and saying: "He's not bloody coming, is he?"

'We'd go to the Stanley Conservative Club behind Gigg Lane for a drink. You recognise everyone who walks in, put your hand up to greet them. It wasn't so much about the game. It was about the million tiny interactions you'd have. The woman selling Golden Gamble tickets in the car park is not my lucky seller, so I'd go to Susan, who is selling them under the stand. I have to buy one from her.

'I'd see Joan, who had worked for the club for 47 years. Joan's dad is Bury's most-capped player of all time, a fella called Bill Gorman. Lynne is her daughter. She'd worked for the club for 30 years. Mike, her brother, is the groundsman, but has done all sorts of jobs for the club over 33 years. They've watched me grow up from a snot-nosed kid.

'You know everybody around you. You know every nuance of it. It's learned behaviour. You are not taught matchdays. My dad didn't say: "You're going to experience this, this and this." You just take in all these sights and sounds of a place where you are made to feel comfortable, made to feel wanted. You are not a commodity. You are a supporter. Individually you can be important to your club.'

He paused, pulled a laminated membership card out of his brown leather wallet and introduced me to his eight-year-old self. The boy had short black hair. He was smiling broadly and wearing a white Bury shirt. 'I love the fact the signature is so haphazard,' he said tenderly. 'It's just me, wobbly writing my name. We wore that shirt when we took the lead at Old Trafford in the fourth round of the League Cup on the night of the King's Cross fire. I've still got the *Sportsnight* coverage, transferred from VHS to DVD.'

The Conservative Club, reached along a cobbled lane and a stone-walled entrance that led to a bowling green, had the musty air of a provincial museum. Team photographs from the Sixties nestled alongside grainy reproductions of goals scored by Bury legends like Northern Ireland striker Derek Spence. A panoramic colour portrait of Gigg Lane, pristine in pre-season, had been signed by 16 players.

A brass plaque, framed by two posies of plastic red roses and holly leaves, commemorated members lost in the First World War.

Allegiance isn't necessarily sustained from cradle to grave, but it confers a certain sense of immortality. Later, at the AFC match, I was struck by a huge union flag behind one of the goals, which proclaimed 'Beardyman Lives On'. This paid homage to the memory of Adrian Webb, a fan whose presence on club message boards was described as 'often irreverent, irascible and politically incorrect'.

Other friendly ghosts emerged for a namecheck: 'Barry Lockley was a friend we'd have a drink with before games. He once turned up to a game over Christmas dressed as an elf. He was a fantastic bloke, but he had cancer and died in 2015. I put something on the Bury message board, saying: "You might not know his name, but if I was to say he was the fella in the South Stand with a big Russian hat you'll know who I mean."

'Straight away I started getting messages, "RIP Fellow Shaker". He had his ashes interred at the side of the pitch. Our little group who drank with him went down to Gigg on a nondescript weekday morning. The groundsman was trimming the grass. There was just the general hubbub of a football club at work. And there we said goodbye to our friend. Gigg Lane was where he was happiest.

'Recognition of those sorts of fans is largely missing from the game today. That little group who drank together didn't sit together. My dad and I went into the main stand and everyone else went in the south stand. You invite those people to the night do at your wedding. You grieve when they die. When we found out that John Buckley who sat behind us had died my dad and I were absolutely distraught.

'In 2009 I lost my job in quite distressing circumstances. It really pushed me to the edge. My dad said: "Do you want me to buy you a season ticket beside me?" I think he knew exactly what he was doing. The restorative power of sitting in that group on that regular basis, with that network around me, really, really helped. When everything else goes to shit you've still got your team.'

Until that team gets taken away.

'What's happened to Bury? We've been punished for the actions of somebody who couldn't care less about connections like that. Steve Dale hasn't been punished. By his own admission he is not a football fan. But I've been punished. I don't want to be glib, but until I met my girlfriend the club was the love of my life. I've had that taken away from me and I've done nothing wrong.

'If you'd have asked me at seven o'clock on a Saturday evening during the last football season what I did between three o'clock and 4.45 I wouldn't have been able to tell you because I didn't watch *Football Focus* any more; I didn't read the sports pages, I didn't buy football magazines. I'm sure Mr Ladbroke won't be quivering at losing my two pounds every week, but I didn't put a bet on.

'Your whole interest in the game just disappears. You can't look at the League One or League Two tables if it doesn't affect you in any way because you don't have that emotional investment in it. It's extremely frustrating when all you want is something concrete. AFC are doing something concrete. They have been transparent from day one. It upsets me that we can't all work together.

'Gigg Lane is like a ghost town. When I go there now, it physically hurts. I could do the walk there with my eyes closed. I know every bump in every paving slab. Until expulsion, it was part of my life for 31 years, to the day. I know it sounds clichéd but you just stand there, go through all the goals, the saves, the great moments you had with your mates when you were a teenager.

'Bury won the Second Division championship when I was 16. Is there a better age for something like that to happen, for a club to really get the talons into you? You just remember the best times of your life you had in that square mile near Bury Cemetery. You remember Tony Rigby scoring the goal against Preston that got you to the play-off final, and the absolute joy you felt, aged 14, that night.

'To be able to ask Tony Rigby: "What did it feel like?" Imagine that. Players always used to go into the social club after games. You could get their autograph and they'd say: "How do you think I played today?" You could talk to them. I used to run on the pitch after every game and slap them on the back.

'When Manchester City launched that tunnel club they said it would be the closest you'd ever get to the players. You were separated by a massive perspex sheet and the players all had headphones on. That is not what being a football fan is all about. Now I stand there at Gigg, looking at this shell that hasn't been used for a year.

'We actually got into the ground in the summer. I sat in my old seat in the South stand, V152, and my seat in the main stand, J15. The fact I know those seat rows and numbers off the top of my head tells you how important it is to me. You sit there, thoughts echoing. All the Tuesday nights we spent there. There were 1,396 of us against Stevenage. Again, that's imprinted on my mind.

'On a night like that you're thinking: "Jesus, can it get any worse?" But you keep going to games because you hope that one day it will be like it was before. In the promotion season under Ryan Lowe we were 3-1 down at home to MK Dons with 18 minutes to go. We won 4-3. I'll be talking about that game when I'm 80, and a prisoner of my own degenerating mind.

'I am not a football fan. I am a Bury fan. I'm not one of those who say I'll go anywhere to watch a game of football. If the football is on in the pub, and it is a Champions League semi-final, I wouldn't really watch it. It was all those interactions at Bury that made me a Bury fan. They welcomed me in as a kid. It was like being welcomed into a secret society.

'When I was a kid everyone supported Liverpool. Why? Because they were good. There weren't many Bury fans at school. I supported them because I could actually go to a live game. I'm very proud to come from the town. So I see Bury football club as my link to my town and my family. I want dignity, pride, a sense of self from my football club. Steve Dale doesn't give me that.'

That afternoon's match was typical of the level, tier ten in the football pyramid. It featured flawed decision-making and lack of composure, flashes of natural skill and instinctive movement. These part-time players, paid around £80 a week, were relatable to the 150 fans, a capacity crowd under social-distancing protocols.

They rested their pints on a whitewashed, four-tiered breeze-block wall around the pitch, and were visibly and vocally glad they had something to watch. AFC were profligate in front of goal, having worked the majority of their opportunities down the right-hand channel, where the relative quality of Lewis Gilboy, a young winger released by Accrington Stanley, stood out.

Liam MacDevitt, whose goal separated the teams at half-time, is a former sprinter turned children's television presenter, whose football career was derailed by untimely injury. He ruptured quadriceps muscles at the age of 20, and became AFC's second signing following spells at Yeovil, Swindon, Bristol City, Farnborough, Stoke City, Livingstone, Gosport

Borough, St Albans City, Stalybridge Celtic and two clubs in New Zealand, Southern United and Tasman United.

He did media work for the PFA and had evidently developed a strong sense of narrative. 'I was never going to play in the Champions League, but what I got from football has not changed,' he said in a Football Shorts film that accompanied his arrival. 'I loved the idea of playing in front of fans, representing the lifeblood of a community, becoming part of something bigger than myself. If you could be part of something this meaningful, you'd sign too, wouldn't you?'

Nostell equalised seven minutes into the second half through Amir Berchil, and the game petered out in a flurry of inconclusive substitutions. Arlo Young didn't appear to care. A bright-eyed boy, aged three and a half, he played between blue plastic seats with a green toy bus, produced from his miniature Star Wars backpack. In the car on the way home, he told his father Phil he loved the half-time chips and the way people smiled at him.

A rite of passage, attending his first live football match, had been completed. Phil, one of the pivotal figures in the new club's creation, did not attach any grandiose importance to the occasion since his attachment to the sport was more measured than most of those around him. He took quiet pleasure in being a Bury fan and became involved with AFC almost out of a sense of civic duty.

'I thoroughly enjoyed the anonymity of being a football supporter,' he reflected as we sat at the back of the small stand behind the goal. 'I didn't go for a beer before or after the game. I don't live in Bury any more. But when I saw some of the things that would be required for AFC, I knew I would have to help. We needed to create a governance structure, put a proper financial structure in place so the club could be sustainable.

'I work heavily in financial services and regulation. I sold my own business to a FTSE 100 company, so I know what systems and structures and governance look like. The club, in the way we have organised it, is effectively a business with a £300,000 turnover. Because of what happened previously to Bury FC we have to be absolutely squeaky clean.

'Football is a world of excess. It attracts people with money, and attracts people without money, who want to look like they've got it. There are a lot of people out there who are driving very expensive cars, or living in very big houses, who have borrowed money they can't afford to repay. That's the equivalent of what we've seen at Bury.

'Intellectually, I knew I had the skills and experience to help. On an emotional level, I kind of got fed up with the powerlessness of the fans who were hurt by the expulsion from the Football League. They were moping about. Maybe that's a typical northern thing, tipping the cloth tap and waiting for someone to save them from the mill owner.

'I don't mind admitting that I've felt like jacking it in a few times over the last six months or so. The lack of belief in the community from the fanbase really frustrated me because I knew the talent, ability, effort and application required was there. It just needed a few people to push things together.'

This embryonic, modular organisation was operating on old school enthusiasm and millennial marketing skills. Older volunteers, acting as matchday stewards, exuded the kindly concern of lollypop men and ladies. Younger helpers devised a slick, interactive social media operation that sold 1,500 newly designed, fan-approved shirts in the month leading up to the season. Those shirts funded a fitness and conditioning coach through the lockdown.

Three internal teams, covering commerce, media and governance, were overseen by club chairman Chris Murray, who became a Bury fan as a teenager despite 'the weird dynamic' of having various factions of his family urging him to support Manchester United, Liverpool, Everton, Bolton and, most improbably, Sheffield Wednesday.

His tipping point came when a neighbour took him to see Bury beat a second-string Manchester United team, containing the Class of '92 in its earliest incarnation, 4-0. 'From then on, I was screwed,' he admitted, with a gentle chuckle. 'I've tried all the way through this to take sentiment out of it, and look at it from a business perspective, and I can't. There are a lot of people who struggle to talk about it. They're hurting.

'It's really weird. I told everyone from the start I would be respectful to their opinion, and listen regardless. Social media can be horrible, especially when you see the names some of the volunteers are being called. They're Bury fans who've lost their club, and decided to do something about it, rather than tweeting "Fuck the EFL" every day. How long can you go on having your club held hostage?'

Each fan had his or her individual journey to make towards acceptance. Bentley's Damascene conversion came at AFC's opening North West Counties League match, a 3-2 victory over Steeton, secured by two goals in added time at the end of the second half by Tom Greaves, who wore the number nine shirt sponsored by him and his father.

The 95th-minute winner, a classic goal-line scramble from a right-wing corner, sparked unbridled, long-supressed scenes of joy; a fan, in an exultant time warp, even cranked up an old school rattle in celebration.

'My throat was red raw,' Bentley admitted in an entranced tone which suggested he could barely believe his good fortune. 'It was one of those games you felt was written in the stars.

'I had been wavering about whether it was for me, but it soon became apparent that this club is just as "Bury" as the one formed in 1885 because it's all about the spirit of those watching. Your ancestors, my ancestors, just wanted to watch football. It's not about the level. It's about the familiar faces, familiar conversations with an extended family you haven't seen for too long.

'I hadn't seen my dad so excited for years. He said when he woke up that morning he felt like a football fan for the first time in a long time. This story has more twists and turns to come. This could be the start of a journey that ends like AFC Wimbledon, or it could level out in the upper reaches of the pyramid like at Chester or Darlo, but I loved it and feel like I've got something back at my core.'

AFC are paying £30,000 to ground share with Radcliffe Boro for two seasons, during which manager Andy Welsh is expected to secure at least one promotion. Despite Dale quoting Voltaire, rambling on about 'Calvin Cline (sic) boxers' from Bury market and excoriating 'people trying to pass off fakes as the real thing', the ultimate aim is to purchase the charge on the original ground at Gigg Lane, which will cost up to £3million.

For Murray, football became a deeply personal, dauntingly painful experience: 'My son Ryan is buried in the cemetery right behind the ground. He was buried in a Bury shirt. His headstone faces Gigg Lane. When I went there, I had this overwhelming feeling that "This couldn't and shouldn't happen to a football club." I said, both on the day we got expelled and the day they refused to reinstate us in the League, that I have a duty for my son to get us back there. People want to go home.'

Fans in that situation have the desperation of a drowning man, scanning the sea for driftwood. David Hilton, another would-be saviour, a stranger with an indistinct background, was touted as the potential owner of a reformed Bury FC, inserted into the National League North.

When his initiative collapsed, some fans groundlessly blamed the phoenix club. Murray resigned after he and his family was subjected to 'vile' online abuse which prompted this Cri de coeur: 'Regardless of opinions the abuse of everyone needs to stop for people's mental health before someone ends up getting hurt, arrested or worse, committing suicide.'

Life, death and football: interlinked, and spanning the canyons between hope, uncertainty and despair. Unexpectedly, heading into a fearfully unpredictable winter, my head was beginning to clear.

Chapter Twenty-One

The Curse of the Quid

ANDY HOLT slept fitfully on flattened cardboard boxes on the garage floor beside a temperamental injection-moulding machine on which his determination to make a better life depended. It would often stall and emit a shrill alarm that had to be answered immediately. He had limited technical knowledge and had no option but to learn, through trial and error, how to keep it running.

Days bled into weeks. He was too consumed to return to the house to eat so, in the early hours, when their baby son was asleep, his wife would emerge in her dressing gown with a tray of food. She paid the mortgage by assembling the plastic products her husband had made and distributing them to retailers across Lancashire.

Nearly 20 years later, What More Ltd is the UK's largest manufacturer of plastic household accessories and storage boxes. Holt, the council estate kid with a driving ambition, employs 400 people and is worth between £80 and £90million. The money he has made gives him commercial credibility and an entrée into certain strata of society. At one gathering of the great and the good, he was asked whether he liked paintings.

He made small talk that he admired art as much as the next man. His acquaintance, a prominent businessman, told him: 'I paid 23 quid for a painting last week.' The painting was by Pablo Picasso. The word 'quid' was used as shorthand for a million.

The arrogance and egotism implicit in such indulgence is anathema to him. Holt pays himself £250 in cash, in a brown sealed envelope, each Friday. On the bright and blustery September Saturday I spent with him, the first of the League One season in 2020/21, he was wearing a flat cap, a £20 pair of chain store jeans and a crisp but relatively cheap shirt.

'I started in that garage with nothing, just my hands, my time. You build it, chase it, grow it and keep getting bigger over time. It has taken my life to do that. The truth is I keep spending the cash I make on more cash generation, through the business. We make money every month. I don't need it. What football has done for me has put me back in touch with people, my roots, where I belong, where I'm comfortable.'

As chairman and major shareholder of Accrington Stanley – he isn't keen on the connotation of the more obvious title of owner – Holt has unnerved the game's hierarchy. He doesn't obey convention, or recognise the code of the gentlemen's club for ungentlemanly people. Administering common sense and financial logic, in a distinctive Burnley accent, isn't football's way of winning friends.

As they say in those parts, 'tek mi's thi' find mi'. If they don't like him, he doesn't particularly care. The club he rescued when 'they caught me at a weak moment' perennially overachieves, regardless of results. It is a throwback, a reminder of football's lazily squandered heritage that offers hope for the future. Its ethos is captured by the inscription on the badge: 'Industry and Prudence Conquer'.

Accrington, set in a valley between a Scalextric track of motorways, is a faded former mill town. Stanley, formed in 1878, dissolved in 1962 and revived in 1968, is one of the few strands of social fabric that have yet to be unpicked by modernity. Holt talks fondly of community, family and football in its natural setting, a small ground 'surrounded by chimney pots' and renovated beyond recognition:

'My dad always told me: "Son, money goes to money and that's why we'll never have any." He died when I was 16 and it broke me. I had more money in my pocket than him. In fact I'd lent him a tenner so he could go to the pub three days before I lost him. It still hurts. He was right though, money goes to money and I had to earn some.

'Now that my money is doing what he said it would do I won't waste it. I've done a variety of things that makes me proud of my roots, and I hope my dad would be proud of me. One of them is sorting our community club out. I'm not a football man and never want to be. Football needs non-football people running it with a clear mission statement and mandate, openly run and publicly judged.

'Capitalists make the rules in life and in football. The job's fucked for the vast majority as a result. If the rich believed in fairness, they wouldn't shelter all their "money goes to money" gains offshore. They should not be running football via the Premier League's dominance. They should have very limited influence over our national game.

'I know capitalism isn't the answer to anything, especially football, but neither is rampant socialism. Everyone was Labour on our estate. Most blokes worked down the pit and Thatcher would have been lynched if she'd turned up there. But they were wrong. If a nice car went down our street, my mates wanted to scratch it. I told them I'd get a better one.

'I spoke to Keir Starmer when he came to the club and told him he should encourage cash generation, tax it fairly and spend it wisely. When I was a kid, it was more about destroying the cash generators. It's about supporting our economy and making everyone contribute fairly to a great nation and society. That's also how football should be run, for me.

'The rich clubs make the rules. Re-running the Premier League breakaway with a top-six breakaway into some sort of Super League is just pouring petrol on the fire. There is no way the top six should be making the rules. They will never do the right thing. They're self-interested, selfish fuckers. When you have money, you are used to getting things done for your benefit, and that dynamic is hard to stop. Wealth becomes meaningless, an extension of ego.

'I genuinely care for the game and the impact it has on millions socially. Some of these owners, the sort who think about a million as a "quid", should go and stand with the crowd. What they've lost is that grounding. I don't enjoy it in boardrooms. I care not what league Accy is in. I only insist on it being run in a manner that ensures it survives. I love winning: I define winning differently to 91 other owners, that's all. Accy is winning regardless of what happens from time to time on the pitch.'

As if on cue, John Coleman, starting his 19th season as Stanley manager, returned to his office, a portakabin behind spartan changing rooms, after handing in the team sheet for that afternoon's match against Peterborough United. 'Another beer, boss?' he asked, pulling a cold bottle of Estrella out of a small refrigerator in the corner. 'Come on. I've seen your school report: "Easily led."'

The next half an hour or so, from 2.10pm, would be his golden time. The gameplan would require little tweaking; with the exception of the injured Siriki Dembélé, Posh would be at full strength. Jimmy Bell, his assistant, was outside, overseeing the warm-up with John Doolan, the other senior coach. All three had signed new four-year contracts; an announcement was made four days later.

Holt light-heartedly warned his manager 'the tape's running' and launched into a robust defence of the salary cap system that was scheduled to limit League One clubs to an annual budget of £2.5m until the PFA won a legal appeal against its imposition. 'You have to have some control over it,' he argued. 'What some are doing might benefit their club, but it is damaging the industry. They are creating an environment where nobody can compete. In order to try and compete, people get themselves in trouble.

'Take that supposed £200m play-off game to get into the Premier League. If I put a one-armed bandit in the middle of Burnley with a £200m prize, it wouldn't be long before half the town were fighting, skint, because they'd poured all their money into the machine. That's what is happening in the Championship. They're all blowing their brains in on the £200m bandit.

'Look at what has happened to Wigan. I talked to them, and their budget was to lose £10m a year for five years. It repels my mind. I couldn't have a business like that. It goes against all the principles I hold dear. You need a cap and you need to maintain it. Clubs should be relegated two divisions if they are cheating. No appeal. I'd kick 'em straight out of the EFL. I wouldn't give a shit. I'd bludgeon them, to get control back in sensible hands.

'Without Covid-19, there would never have been a salary cap. I will listen about the numbers, but not the principle. What has gone before hasn't worked, so let's try something new. What

I don't get is why wouldn't you want to welcome a salary cap and make a profit? Cut ticket prices, fill grounds. Cut prices for merchandise. Don't rip people off for pies and pints.'

Coleman, half-watching the final stages of Brentford's defeat at Birmingham on TV, seamlessly joined in the debate. 'You'll look at us later,' he said. 'What I always say is that at three o'clock it doesn't matter what fancy car you're driving, a 4 x 4 Lotus, or a Tesla. You might have eaten a better steak than me last night, but it doesn't make you a better player than me.

'So when we get fans in, if God spares us, they'll pay £4.50 for a pie and a pint. If I go to Anfield, a pie and a pint costs me nine quid. It's not a Premier League pie. It's not made of better ingredients. It's not a super-duper ale that I can't get anywhere else. It's a bog standard bottle of fucking Carlsberg and a Holland's pie. So why is it nine quid? They've got a captive audience, we haven't.

'There has been no equalisation of wages in our league so far. Look at the wages Peterborough will be paying here today. Sammie Szmodics has come in from Bristol City for a million. He's not going to do that for less than six grand a week is he? Same with Jonson Clarke-Harris. He's cost a million from Bristol Rovers, had many suitors. He'd have gone for four, five.'

Coleman's perspicacity reflects his background in non-league football, where talent is worthless without application. A former schoolteacher, he is accustomed to working on a low budget and spoke about recent rejection by a League Two player: 'The lad started at three grand a week. I told him: "You're way out of our league, son. There's no point in us having a conversation." Salford wouldn't have told him that.

'If you look at League Two, Bolton are paying Eoin Doyle four, four and a half grand a week. They've got themselves into a terrible financial situation. They're trying to get themselves out of that situation by doing the same thing that got them into it. So you can have no sympathy. Where does it all end? If they have a salary cap, and clubs go over it, how are they going to monitor it? How are they going to punish it?

'Points deduction is the only thing that people are fearful of. If everyone knows the rules, that one breach is three points, the second six, a third nine, they will stop doing it. Think about it. If you've got 12 points on your licence, you're driving down the motorway like Miss Daisy aren't you? You're petrified of losing your licence. It's the same thing. Clubs should be petrified of losing their status.

'The problem you have got – and he will tell you, because he is the owner and he who pays the piper calls the tune – is that it is a double-edged sword. Say Andy goes to me: "C'mon John, I'm fed up of us being at the back of the queue. Go and sign four players on four, five grand a week." That's all well and good. But what does that do to the rest of the players who are on a fraction of that?

'He knows I wouldn't do that unless I can give them a lift up as well. But more than that, if I sign big money players on three-year deals and we go down, or he fucks off, the club is stuck with those contracts. That's what indirectly has led to the biggest problems in football. Clubs haven't built in the failure factor.

'I agree with Andy. As he says, everyone gambles. They are chasing an impossible dream. They don't put failsafe, worst-case scenarios into their contracts. The cap protects them against themselves. It's like a punter can set a limit on how much he bets. It protects him from doing his brains in if he is having a bad day.'

Coleman sees Premier League 2 as 'a fait accompli', given the undercurrent of self-interest that is likely to result in the formation of a pan-European Super League, or a bloated version of the Champions League, in this decade. He nevertheless insists a 'vibrant Championship' is possible, beneath two elitist divisions of 12 or 14 clubs, providing relegation and promotion is maintained, even in a limited form.

Unchecked desperation is a systemic cancer: 'The clubs who get themselves into trouble do so through mismanagement at the top. That might include a manager saying we need this, this and that. Look at Rangers. How did they get themselves into trouble? They are virtually in a monopoly situation in Scotland. How could they go pop? It doesn't bear thinking about.

'Well, before Andy came here, we played Notts County in League Two. We beat them 2-1. Kasper Schmeichel was on more than our whole squad. I'm thinking: "How can this be right?" In the end, they won the league, but it all went wrong, didn't it? One of the other chairmen made a great point. He said County won promotion with all these big hitters no one else could afford. The problem was neither could they …

'That happened ten years ago yet they still let it happen again with Bury. Bury couldn't afford the players that won League Two in 2019. No chance. They were giving them four, five grand a week. I feel sorry for the fans, but they didn't deserve to get promoted because they cheated. They spent money they didn't have. We could have all done that.'

Our discussion meandered, into the minutiae of change. Holt spoke of the need for football to appoint a central auditor, to monitor contract payments 'on a day-by-day, week-by-week, month-by-month basis'. The imposition of B teams into the pyramid, a possible reciprocal gesture as part of the negotiations for Premier League support for EFL clubs during the pandemic, would be 'a disaster'. The FA was impotent.

The Father of a Nation, with a coming of age present. Nelson Mandela helped heal South Africa with the rugby version, but football's World Cup united the townships.

'A few people were singing and dancing.' Mike Gatting's reference to a protest outside a cricket ground, brutally repressed in the dying days of apartheid, summed up the shameful rebel England tour he captained. It was a political and sporting embarrassment.

Albania was a closed
nation when Barcelona
played a first round
UEFA Cup tie against
Flamurtari in 1986.
I was smuggled in
as Terry Venables'
interpreter. Globally
renowned players like
Gary Lineker were
treated like visitors
from outer space.

Dwarfed by the power
of the state. Barcelona
staged a chaotic
photoshoot here, at
an independence
monument in the
Adriatic port of Vlore,
stronghold of the
Sigurimi, the Albanian
secret police.

Ari Vatanen has an al-fresco massage after a long day of desert driving in the Paris–Dakar Rally.

Co-driving Ari Vatanen through Kielder Forest in Northumberland in the 1996 RAC Rally. Since both front wheels are meant to be pointing in the right direction, it didn't end well.

More boys with toys. Highest foreign finishers in the Arctic Rally. Driver Tony Jardine was remarkably sanguine as we headed down an ice chute, towards a Moose, at 120mph.

Off to sail around the world the wrong way. The yellow spinnaker of my yacht, Hofbrau, *stands out in the flotilla of small boats escorting us towards the Channel, and the adventure of a lifetime.*

Working on the foredeck as a storm begins to build. It's no place for the faint-hearted. Trust in your lifeline, and get back to the cockpit as soon as possible.

Team Philips was beautiful, thrilling, fragile and fatally flawed. She was a nautical version of the Starship Enterprise.

Team Philips *leaving Dartmouth for sea trials in the North Atlantic. Bigger than Wimbledon's Centre Court, the catamaran had twin masts the height of ten double decker buses.*

The Way We Were. Press conferences for England managers are now multi-media, interactive showcases. This, one of my first, was an impromptu gathering with Ron Greenwood in the café at Barcelona airport, the morning after a 2-0 win over Spain in Camp Nou in March 1980.

David Forde, the former Millwall goalkeeper, is now a performance coach with a distinctive insight into the human condition. I forgot myself when promotion to the Championship was assured at Wembley, and leaped into his arms.

A Man Alone. Bobby Robson watches his England team lose the penalty shoot-out in the semi-final at Italia '90. Endearingly human and endlessly absorbed, he made the best of the Impossible Job.

Marcus Rashford, a modern role model who speaks truth to power.

'All these superhero clubs were shit at one point,' Holt argued. 'There is no future for many clubs unless we get these issues ironed out. The problem with football is it doesn't consider the long-term outcomes of its actions. If it did, there would never have been a Premier League breakaway. We're facing an existential crisis due to Covid, and we're not being helped by piss-poor regulation.

'As an industry we are weak because the belief is that clubs should blow every penny available at all times, leaving little wool on our backs for times like this. When you talk about survival you need to keep it in context. It's not about surviving in the Championship, or at this level. It's about surviving, full stop.

'A club survives by running a sustainable budget year in year out, whatever league it is in. So, if we went down to League Two we'd have to work on a lower budget, work hard to attract fans, do all the things we are already doing to compete as best we can on the pitch. That's good business. That will improve standards.

'In business 80 per cent of my time is spent assessing downside risk. Only 20 per cent is spent looking for opportunity. I always look at a range of outcomes when budgeting. This makes me prepared for anything that happens within the ranges planned for. The range of outcomes for football is too wide now.

'It ranges from a government bailout to the collapse of the entire pyramid. My central view is that there will be some assistance, but no golden bullet, and we will be OK. It is easy to see the other extreme if clubs start falling over, rendering competition hopeless, followed by a rapid loss of TV cash.'

When the first wave of the pandemic was building in the spring, and his company was voluntarily making plastic parts for single-use protective masks for NHS staff, Holt had taken the precaution of having the stadium valued. 'It's ours, and it's paid for,' he reiterated. It could be sold to a third party as a last resort, but not without legally binding agreement from supporters.

Their banners, colourful symbols of frustrated allegiance, festooned the Clayton End of the ground. '1962 – Never Forget' read one. 'Stand Up and Be Counted' proclaimed another. Holt had tried, and failed, to get permission to stand on the terracing and bang the bass drum that remained, tied to one of the crush barriers. I couldn't help laughing when Holt confessed the goalposts were cast-offs from Manchester City.

'I'm right excited,' he confided, as we headed for the mothballed Supporters Club bar, where victories were once celebrated with £1 pints by unsegregated fans. Fish, chips, mushy peas and Barry Fry were on the menu. Peterborough's director of football, at 75 a self-proclaimed 'fossil', was, true to form, a human whirlwind. I'll leave it to you to guess his favourite word.

The meal, served to the few temperature-checked guests permitted by the new protocols – mine, taken by a paramedic at the Redz Bottle Bar, was 36.6° – came in boxes from the Whalley Road Fish Bar, nearby. It was the least Holt felt he could do, since they were denied matchday takings. 'Fucking lovely, Andy,' Fry cackled. 'This'll do for me. Fuck me, mate, do you know this is my 60th season? Can't fucking believe it …'

Holt loved it and asked David Burgess, Stanley's managing director, to take a photograph of the pair, arm in arm, in defiance of the new normal. It's not every day you meet a football artefact, a former Busby Babe born 24 hours before VE Day. 'Fucking strange with no fans, innit?' Fry said as he headed towards his socially distanced seat in the stand.

It was film-set football, a familiar ritual enacted in a vacuum. It was a contradictory experience, soulless yet intimate, forbidding but fascinating. The unreality of the atmosphere encouraged hyper-sensitivity. Each kick, clash and obscenity had rare resonance. The touchline tableau, featuring managers and coaches, was magnetic.

Coleman lounged against a wall, arms folded, while Bell and Doolan double-teamed Steven Copeland, the fourth official. Darren Ferguson, his opposite number, had clearly attended Fry's language school. 'Fuck off,' he screamed in Copeland's face. 'How is that a fucking foul?' As the first half wore on, he became increasingly agitated. 'Come on,' he shouted at no one in particular. 'This ain't a fucking pre-season game.'

I was particularly impressed by Stanley's academy graduate Ross Sykes, who played on the right of a defensive three. Scouts dismissed him as 'Bambi on ice' and 'a horror show on the ball'. I saw a 6ft 5in youth growing into himself, after paying a personal trainer to improve his upper-body strength during the lockdown. He was assertive in the air and in possession. Coleman had sensed leadership qualities; at 21, he captained the team in the lesser cup competitions.

Dion Charles, who gave Stanley the lead on the stroke of half-time with a wonderfully instinctive volley from the edge of the box, is a typical reclamation project. Released by Blackpool in 2014, he retrieved his career in non-league football at AFC Fylde, Skelmersdale, Fleetwood Town, Halifax Town and Southport.

Tariq Uwakwe, who sealed victory in the 85th minute with an equally audacious curled shot from similar distance, represents the other strand of Stanley's recruitment strategy. He joined Chelsea's academy at the age of eight; at 20, in his first loan spell, he had been repurposed as a left wing-back by

Coleman, who paid him £400 a week. The Premier League club had fruitlessly asked him to contribute £1,500.

Uwakwe's goal was my moment of surrender. Standing next to Holt, in front of an open doorway at the back of the stand, I involuntarily celebrated with both arms in the air. For a supposed neutral, it was conduct unbecoming. For a football fan, it was as natural as breathing. I realised, then, how much I had missed the release of emotion that accompanies a beautifully struck leather ball, hitting the taut side panel of a net. Club colours didn't matter; this was an Everyman experience.

Sometimes, it takes a stranger to point out what is in front of our noses. I recalled the words of Marcelo Bielsa, a singular football man and economic migrant to the Premier League: 'If anything describes English football, it is League One and League Two. If there is anything to distinguish English football, it is the spirit you compete with. This spirit is no better represented than in these lower categories. It's the nucleus, the heart, the essence of football in this country.'

When the hapless fourth official signalled six minutes of added time at the end of the match, Fry leaned across the gangway with a smile: 'We wouldn't score in 25 fucking minutes. Since we're going away with fuck all, any chance of a bottle of water for the car on the way home, Andy?' Holt beamed, and brought him two.

He punched the air at the final whistle. 'Got goose pimples,' he confided. 'That were brilliant.' Reality could wait. It returned soon enough; Macclesfield Town were wound up in the High Court four days later, the night after winning 2-1 in a friendly at Witton Albion. Another name had been etched on football's tombstone.

The scenes of distraught fans, gravitating towards Moss Rose, a padlocked stadium, were irredeemably sad and terribly familiar. A 146-year-old club had died for the want of a £500,000 debt. Phil Young and Chris Murray, from Bury AFC, showed their solidarity by immediately offering to assist the formation of a phoenix club.

A note at the ground, left in a plastic envelope and highlighted by Philip Buckingham, a football news reporter for the Athletic who had gone to school with James Bentley, read: 'To all Macclesfield Town fans. We know how you feel. We were betrayed, now you too. Yours in sympathy, the fans of Bury FC.'

The indignity of the stadium being subsequently advertised for sale at £500,000 on the Rightmove property site was eased when Macclesfield Town's assets were bought out of liquidation in early October by local businessman Rob Smethurst, owner of Stockport Town and 40 academies, involving more than 2,000 junior footballers across England. Robbie Savage, football's Mr Marmite, joined the reclamation project.

What is a football club? The mental gymnastics might have been predictable, but I immediately thought of Accrington Stanley. Each of their 1,100 season ticket holders is a recognisable human being, rather than an anonymous statistic in a customer relationship marketing database. Club staff had proactively been helping older fans through the technical minefield of streaming live matches.

Stanley's supplementary programmes cover physical literacy lessons for primary schoolchildren and walking football sessions for pensioners. The club runs a disability team and initiatives for the unemployed. It is a priceless point of contact, a voice on the end of the phone for the lonely or the infirm. It lives by ten club values: honesty, integrity, trust, commitment, pride, respect, quality, value, collective success and character.

I was given a glimpse of sustainability that September Saturday, which began in a newly constructed Memorial

Garden at the back of the ground, where supporters' lives were recorded on a series of grey metallic plaques and Holt watched Burgess draw the monthly raffle live on local radio. Against all odds, and in defiance of a gathering storm, it made complete sense.

I should have known better. Coleman had built a squad capable of mounting another unlikely promotion challenge, but within a month, the club was paralysed temporarily by a coronavirus outbreak. Right on cue, English football indulged in another bout of self-harm. The aristocracy were ready to exercise what they regarded as a feudal right to burn down the tithed cottages of the lower classes. To make matters worse, my childhood hero was dealing with the cruellest of diseases.

Chapter Twenty-Two

Everyday Heroes

ONE BY one, the brightest lights of childhood flicker and fade. As shadows lengthen and darkness descends, heroes lose their definition. In too many cases, they are gone before we know it. They are unlikely to be forgotten, since their impact is invariably profound, but the sense of loss is stark because it is so personal.

News that Bobby Charlton had been diagnosed with dementia, released by his family last November following the death of his brother Jack and World Cup-winning team-mate Nobby Stiles, was another fragmentation of legend. Bobby retreated a little deeper into the imagination; sightings of him in the main stand at Old Trafford, alongside his wife Norma, were increasingly rare.

His benign influence endured through a charitable foundation, set up to ease conflict recovery following a visit to Cambodia 20 years previously. It covered all aspects of humanitarian assistance, including rehabilitation from childhood trauma, physical and mental therapy, to the supply of a range of modern mobility aids, including prosthetics and orthotics.

His own plight was especially poignant for me because it was not entirely surprising. I had known of his decline for a couple of years, following a friend's confirmation of a public show of confusion at a Munich memorial event in Germany, but kept my counsel as a mark of respect. It was the family's right to provide confirmation in their own time.

Six of the Boys of '66, Ray Wilson, Martin Peters, Peter Bonetti, Gerry Byrne, Jack and Nobby, had already been taken by Alzheimer's or dementia. A *Mail on Sunday* survey of the 475 First Division players in that 1965/66 season found that of the 185 who had passed away 79, or 42 per cent, were victims of neurodegenerative illnesses or conditions linked to traumatic brain injury.

Evidence, resisted by the football establishment for generations, was overpowering. Former footballers were found to be three and a half times more likely to develop dementia. Dr Willie Stewart, the neurologist who raised awareness of the significance of Jeff Astle's premature death, concluded they are five times more likely to die of Alzheimer's, four times more likely to die of motor neurone disease and are at twice the risk of succumbing to Parkinson's disease.

It is a complex problem. Dr Stewart's research has defined combinations of up to four different types of dementia, suffered simultaneously by former players. Billy Bingham, at 89 Everton's oldest surviving player, was first diagnosed in 2006 as suffering from percussive dementia, the type most prevalent in contact sports.

As an emerging player in Belfast with Glentoran, Billy suffered three traumatic head injuries before his move to Sunderland at the age of 18. On one occasion, he woke up in hospital without any conception of how he got there. David, his son, was his principal carer for 12 years from his initial diagnosis before he moved into permanent, residential care.

Billy embodies the ease with which we create personalised time warps. I got to know him in the build-up to the 1986 World Cup, when I covered his Northern Ireland team in the opening phase from their base in a castellated hotel overlooking Guadalajara. Relationships with players, formed in the pub in the grounds of their domestic training base, overlooking Belfast Lough, flourished despite the deceptively complicated nature of the group.

Kate Hoey, who decades later became the Pantomime Dame of Brexit, insinuated herself into the camp as companion to Robert Armstrong, the *Guardian*'s correspondent, who distinguished himself, in temperatures of 90 degrees, by persistently wearing the same woollen plaid shirt. Armstrong's background was typical; a union activist, he was brought up on a tough Protestant estate. His father worked in the shipyards; his mother was a former music hall artist.

Bingham identified with his upbringing. He began as a marker boy at Belfast's Harland & Wolff shipyard, drawing chalk lines on steel plates before they were cut into shape. His combination of charm and cunning made him a perfect figurehead. He knew the totemic value of Norman Whiteside, the Manchester United striker he had selected for a record-breaking World Cup debut against Yugoslavia in 1982 at the age of 17 years and 41 days.

Whiteside, hardened by boyhood on the Shankhill Road, loved a goal and a Guinness. He was uncannily assured for someone so young, a perfect fusion of technique and temperament. Sir Alex Ferguson described him as 'being close to genius', but recognised the warning signs of the knee injuries that would lead to his premature retirement at the age of 26 and sold him to Everton.

Footballers offer us an insight into the fragility of the human condition. They are prisoners of fate and their respective generations. A player of Whiteside's presence and personality would be a multi-millionaire in this brand-aware modern era; he retrained as a podiatrist, became a United ambassador and felt compelled to sell his medals, in July 2020, to supplement his pension.

What. If. Strung together, they remain two of the most toxic words in sport's lexicon.

Who knows what would have happened had Northern Ireland held on to the early lead Whiteside gave them in the opening match against Algeria? They drew 1-1, lost narrowly to Spain and were fortunate only to be beaten 3-0 by Brazil. Whiteside was awestruck by the experience of facing Julio Cesar, the central defender who would miss the critical penalty in the shoot-out against France in the quarter-finals.

'Man,' he said, as the players wound down in the tiny hotel nightclub. 'That bloke was something else. He had so much time. He glided about like a head waiter. He could have been playing in full DJ and dickie bow, and carrying a tray of drinks.' Reverence softened the clipped tones of west Belfast, signalling that the boy had finally been freed from the barbed wire of fame.

World Cups do that to people, but they cannot change them completely. Football was rightly celebrated as a unifying factor, but that night ended with a sobering reminder that the squad, inevitably, was divided on sectarian lines. As the lights went up, a group of players from the Unionist community gathered in a square on the dancefloor and sang the national anthem.

That image seemed horribly relevant in Bingham's final match, after 15 years as manager. The World Cup qualifier against the Republic of Ireland in Belfast on 17 November

1993 had the most vicious undercurrent I can remember. The Troubles were at their height; 23 people had been killed in the three weeks leading up to the game.

British Army helicopters had been shot out of the sky, and nine Protestants died in the Provisional IRA bombing of Frizell's fish and chip shop on the Shankhill Road. Eight civilians, aged between 19 and 81, were killed in a retaliatory massacre by UDA members at a Halloween party in the Rising Sun bar in Greysteel, County Derry.

Windsor Park was at the heart of the Loyalist stronghold of south Belfast, a traditional no-go area for Catholics. Linfield, the host club, had continually to deny the existence of sectarian bias in its selection policies. On this occasion, uniquely in my admittedly limited experience, the conventions of journalistic neutrality were not observed.

Alex Toner, the *Daily Mirror*'s veteran Northern Ireland football correspondent, was normally impeccably dressed; he was accustomed to taking light-hearted stick for his range of wide chalk stripe suits. He arrived in the overcrowded press box looking dishevelled and, frankly, terrified. A readily recognised Catholic, previously afforded safe passage because of the respect in which he was held in the football community, he was abused and threatened on the way to the ground.

Crowds on the Lisburn Road were singing sectarian songs that celebrated bathing 'in Fenian blood'. Children pointed imaginary guns, random pieces of wood, at the Republic's team bus on which the lights were turned out. Players, protected by armed, plain-clothed Special Branch operatives in a convoy flanked by armoured cars, were warned not to sit next to the windows.

The Republic's national anthem was not played; a brass band recycled its version of 'God Save the Queen' as police, with dogs, ringed the pitch. History felt oppressive, but Bingham, who would lead tributes to the 'gentlemanly' Toner when he passed away in 2006, had helped to set the incendiary mood by branding Jack Charlton's UK-born players as 'carpet baggers'.

His contemptuous comment that 'they couldn't find a way of making it with England or Scotland' would not be forgotten. Jimmy Nicholl, his assistant, screamed 'up yours' at the Republic bench when Jimmy Quinn, ironically a Catholic from west Belfast, put Northern Ireland ahead, only for Manchester-born Alan McLoughlin to secure World Cup qualification with a 78th-minute equaliser.

Charlton confronted Bingham at the final whistle, quickly regretted his taunt of 'up yours, too, Billy' and ended, bizarrely, being given an ovation after presenting his opposite number with a retirement gift in the post-match press conference. I once bumped into Billy on the scouting circuit when he was working for Burnley in the early stages of his illness, but he had only one more managerial job, a brief spell at Al Nassr in Saudi Arabia.

As is the way of things, I lost track of him. It was only by chance, researching case studies of former players with dementia, that I came across an interview with his son by Paul McNamara for the Everton website. David spoke compellingly about Billy's lack of self-pity and his innate pride in his father's character and achievements, even if there was a tinge of sadness in his admission that he was no longer interested in the game.

'He is not caught up with the idea he has a problem and is not feeling sorry for himself,' David told McNamara. 'People who have dementia don't want to believe they have it. They feel they are fine and can function and their memory loss is simple forgetfulness. If you are used to being director of your own life, you don't want some other orchestrator coming in and telling you what's what.

'At the mid-stage of the illness, the person can be quite distressed with it. Things are not as they want them to be and they don't understand why. It becomes a deeper pool of confusion. I gradually built a series of carers, until someone was always with dad. He had help with medication and assistance to cope as long as possible in a home environment.

'I knew that's what he would want. He would probably look around and think: "I am fine." He was being looked after and in his own home, able to potter in the garden. All the things were in place that made him think life was continuing and he was okay. If you'd taken away those props, he wouldn't have been able to sustain himself.

'It maintained an illusion that all was well. That is beneficial for someone who has that kind of illness. Why should you be pondering your deterioration all the time? It is nicer to think you are on top of things. There is no point in sharing the truth if the truth is unhelpful to the person experiencing the illness.

'I think all carers feel they will be dragged down by the decline of someone they care for and are worried about. Families and relatives feel the anxiety for the person who is not well. It was deeply worrying, but it turned out to be surprisingly different. I think only positively about it now. It was a personal and spiritual transformation.'

Yet witnessing the disease 'stripping away' a loved one's mind, to use David's phrase, is a relentless, debilitating experience. Its terrible mundanities and indignities can only be truly understood by those everyday heroes dealing with a distorted version of a father, husband or lover. Afflicted families huddle together as if starved of the warmth of human kindness.

Dawn Astle, who dragged the disease from the shadowlands during an 18-year campaign marked by resistance, ignorance and obfuscation, is at the centre of that unofficial self-help network. She barely slept for a fortnight after the revelation of Bobby Charlton's illness, and the bitter criticism of 'football's cancer of denial' by John Stiles, Nobby's son.

Her landline at home rang constantly; during one of our conversations, which lasted no more than 15 minutes, six messages were left on her mobile. She shared relatives' tears and fears without respite, and was being worn down by the intensity of reflected grief because of her determination to honour her father Jeff's memory.

'The families are prisoners of this,' she said, with familiar, quiet intensity. 'It has devastating life-long influence. It impacts on a daily basis on everything you do, everything you feel, everything you think. Bones can mend, scars can heal, but brain injury stays with you. It's a constant process of deterioration. There is no light at the end of the tunnel.'

The public's response to such selflessness is heartfelt. Penny Watson, who described her husband Dave, the former Sunderland and Manchester City defender who won the last of his 65 caps at the age of 35 in 1982, as 'England's forgotten captain' in outlining his daily struggle, was swamped by hundreds of letters from all corners of the world.

The stories Dawn hears are bleakly comic, occasionally disturbing. They range from the former player who stole downstairs in the middle of the night before being caught gorging on Haribo sweets like a naughty child, to the devoted father who was so mentally unbalanced he threw his adult daughter on to the bed and began simulating sex with her.

It was hard to suppress scorn as the players' union, the Professional Footballers' Association, sought to position itself as a central pillar in the response to an overdue outcry. This is an organisation that, under the notoriously adhesive leadership of Gordon Taylor, has serially failed in its central duty of player welfare.

The PFA charity, already under independent investigation by the Charity Commission, has received almost £54million in the last two years, mainly from a share of broadcasting income. In that time, Taylor was paid £4,043,090. A mere £325,000 was allocated to dementia and concussion research. That represents an enduring disgrace, hardly eased by an admission by Taylor's assistant, Simon Barker, that criticism of their conduct 'hurt'.

His promise to 'change and improve' was rejected by Chris Sutton, another influential campaigner. Dawn's price for joining a PFA-branded dementia task force was a commitment for the union to fund up to ten weeks' respite care a year for families of former players with neurodegenerative conditions. As one relative told her: 'Even half a day a week would help because it would give us a chance to get to the supermarket.'

Mark Bullingham, the Football Association's chief executive, stretched credulity still further by insisting to the BBC's Dan Roan that the governing body 'led the way' in investigating the disease. Greg Dyke, a former FA chairman, expressed some sympathy to the Astle family, and although his successor Greg Clarke made similarly soothing noises about the provision of a care facility for footballers, no advancement was made.

This is not entirely surprising since the FA's self-protective line, as expressed by head of medicine Charlotte Cowie, is to highlight uncertainty about the side-effects of persistently heading a football. She argues, unconvincingly in the view of this layman, that, since it could take decades for clarity to be established, risks should be mitigated without resort to knee-jerk reactions. Meanwhile, examples of what Dr Stewart refers to as 'traumatic brain injury' are becoming forbiddingly familiar.

British sport is unprepared and ill-equipped for the legal tsunami that is about to engulf it because of the consequences of concussion. Rugby is facing individual seven-figure claims from an initial batch of more than 100 ex-professionals, diagnosed with early-onset dementia and other neurodegenerative diseases, as part of a class action suit. Football will inevitably be confronted by the same calamity since its provision for after-care appears to be similarly flawed.

Governing bodies, like many membership organisations, are infested with ego-driven mediocrities. One senior figure in a funding body welcomed me to the English Institute of Sport by saying: 'You'll last 18 months and then tell the world how useless we are.' I lasted four years until growing tired of the petty politics, but glad to be of service.

Professional sport is assumed to be about wealth, when it should concentrate on health. Denial of its physical and mental impact is a by-product of the hypocrisy typified by the chief executive of a major Olympic sport. He sat next to me, in a planning meeting for London 2012, and insisted: 'We all know these Games won't result in a single extra kid taking up sport,' before going out to insist, to the assembled TV crews, they would be uniquely inspirational.

The FA is unfit for purpose. Its inability to act quickly and decisively, regardless of the gravity of the problem, is notorious. The independent inquiry into child abuse in football it commissioned in December 2016 entered its fourth year, with victims seething at the lack of urgency and outcomes. Families were left in limbo. Lives were being compromised. No one seemed to care.

Football's prevarication over the introduction of concussion substitutes, adopted smoothly and effectively in other major sports, emphasised institutionalised indolence and counter-productive caution. Anton Ferdinand added to the sense of unease by highlighting historic shortcomings in the FA's investigation of alleged racism by John Terry.

Stacey Cartwright, the senior independent director overseeing the FA's appointment of a new chairman following Clarke's departure, resigned when backwoods members of the National Board insisted on Brian Jones, a council member forced to resign after an Islamophobic social media post, being given 'fellowship rights', two tickets for England games and occasional access to the Royal Box.

Clarke ultimately became a symbol of football's dysfunctional leadership at a time of global crisis. His self-importance was excruciating, but he would have been safe from the consequences of parliamentary scrutiny had he continued to boast of being a pivotal powerbroker, shaping the future of the game. Instead, he talked himself out of several jobs.

'I'm a big boy. Football is a contact sport,' he told MPs, inadvertently framing his epitaph. By the time he had rambled through a mind-numbing sequence of archaic ignorance that touched on themes of unconscious racism, sexism and homophobia, he had the puzzled look of a bulldog chewing a wasp, wondering where the pain was coming from.

For someone evidently enraptured by the sound of his own voice, Clarke was unaware of the power of language. In referring to 'coloured' players, the 'career choices' of South Asians, suggesting being gay was 'a lifestyle choice' and recycling stereotypical nonsense about girls not liking balls hit hard at them, he unwittingly made a powerful case for football to be run by an independent regulator.

Despite an immediate apology, there was no realistic option for him but to resign from the FA. Following a graceless, characteristically pompous attempt to limit the damage, his lucrative sinecures with UEFA and FIFA also proved unsustainable. The chances of being knighted for services to football, an honour his critics within the FA hierarchy quietly suggested he craved, were atomised.

He had unwittingly acted as useful idiot for the two other administrators called before the DCMS select committee, Rick Parry and Richard Masters, respective past and present chief executives of the Premier League. They might have been labelled 'pitiful' by committee chairman Julian Knight, and accused of leveraging the pandemic to get their 'pound of flesh', but their corporate doublespeak and evasion of responsibility were largely overlooked.

With Clarke out of the way, they were free to pursue the time-honoured diversion of a consultant-driven strategic review of the structure of the English game, which was due to report in March 2021. The shameless elitism of the covertly conceived original plan, Project Big Picture, was unlikely to be compromised.

Premier League 2, the insertion of B teams into the Football League and the prospect of regionalised semi-professional football in the lower divisions were back on the agenda. Any support package for the base of the pyramid from the Premier League would contain more penal fine print than an application for a pay-day loan.

As ever, perceived progress was only visible through a cracked mirror of conflicting interests, secrecy and hypocrisy. So much for the 'moral authority' the plan was supposed to ensure. The overwhelming impression of a defective sport, in which everyone mistrusts anyone with whom they come into contact, was depressingly recognisable.

Further details of the proposed European Super League, as envisaged by Manchester United's Joel Glazer, the principal agitator, emphasised its formative greed, amorality and desperation. Fifteen founding clubs were promised an initial £310m, and seasonal income ranging from £100m to £200m, dependent on supposed status. Five further clubs, qualifying on competitive merit, were identified as the poor relations in two groups of ten.

The Premier League's so-called Big Six cravenly bought into the concept of such lucrative sterility since, at worst, it promised greater influence in domestic negotiations. The other Premier League clubs sought to protect inherent advantages. All concerned expected the lower orders to tug at their forelocks and be grateful for whatever crumbs fell from the table.

Ferran Soriano, Manchester City's chief executive, used the financial challenges of the pandemic to renew pressure for B teams, the natural precursor to feeder clubs, to fill a supposed 'development gap'. It was a novel approach from someone whose club's net spending in the transfer market under the ownership of Sheik Mansour was close to £1billion.

Already allowed to harvest talented young players from smaller clubs for minimal outlay because of the one-sided Elite Player Performance Plan, and with a global network across which to loan products of an overstocked academy, Soriano clearly had no conception of the culture he was threatening. In his eyes, the pyramid was nothing more than a talent pipeline ready to be adapted to serve his purposes.

Even by their standards of insouciance, which would make Marie Antoinette blush, Premier League clubs, with the honourable exception of Leicester City, excelled themselves by ignoring the economic hardship being endured by their supporters as the second wave of the pandemic hit. They voted to charge them another £14.95 to watch pay-per-view coverage of individual matches on top of already exorbitant subscription fees.

It is probably unfair to single out Arsenal to illustrate big football's fundamental hypocrisy, given the activities of gnomic predators like the Glazers and the plague of opportunists infesting other areas of the English game, but, under the ownership of Kroenke Sports & Entertainment, who have imposed the highest season ticket prices, charity is in short supply. What goes around comes around.

Stan Kroenke is worth in excess of £6billion because he ruthlessly exploits seven professional sport franchises, four major stadia, four TV channels, four radio stations, two e-sport franchises and a group of 19 magazines, which includes such wholesome offerings as *Bowhunter*, *Firearms News*, *Guns & Ammo*, *Shooting Times* and *Walleye Insider* (which tells you everything you were afraid to ask about a certain species of game fish).

His minions mercilessly sweat the small stuff, which tends to include fellow employees. Arsenal already refuse to pay agency staff the London Living Wage; in a post-truth, post-shame society, the board blithely assumed they could avoid the fallout from making 55 support staff, including senior scouts, redundant as a result of losses accrued during the pandemic.

Claims 'we are operating in a sustainable and responsible way' were risible since they simultaneously signed Willian on to a three-year pension plan contract worth in the region of £20million. The infantilism of the debate ensured attention was focused on the brief redundancy of Gunnersaurus, the mascot, rather than the crisis into which many families had been plunged.

Andy Holt's Curse of the Quid applied. I understand the logic of the counter-argument that football is the most capitalist of businesses, but cannot come to terms with the insincerity of a marketing strategy based on the fantasy that supporters are blood brothers and sisters, rather than one element in a network of club stakeholders.

Notions of loyalty and family have been usurped and cheapened, most visibly, in Arsenal's case, in the promotion of the ultimate frivolity, a new third kit. The so-called authentic edition of the shirt sells for £100 as 'a technical version' of the one 'worn by your heroes on the pitch'. Fans are urged to wear it 'with pride and show your support for the Gunners'.

Those ludicrously expensive shirts are not aimed at my generation, despite plenty of my contemporaries, entering their third childhood, deluding themselves that they look stylish as they squeeze into them. They put unfair pressure on parents, whose children are sucked into a culture of false expectation.

Clubs have been finding ways to exploit loyalty for decades – my first national newspaper byline, in the *Daily Mail*, was on an investigation into exorbitant replica kit prices in 1979 – but Arsenal's sales pitch, a disingenuous promotional video that used the F-word profusely, reduced Mikel Arteta, a principled man and a progressive manager, to a marionette.

It's worth describing in tacky detail. It begins with a stylised version of a dressing room celebration that bleeds into an equally inauthentic recreation of a press conference. Arteta, starkly lit, then addresses the camera directly: 'I want to tell you what I talk to the lads about every day, and what it means to be part of our family.'

A car driver in an Arsenal away shirt fiddles with the radio and exclaims to his passenger, who is wearing a bucket hat and an officially approved club sweatshirt: 'Are you listening, bruv, are you listening?' The camera lingers on another fan, in a blue Arsenal third-kit shirt with orange piping, before returning to Arteta.

'A strong family,' he intones. 'First there is the non-negotiables, respect, humility, belief. It's OK to get angry, to raise our voices as long as it comes from the right place.' Another fan, in another third kit, places his hand over his heart as the manager drones on: 'And even though family can hurt us like nobody else, remember they are the ones who raise us up.'

Curtain is clearly up in the theatre of the absurd. A fan in first-team kit is captured, by a long lens, on the balcony of a fourth-floor flat. He is, perhaps, the only supporter to have a home-made banner of the club motto, 'Victoria. Concordia. Crescit.', hanging over the railings. Latin scholars will have spotted the link: it translates as 'Victory grows through harmony'.

Arteta (or to be more precise, his scriptwriter) takes up the cue: 'When people come to our house, they try to divide us because they know our family and what our shirt means.' He is stopped in full flow by Nwankwo Kanu, who appears to be 44 going on 64. He throatily repeats 'Gunners for life' over an image of his younger self, superimposed on an old-fashioned TV monitor.

'Let them know we can't be divided,' insists Arteta, before he is usurped by a female fan in an estate setting, wearing the ubiquitous third shirt. 'Aubameyang,' she trills, 'best striker in the league, come on.' This dissolves into a freeze-frame image of a man attempting to feed three thin-cut chips into his mouth with a wooden fork and a soft-focus view of a Thierry Henry statue.

Arteta continues: 'It will take all of us, together, because we know where we belong. So when the challenges come, you will tell them ...' Half a dozen fans, wearing the contents of the club shop, take up the invitation, and repeat: 'This is family,' in succession. The money shot involves the manager walking down the tunnel at the Emirates; when he emerges into the light, he is followed by a 360-degree gimballed camera.

He mercifully concludes the sequence by saying, 'This is Arsenal,' in tones that suggest he has revealed a cure for the common cold. I don't blame him for fulfilling his contractual commitments; whether a club should be excused such an overblown intimation of intimacy is another issue. The methods are crass and the messages are stereotypical, but they conform to a pattern.

You can peddle the pretence of togetherness and promote a cult of unquestioning allegiance, but the death of the greatest footballer of my lifetime proved you cannot manufacture perfection because it simply does not exist.

Chapter Twenty-Three

Shades of Grey

IT BEGINS with a ball.

In places of privilege, it is soft and small, and placed in a baby's crib as a symbol of a father's intent. As the child grows, pushing or kicking it instinctively across a back garden or a suburban park, the feel of it against the foot becomes familiar. By adolescence, it will be made of leather and a size 5, a gateway drug to adulthood. In places like Villa Fiorito, a slum in Buenos Aires that lacks running water, electricity and basic sanitation, it is a symbol of desperate hope. It is created by necessity, a ball of compressed rags, discarded newspaper or a piece of rotten fruit. Diego Maradona made it his accomplice, teacher, pet and feckless lover. It was a meal ticket that ultimately poisoned him.

It ends with a ball.

We all place the passing of greatness into a personal context, but the ball was a constant feature in impassioned commentaries on the nature of Maradona's life, and death. Presented by writers of the quality of Marcela Mora y Araujo, Rory Smith, Jonathan Wilson, Miguel Delaney and Jorge Valdano, they were *billet-doux*, notable for their lyricism and insight, longing and sadness, sparseness and regret.

Here is Maradona, on his final appearance at La Bombonera, the cockpit that houses Boca Juniors: 'La pelota no se mancha,' he tells a fevered crowd. (The ball does not show the dirt.) Later, depicted in a TV studio, he refers to football as 'the sport that gives me the greatest joy, the greatest freedom. It is like touching the sky with your hands. Thanks to the ball.'

Valdano, writing in *El Pais*, celebrates its constant presence. His image of 'a poor boy in a humble setting, controlling a ball with the concentration of a bureaucrat and the happiness of a child' leaps from the page. He describes the scene as 'an amiable discussion, a gentle argument with a ball that still occasionally rebels against him, still resists but will soon join him'.

The ball becomes principal mourner, acquires texture and emotion in human form. Valdano sprinkles words, like grains of soil, on his former team-mate's coffin: 'Today even the ball, the most inclusive, shared of toys, feels alone, inconsolably weeping for the loss of its owner, its master. All of those who love football, real football, cry with it.'

Sometimes, life isn't fair. This is a man who led Argentina's attack in two World Cups, played for and managed Real Madrid, writing with the skill of a surgeon and the freedom of a poet. My immediate instinct after the announcement of the death of his 'great captain' was merely to return to a 99-second film clip, and play it on a loop.

We all have our reference points. The film was shot in Naples more than 35 years previously. Maradona had stayed behind after training in sodden kit supplemented by a red bib. The penalty area was a swamp, puddles and tributaries of recent rain merging with glutinous mud.

Fans gathered, out of focus, behind bars and pitted concrete walls that somehow sustained the skeletal frame of a summer vine. They cackled with delight as Maradona lobbed the goalkeeper, who advanced two paces before thinking better of his initial impulse, to chase and kick his backside. He repeated the trick, fell to his knees, beamed and clenched his fist with childish glee.

Sequences of caressed chip shots and vicious left-footed volleys helped to form sumptuous passages of skill that defied conditions and, occasionally, the laws of physics. He exuded the joy of a boy whose Groundhog Day is Christmas Day. When he left the pitch, playfully kicking rainwater after hugging the goalkeeper, he crossed himself.

We didn't think to pray for him.

Heroes might be sanctified by memory, but they are mortal. Maradona's excess was theatrical, tragic and strangely divisive. Those who never saw him play viewed him principally as a toxic version of a reality TV star, but those of us who followed his career until its implosion were more forgiving. We had been baptised by his brilliance.

Attempting to measure his greatness, across cultures and generations, is as pointless an exercise as trying to bottle sunshine or count imaginary angels on a pinhead. The essence of Maradona was how he made us feel rather than how he made us think. It was a devotional experience, barely impacted by first-hand knowledge of his faults.

On the few occasions I was in close proximity to him I was struck by his sourness. He had no time for the process of fame, the natural enemy of authenticity. Formal access to the best and brightest talents tends to involve commercial expedience, corporate caution and the tragic vanity of self-appointed experts.

Pele is more comfortable with the charade. Perhaps that is why his tributes to his 'great friend' after his fatal heart attack ('One day, I hope we can play football together in the sky') were verbal candyfloss. Bizarrely, a photoshopped image of him supposedly leaving flowers on Maradona's grave went viral before it was exposed as a fake by a reverse-image hunt on Yandex, a Russian search engine that revealed it was a standard shot issued to funeral directors.

Within a week, he was posting an open letter on his Facebook account: 'Many people loved to compare us all their lives. You were a genius that enchanted the world, a magician with the ball at his feet. Your trajectory was marked by honesty. And in your unique and particular way, you taught us that we have to love and say "I love you" a lot more often. Your quick departure didn't let me say it to you, so I will just write it: I love you, Diego.'

We're going to have to order bigger fortune cookies.

At 80, Pele remains a world-class pragmatist. In recent years he has been prepared only to speak as global ambassador for Pfizer, makers of Viagra. The last time I saw him he made his pitch about the mental health benefits of a product that confronts a global taboo with brisk efficiency before submitting to the inevitable with a gentle, world-weary smile.

The topic of the day, he learned, would be familiar: the relative merits of legendary players. He knew that we knew he had history with the ruffian-genius and was smart enough to come up with what seemed to be a suitably mystical money quote. 'Maradona?' he mused. 'The Angel Walks with the Devil ...'

Since it suited creative circumstances, I kept a little secret to myself. I had heard him use exactly the same phrase to sum up Michael Owen, of all people, during a previous audience at Old Trafford. The mind duly boggled at the improbability and incongruity of the recycled image. It was like linking Scarface with Captain Sensible.

The most affecting tribute was *L'Equipe*'s stunning front page, featuring a young Maradona in Argentina's iconic sky blue and white striped kit. Since it encouraged association with the famous Friedrich Nietzsche quotation, the headline 'Dieu est Mort' (God is Dead) could be taken as a simple act of reverence, or as a social comment.

The German philosopher's expanded observation was: 'God is dead. God remains dead. And we have killed him. How shall we comfort ourselves, the murderers of all murderers? What was holiest and mightiest of all that the world has yet owned has bled to death under our knives: who will wipe this blood off us? What water is there for us to clean ourselves? What festivals of atonement, what sacred games shall we have to invent?'

Were we being invited to dwell on the potentially fatal consequences of the hysterical attention he received? I thought that fanciful until I chanced upon a YouTube clip of Lionel Messi caught at an intersection in his car. It was surrounded immediately by fans pressing mobile phones against the windows. Messi's attempted grin is a wince; he waves distractedly a couple of times, but his eyes register recurring alarm. He glances continually over his shoulders, as if he is checking the security of the door locks.

He's an exhibit in a human zoo that never closes.

Peter Shilton, meanwhile, emerged as the UK's resident philosopher. His graceless reflections on the Hand of God goal were unworthy of him, but unsurprising. They served to emphasise the impact on the collective English psyche of events which unfolded in 11 seconds less than four minutes at the Azteca Stadium in Mexico City on 22 June 1986.

Football's biggest occasions are laced by legend and defaced by nationalism. The World Cup quarter-final against Argentina, England's 618th official international, was trailed, in true Orwellian spirit, as war by other means. Memories of the Falklands conflict were fresh and eagerly summoned by those, on both sides, who sought to make commercial, sporting or political capital out of the sacrifice of young lives.

It was the first World Cup meeting between the nations since 1966, where, at the same stage of the tournament, Sir Alf Ramsey refused to allow his players to exchange shirts with 'animals'. Generations of England supporters had been weaned on the iniquities of Antonio Rattin, the Argentina captain, sent off for 'violence of the tongue' by Rudolf Kreitlein, a German referee who spoke no Spanish.

Rattin infamously refused to leave the pitch for eight minutes, created an international incident by sitting on the red carpet reserved for the Queen and screwed up a pennant bearing the union flag. Viewed through a South American prism, his contempt reflected an enduring suspicion of British colonialism and a cultural fondness for conspiracy theories.

We, as victors, have written a cheating, spitting, spiteful Argentina team into our version of history. Statistics, which are infinitely more difficult to wrap in a flag of choice, provide an inconvenient reminder that England committed 33 fouls to their opponents' 19. The solitary goal, 12 minutes from time, captures the contradictions of a match known in Argentina as 'el robo del siglo', the robbery of the century.

Those in Basildon will say Geoff Hurst's near-post run on to Martin Peters' left-wing cross to flick a header beyond Antonio Roma, the static Argentina goalkeeper, was a masterpiece of timing and marked the moment West Ham began to win the World Cup. Those in Buenos Aires will recall him as being offside, an indication of bias towards the hosts that preceded the Russian linesman who entered football folklore in the final by allowing Hurst's dubious second goal.

Rattin, 83 at the time of writing, still talks mischievously about eating the chocolate thrown at him by outraged England fans, yet his legend, as *El Caudillo*, the leader, helped to set the tone of Maradona's performance at the Azteca. They share a bloodline and a strong sense of tribal identity that defines South American football.

Rattin won the Argentine league three times in four years and is revered for giving 14 years' service to Boca Juniors. Fiercely loyal and loyally fierce, he was emblematic of the club Maradona longed to play for before he won his only domestic title for them in a solitary season before being transferred to Barcelona after the 1982 World Cup.

Ironically, Rattin believes Pele was a better player than his compatriot, voted the people's Player of the Century. Their relationship was captured by an exchange between them before a match between Boca and Santos: 'I approached Pele and he said to me: "Rattin, with the ball yes; without the ball, no." "No problem," I said, "if I kick you, I'll kick you when you have the ball. You just play."'

Malevolent intent invested with dignity. That's a different perspective, an affront to the spirit of the patricians who grew the game in a different petri dish in Europe, but complementary to the self-image of the boy from the barrio: 'I am Maradona, who makes goals, who makes mistakes. I can take it all. I have shoulders big enough to fight with everybody.' In Spanish, such spirit is known as *Branca*.

The kick-off time at the Azteca, high noon, felt appropriate, but walking up to the stadium that morning nearly 35 years ago, past churches spilling out communicants and children in their Sunday best, had a surreal serenity. Tensions took time to surface before rival supporters, fuelled by beer-sellers who wobbled through the 114,580 crowd carrying a dozen or more drinks on a tray, began to scuffle. One banner, unveiled by four English fans, read: 'Make love, not war'. Its message did not appear to have been registered by a fellow countryman with the cross of St George painted on to his shaven temples. Dullards who unveiled another banner, which hailed Gary Lineker as 'Exocet Lineker', did not appear to understand that they had referred to the type of missile that sank HMS *Sheffield* in the Falklands war with the loss of 20 crew members.

High up in the main stand, parallel to the right-hand penalty area in which Lineker was to poach a typical but quickly forgotten consolation goal, I was entranced by the coiled shadows cast by the stadium's public address system across the centre of the pitch. The heat was stultifying. The smog, which shrouded the city, scoured the throat and occasionally stung the eyes, did not clear until late morning. We continued to suffer from what we had christened the Mexico Cough.

Maradona created a chaotic cottage industry out of the glory and infamy that characterised that afternoon in the Azteca. He had been brutalised by far more accomplished enforcers than England's Terry Fenwick, a work experience goon who began his assault as early as the ninth minute when he was booked for a challenge that arrived from a different time zone.

After being reduced to a puddle of frustration due to his failure to stop a run that left him on his knees, he elbowed Maradona in an off-the-ball incident that the hapless Tunisian referee failed to spot. When Fenwick avoided censure for another head shot, delivered like a burglar's cosh in the centre circle five minutes into the second half, his tormentor took fateful, contemptuous revenge by scoring twice between the 51st and 55th minutes.

Brutality is part of the price paid by timeless talent expressed on the biggest stage. Ferenc Puskas had the main ligament in his left ankle almost severed by a vicious late tackle by West German defender Werner Liebrich in the 1954 World Cup. Pele was kicked out of the 1966 tournament. Berti Vogts beat a tattoo on Cruyff's shins with his studs during the 1974 final.

Maradona, elegantly mugged by Italy's Claudio Gentile in 1982, made sure to get his retaliation in first three days later, when he was sent off for kicking Brazil's defensive midfield player Batista in the groin. Though accustomed to absorbing punishment in his squat frame, he was revealingly protective of Lionel Messi as his national team manager in 2010.

The delicacy of the build-up to Argentina's first goal was buried by debate about its morality. Maradona, cutting in through the vestiges of England's midfield from the left, beat Glenn Hoddle, Peter Reid and the hapless Fenwick before drawing covering defenders towards him. He passed to Jorge Valdano, who panicked Steve Hodge into slicing an attempted clearance towards his own goal.

Time slowed down and confusion reigned as Maradona directed the ball over the head of a leaden Shilton. Something was obviously not right since Argentina's captain had evidently grown six inches or learned to levitate, but if I were to tell you I knew immediately he had punched it into the net, I'd be lying. In such moments, the press box becomes a self-help group and I offer a silent prayer of thanks that I'm not a TV or radio commentator.

Terry Butcher, Shilton and the inevitable Fenwick, a bystander at his own car crash, were advancing on the referee, arms waving in a semaphore of outrage. Maradona scuttled towards the right-hand corner flag and a Bulgarian linesman who, it transpired, was too scared to believe the evidence of his own eyes. Maradona, mobbed, hissed 'shut the fuck up and keep on celebrating' at his bemused team-mates.

The BBC's Barry Davies tried to solve the puzzle in real time. 'They're appealing for offside, but the ball came back off the boot of Steve Hodge,' he reported, as if mentally running through the laws of the game. It took a couple of minutes, several TV replays and the sight of colleagues on the left-hand end of the press box, who were closer to the action, punching their palms, signalling handball, before we sensed the magnitude of the story.

Maradona was finally untethered from the conventions of morality. This was an early manifestation of the bug-eyed cheat thrown out of the 1994 World Cup for failing a drug test. He did not dispute the veracity of that charge, but fought it on the basis there had been a conspiracy against him. Before we knew it, in charge of Argentina for the 2010 tournament, he was grabbing his crotch and inviting the world's media to 'suck it and keep on sucking'.

FIFA banned him for two months, but were powerless to prevent the circus in South Africa. The big top had barely been pitched before Maradona was telling Pele to 'go back to the museum' and dismissing Michel Platini, the UEFA president, because 'we all know what the French are like'. His press conferences were simply surreal. He made us wait for an hour in a dangerously overcrowded, intimidatingly claustrophobic and insanely hot room at Argentina's training base in Johannesburg before delivering the following lecture: 'I am a grown-up, an adult, I don't hold grudges. But what makes me mad is when people lack respect. Those journalists who had been saying we are nobodies before the tournament should just come forward and apologise. Apologising doesn't mean getting naked in front of everyone. It's just the noble thing to do.'

With that, he leaped over the crash barrier to hug former Napoli team-mate Salvatore Bagni. Truth be told, we loved him for his impetuosity, forgave him his crudity and cruelty and feasted on the repeatability of his quotes. He unlocked the child in us all because, buried beneath the calcified layers of celebrity and notoriety, he remained a child himself.

That second goal against England in Mexico City is his ultimate excuse. It remains the greatest goal I have seen live, but rather than describe it, I'll leave the summaries to others. Bryon Butler, on BBC radio, began a memorable monologue by conjuring the image of Maradona as 'a little eel'.

Davies's voice rose in excitement: 'He has Burruchaga to his left and Valdano to his left. He doesn't … he won't need any of them … Oh, you have to say that's magnificent. There is no debate about that goal. That was just pure football genius.' On ITV, David Pleat was simultaneously exclaiming: 'He's dethroned Pele!'

On Radio Argentina, Victor Hugo Morales was entering legend: 'Maradona has the ball. Two mark him. Maradona touches the ball. The genius of world soccer dashes to the right and leaves the third and is going to pass to Burruchaga. It's still Maradona! Genius! Genius! Genius! Ta-ta-ta-ta-ta-ta-ta. Goooooaaaal! Gooooooaaaaal! I want to cry! Dear God! Long live soccer! Gooooooaaaaalllllll! Diegoal! Maradona! It's enough to make you cry, forgive me.

'Maradona, in an unforgettable run, in the play of all time. Cosmic kite! What planet are you from, to leave in your wake so many Englishmen, so that the whole country is a clenched fist shouting for Argentina? Argentina 2 England 0. Diegoal! Diegoal! Diego Armando Maradona. Thank you, God, for soccer, for Maradona, for these tears, for this. Argentina 2 England 0.'

Follow that. Fenwick attempted to do so, again escaping a red card for another assault on Maradona midway through the second half, but there was an overwhelming sense of futility to England's response. All that remained was for Hodge to swap shirts with the man who invoked the Hand of God. He even entitled his autobiography *The Man With Maradona's Shirt.*

His team-mates were far from impressed. As the day's colour writer, it was my job to amplify the mood of the England camp. Bobby Robson was incandescent. His players raged in the dressing room, demanding the FA seek a replay. Terry Butcher was tempted to punch Maradona when they met in the drug-testing area. Even the normally mild-mannered Ray Wilkins told Argentina's kit man to 'fuck off out of here' when he came into the room to organise shirt swapping.

Fenwick, a likeable if politically cute individual off the pitch, appeared resigned to his fate as history's fall guy. He has spent the majority of his subsequent coaching career in the Caribbean and now admits to being awestruck by Maradona's talent. Others find it harder to let go. More than 30 years later I had lunch with Butcher and a mutual friend, my former sports editor David Walker.

Terry needed a walking stick since he had just undergone a knee construction operation to counter the creeping arthritis that torments many players of his generation. He is a friendly man, with a gentle sense of humour, but it only took a mention of Maradona's name to remind us that here was a man who had photogenically shed blood for his country: 'Fucking cheat'.

Case closed? Life is rarely so black and white. Choose your shade of grey.

Chapter Twenty-Four

Truth to Power

NELSON MANDELA learned a fundamental lesson in leadership from his guardian, Jongintaba Dalindyebo, a tribal king who held court in the Great Place, a royal homestead in the village of Mqhekezweni. He gathered supporters and supplicants in a circle and refused to speak until they had aired their views.

The Thembu monarch understood the power of his example, but knew humility conferred legitimacy. He used his authority subtly, to build consensus, confidence and positivity. He taught his young charge the value of leadership as a collective activity. By allowing followers to forge forward, without realising they were being quietly influenced, he retained control and perspective.

It may seem far-fetched to draw a comparison with a 23-year-old footballer, but, in setting the narrative for a new age of athlete activism, Marcus Rashford emulated Mandela in listening to others and leading from behind. By stressing the significance of community and encouraging others to act on complementary values, he became a beacon of hope.

North American athletes have a tradition of political engagement. Tommie Smith protested against institutional racism on an Olympic medal podium. Muhammad Ali was empowered by the consequences of his pacifism. Michael Jordan and LeBron James were proactive presences in a presidential election. Colin Kaepernick emulated Rashford in the simplicity and starkness of his delivery of a single-issue message.

In the UK, roles have been reversed since Margaret Thatcher viewed football as part of her command and control culture. Rashford led a generation of Premier League players that evolved rapidly once they realised the extent of their reach. Their moral authority, societal experience and communications skills exposed the degeneracy of the modern political classes.

This was sport on a social mission.

Raheem Sterling, an early voice in the debate about ingrained racial abuse, established a charitable foundation to assist disadvantaged children. Trent Alexander-Arnold launched a 'Football for Change' initiative. Andy Robertson, his Liverpool team-mate, set up a charity 'to give people a first chance at life'. Chelsea's Reece James campaigned against food waste. Wayne Rooney, whose charitable foundation has raised £2.3million, funded Christmas campaigns for the NSPCC.

Club captains, co-ordinated by Jordan Henderson, Mark Noble, Harry Maguire and Troy Deeney, supported NHS charities. Portentously, players, led by Borussia Dortmund's Marcus Thuram in a match against Union Berlin six days after the killing of George Floyd, adopted the symbolic gesture of taking the knee. Galvanised by Virgil Van Dijk and his Dutch team-mate Gini Wijnaldum, the Liverpool squad did so at Anfield the following day.

Superheroes don't necessarily wear capes, masks or questionable undergarments over spandex tights. Rashford wore football boots, on which children had written inspirational messages. The laces were inscribed with Muhammad Ali's reminder to 'recognise how every moment of our journey is an important part of the growth of our soul'.

Boris Johnson's resistance to Rashford's campaign against child hunger was laced with institutional ignorance and arrogance. The footballer's response was passionate without being partisan, challenging without being contemptuous. In a popularity contest between a working-class hero and an opportunistic product of the Bullingdon dining club there could be only one winner.

The prime minister made two U-turns, latterly under the pressure of a petition that registered the disapproval of more than a million signatories. His approach was typified by the banality of his news management in choosing to announce the second reversal of his decision to deny additional funding on the day the world was focused on Joe Biden's confirmation as the new US president.

The contrast with Rashford's humanity and authenticity was stark. He had established his social conscience working with the homeless. In learning sign language, to interact with deaf children, he signalled a determination to self-educate. That sensitivity, aligned to the humility required to admit to gaps in his knowledge, gave authority to his actions and amplification to his voice.

He helped to raise an initial £20million for Fare Share, which annually recycles 24,000 tonnes of food that would otherwise be discarded to school breakfast clubs, women's refuges, homeless shelters and lunch clubs for senior citizens. His strategic work with the Food Foundation was underpinned by daily contact through FaceTime calls and emails with underprivileged families.

He controlled the wider narrative through a cyber constituency of 8.5 million Instagram followers, 3.3 million

Facebook friends and 2.9 million Twitter followers, but, at heart, his story was rooted in personal experience. Growing up, in a family shaped by the love and diligence of his mother Melanie, who did not return from work until 7.30 each evening, he relied upon the free school meal programme.

'This is not about politics; this is about humanity,' Rashford wrote in an open letter to Parliament that set the tone of the battle for hearts and minds. 'Looking at ourselves in the mirror and feeling like we did everything we could to protect those who can't, for whatever reason or circumstance, protect themselves.'

Rashford spoke compellingly about parents going hungry to feed their children, and of 'watching a young boy keeping it together while his mother sobbed alongside him'. He had listened to his own mother crying herself to sleep, unsure how she was going to make ends meet and nourish her five children despite working a 14-hour day.

'That was my reality,' he wrote, stressing the importance of removing the stigma of asking for support. 'I spoke to a mother recently who, along with her two young sons, is currently living off three slices of bread a day, soaking them in hot water and adding sugar, hoping that the porridge-like consistency might better sustain the hunger of her one-year-old child. This is the true reality of England in 2020.'

The backlash, from puffed-up MPs and their online orcs, was as puerile as it was predictable. Rashford's presence on the moral high ground was unassailable and did not require the heraldic embroidery of the award of an MBE in the Queen's birthday honours list, since his motives, in a pandemic in which 8.1 million Britons were struggling to pay for food, were consistent and unimpeachable.

His pitch-perfect distillation of anger and concern nailed the old lie about the wisdom of footballers 'sticking to football'. It reached a new constituency, in which 2,000 paediatricians were on the same page as 600 businesses, local authorities and charities. Sir Alex Ferguson pledged £2million to the cause in conjunction with Sir Michael Moritz, the billionaire philanthropist.

It also reawakened the *Daily Beast*. The crudity of bin-rummaging, a literal form of muck-raking practised most obviously by tabloids around the turn of the century, may have been replaced by dog-whistling in a polarised political climate, but the subliminal message to Rashford to know his place, highlighted by a cunningly-crafted piece in the *Mail on Sunday*, was familiarly insidious.

You don't have to have a media studies degree to understand that the tone of such pieces is set by the headline and the principal photograph, especially online, where attention spans waver. In this case, 'What a result! Campaigning star has bought five luxury houses worth more than £2m' was accompanied by an image of Rashford in a dark hoodie. He has an open, notably fresh face; here he was frowning and pensive.

He was patronised as 'school meals Marcus' who had used 'the Queen's bank, Coutts' to mortgage his 'homes empire' in an area referred to as a 'golden triangle'. Readers were reminded of the market value of his house, £1,850,000, and that he had 'splashed out on a golf course in Cheshire where he could build himself a more secluded home'.

More trigger points for envy and middle-class angst followed. The article referred sniffily to modern business practice, the attempt to trademark his name in the US where 'the US Patent and Trademark Office has issued him with a certificate to sell name-branded goods, including clothes, sportswear, books, grooming products and games'.

The boy 'from humble beginnings on a council estate in Wythenshawe' was 'set for global stardom after billionaire hip-hop mogul Jay-Z signed Rashford to his Roc Nation management agency'. A little more research would have revealed that the agency has a 15-strong team in a philanthropy department in New York, advising clients on the most-effective use of their charitable instincts.

Rashford responded in kind, through the most direct form of communication, Twitter: 'Ok, so let's address this. I'm 23. I came from little. I need to protect not just my future but my family's too. To do that I made a decision at the beg of 2020 to start investing more in property. Please don't run stories like this alongside refs to "campaigning".'

This led to some rustling of crinolines at the newspaper, whose editor, Ted Verity, took offence at a brilliantly delivered critique by *Guardian* columnist Jonathan Liew. He made valid points about the publication's support for Rashford's endeavours, but anyone with an understanding of print media culture could read between the lines. Dog should not eat dog.

I was brought up on that maxim on the once-sacred turf of Fleet Street. It is difficult to sustain when the nature of certain publications has changed irrevocably. The world I outline in many of these pages no longer exists, although the principles, personalities and philosophies I describe are timeless and educational. Rashford's unprecedented impact suggests that fundamental change is possible if it acquires sufficient consensus.

Acknowledging hard truths is uncomfortable, for an individual or an institution. Football's approach to racism is typical; it espouses diversity, yet prefers the easy option of symbolism to decisions of substance. It uses the captain's armband as a fig leaf. As a result, it finds itself compromised, morally and culturally. It lacks the dexterity and authority to deal with generational social issues.

Football's Tommie Smith moment duly arrived in a Champions League match at the Parc des Princes on the evening of 8 December 2020, when both teams, PSG and Istanbul Basaksehir, walked off the pitch in response to allegations that the fourth official, Sebastian Coltescu, used a racist term in describing the Turkish side's assistant coach Pierre Webo.

UEFA's response was revealing. It suggested the expedient solution of simply reassigning Coltescu to VAR duties. When it was pointed out that this hardly represented moral leadership, officials effectively let the players decide what to do. The game was suspended after a couple of hours' confusion, and resumed 21 hours later, on Wednesday evening, with both teams and a new set of officials taking the knee around the centre circle.

That gesture, which has its roots in the civil rights movement, had triggered an existential crisis at a complex, singularly defiant club, Millwall, whose fans booed when Derby County players took the knee at the Den the previous Saturday. Huge offence was taken, understandably, and the club's initial response was slow, palsied and vague.

I connected instinctively with Millwall during a year embedded at the club for my book, *Family*. I know it as a huge community asset, a force for good in a diverse, economically disadvantaged urban area. It could not afford another episode of what would be portrayed as collective racism. My immediate thought was that the Den should be temporarily closed for Tuesday evening's game against QPR, to buy time for a cohesive approach.

One senior figure, to whom I spoke within an hour of the incident, felt morally compromised. Others were similarly devastated and were considering their positions. The booing had been predicted on message boards that are no more than cesspits and had not been prevented by a pre-match statement by the Millwall players.

In such circumstances, which reflect a bitter and divided society, it took the moral courage of a young black footballer to crystallise the central issue in a confused, occasionally insincere, debate. Mahlon Romeo, the Millwall full-back, stressed he was speaking for himself, but his words resonated in dressing rooms across the land.

He told Richard Crawley, sports editor of the *South London Press*: 'In society there is a problem, and that problem is racism. The fans who have been let in today have disrespected not just me but the football club, and what the club and the community stand for. They've booed and condemned a peaceful gesture put in place to highlight, combat and stop any discriminatory behaviour and racism.

'For the life of me, I can't understand. I'm almost lost for words. I don't know how they thought that would make me feel. I don't know what they thought taking a knee stood for, but I think I've explained it simply enough. I feel really low, probably the lowest I've felt in my time at this club. It's something I can't wrap my head around.

'People will have their beliefs and views, which everyone is entitled to. I'm not trying to stop or contain them, but if your beliefs and views oppose a positive change in society, then don't come to a football ground and spread them around. A lot of people don't appreciate how much Millwall do and have done in the community. It's a lot, more than most other clubs. It's vital. Today fans have come here and basically fucked it off.'

One of the milder responses on the message board read: 'Should never play for us again after coming out with that. Hope one of the non-kneeling QPR players snaps his legs

Tuesday.' The venom beggared belief and was gleefully spread by far-right politicians, anxious to associate the gesture with Marxist ideology.

The antidote came in the form of a 'United for Change' campaign, crafted during a three-hour Zoom meeting on the Monday afternoon, involving players, staff, directors, representatives of QPR and assorted institutions. Romeo spoke passionately; Kick it Out and the PFA came across as being proactive and empathetic. The EFL was criticised for apparent indifference; the FA refused to dwell on specifics and merely parroted its equity policy.

A letter, handed out to fans at the game, warned: 'The eyes of the world are on this football club – your club – tonight, and they want us to fail.' Criticism of its tone was led by presenters of Sky's live coverage, which would have been enhanced, in ratings terms, by further controversy. That felt premeditated and led to a protracted apology. It also ignored the club's mentality; instead of a Lion Rampant, the club badge should really feature an extended middle finger.

Millwall fans applauded and delivered a Monk's Chant, a definitive extended growl, as players from both teams linked arms behind an anti-racist banner in a pre-match gesture of solidarity. There was no response when QPR players took the knee before the kick-off, and when they took the lead early in the second half. The game, a 1-1 draw, represented a small step forward.

The issues raised on the same evening in south London and Paris are social, political and generational. Experience tells me football, in general, will not change until it is forced to. In the meantime, we must cherish emerging campaigners like Maggie Murphy, whose external experiences are helping to reshape the game from within.

She is general manager of Lewes FC, which, in 2017, became the first club to pledge to pay its male and female players equally. Recruited because of her background as an activist for Transparency International, where she worked on the Panama Papers, FIFA corruption and inter-governmental issues raised at G20 summits, she strives for strategic understanding.

We met at the Dripping Pan, an evocative ground in a natural bowl enclosed by a protected flint wall, on a morning on which the chalky outcrops of the South Downs were still cloaked with mist and fine rain. Lewes would draw 2-2 with Liverpool that afternoon in the sort of incongruous contest that would short-circuit a Premier League fixture computer.

'I've played football since I was a kid,' she said, pausing from oversight of pandemic protocols. 'I always wanted to be out in the garden running around. I was very much the muddy knees type, had a couple of brothers that were older than me, so I always was active, but there weren't any girls' teams when I was growing up. Whenever I had the chance, I would just want to go out and play.

'I was working in anti-corruption when the FIFA scandal hit. A lot of things fell into place for me around the challenges and governance of football. It suddenly made a lot more sense why women's football was starved of resources. The people at the top were not managing things correctly and didn't really care.

'I started to realise the problem with FIFA was replicated in lots of the member associations around the world, right down to the grassroots at local county levels. I thought: "There's something that can be changed here. We don't have to run football the way it's always been run; we can do things completely differently. We can do things better, actually make football for all instead of just a few."

'That really drove me to consider what I could do with this passion of mine, maybe use some of my skills in anti-corruption, human rights and global advocacy to see if we can actually make football better. We just think that the words "football for good" can be thrown around. Actually putting them into action is difficult.'

Lewes marked Rainbow Laces Day last December by posting a video featuring openly gay players. Equality does not diminish the distinction between teams: men wear white shorts; the women wear black or red, since white are unsuitable, given the possibility of leakage during the menstrual cycle. Murphy has also educated herself on eating disorders, which are thought to be prevalent in the women's game.

'Lots of clubs compromise on their principles and values,' she reflected. 'We stick to ours, even when, sometimes, that can hurt us. There's a need for a club like Lewes. You only have to look at the fact that we have 1,500 owners from 33 countries to see there is room for a different model. These people are tired, exhausted at the trappings of the rich you see in the Premier League and other big leagues around the world.

'I think there will be a drive towards clubs that are community-minded, clubs that almost return to the roots. Our club has a personality, and people are drawn to it because of that personality. When they're here, they're treated as an individual, a person in their own right, not just a number on a spreadsheet.'

Chapter Twenty-Five

Whose Game is it Anyway?

TOBI BROWN represents the fan football does not know exists. A quiet, studious boy, he was a fast winger who supported Manchester United from its London heartland. He aspired to be an air traffic controller at his local grammar school, excelled at flight simulation games and studied computing at university. He played FIFA with six friends and, in 2011, joined YouTube.

Those friends eventually coalesced as the Sidemen. Tobi morphed into TBJZL after a spell in which he sought to protect his identity by insisting his real name was Tobi Lerone. His friends, JJ Olatunji, Simon Minter, Josh Bradley, Ethan Payne, Vik Barn and Harry Lewis, also adapted online aliases, respectively KSI, Miniminter, Zerkaa, Behzinga, Vikkstar123 and W2S.

We met in the main stand at Leyton Orient on a December day when headlines were dominated by Boris Johnson's buffoonish posturing about a no-deal Brexit and rising infection rates in the capital. It was a soporific scene; the groundsman's lonely vigil was only interrupted by a couple of workmen preparing a dugout, adjacent to a corner flag, where eight fans would be ceremonially served pizza at half-time during the following Saturday's home win against Newport County.

Tobi laughed gently when I failed miserably to disguise my astonishment at Sidemen's cumulative reach of 111 million subscribers across three YouTube channels. Since their formation in October 2013, they have generated 27 billion views of online content, including global challenges, video game commentaries and vlogs. 'Mad, isn't it?' he said. 'Even we're lost in the numbers.'

Those numbers speak for themselves, though those hidebound by football convention do not appear to be listening. Ownership of the biggest clubs is in the hands of individuals who have no concept of civic commitment and social significance. The marketing strategies they sign off are based on the drug pusher's belief that addicts will keep returning for their fix until it kills them.

Leyton Orient is one of the few clubs to flourish in the pandemic because it understands the way in which that fix must be tailored to a rapidly changing world. It trades off the authenticity of lower league football and an instinct for innovation typified by a mutually beneficial partnership with the Sidemen that reflects the music industry background of commercial executive Josh Stephens.

The deal gives the League Two club access to a huge, unrealised audience, primarily aged between 19 and 25. It is global in nature and demanding in its expectation of football as a 24/7 diet of interactive content. Orient tested the water in the early weeks of the initial lockdown, staging 'The Ultimate Quaran-Team', a FIFA tournament that attracted 128 clubs from 16 countries. It has generated partnership programmes with clubs in Europe, Scandinavia and North America.

The Sidemen, in return, balance the social benefits of helping a local club with the firebreak it provides from fame. Their celebrity has become so overwhelming they can no longer film in easily accessible public areas for fear of being mobbed. The deal gives them access to the ground to shoot a range of videos, including football-skills challenges.

The game bridges the gap between the impersonal aspects of remote gameplay and the humanity of a humble club whose appearance and status are deceptive. Generations collide, but instincts and individuals like Nigel Travis and Tobi Brown are complementary. A new frontier is being established, quietly and irreversibly.

Travis, a Leyton Orient supporter for 61 years, became chairman after leading a consortium that bought out Francesco Becchetti, whose chaotic four-year regime encompassed two relegations and 12 managers. He has harnessed the emotional intensity of the 'horrible' experience of dropping out of the Football League and brought in business concepts developed in the US corporate world.

The club is run on what he terms a 'challenge culture'. This involves giving all employees the freedom to question the status quo, civilly and concisely. The Sidemen deal is a product of that culture, in which ideas flourish because, in Travis's words, 'we question everything without disrespecting anyone'.

Their streaming service is carried in more than 30 countries. Travis insists: 'Our demographic isn't just going to go younger. It's going to go global. I truly think that in three years we will look back and say the future of football sprang from the pandemic, with a fanbase that is different, more diverse and more engaged.'

Tobi acknowledges his group 'now think of ourselves as a business'. They are essentially selling engagement and brand awareness and can command a fee of up to £500,000 for appearing in a 45-minute promotional video. Their merchandise includes their own clothing range. As TBJZL, he created his own clothing line, ILLVZN, in 2019.

Millennials, in this context, are ready for the rocking chair. Every element of the modern football industry needs to recognise that those from Generation Z, born between 1995 and 2009, and even Generation Alpha, born from 2010 onwards, are setting the agenda.

They have been brought up on tablets and computer gaming consoles rather than red top tabloids and *Charles Buchan's Football Monthly*. Since they have no conception of watching a full live game on TV, modern broadcasters are paying billions for a product with built-in obsolescence. Digital entertainment has reduced attention spans and broadened horizons.

Dressing room doors can no longer have 'No Entry' signs. This is the age of the Big Reveal, the all-seeing eye of the embedded camera. Football has become a hybrid product, repeatable content for TV, digital and social media channels. It is the vehicle for documentary series and aspirational lifestyle programmes. Footballers are influencers, whose medium is being constantly refined.

New models are emerging as the evolutionary process accelerates. Teenagers, accustomed to watching several screens, simultaneously, are already being wooed by providers who run quizzes, with branded goods as prizes, alongside sports content on associated channels. A centre-forward scoring a goal in a live match can expect to feature in a question within five minutes.

Tobi Brown, brought up on *Match of the Day*'s diet of Saturday night highlights, believes mainstream television will soon cease to be a relevant form of mass communication. He has a natural affinity with another YouTube content creator,

Spencer Owen, who, in 2016, founded Hashtag United as a group of friends, initially playing a charity match in memory of a childhood companion.

Hashtag entered the tenth tier of the pyramid, the Essex Senior League, in the 2018/19 season. This followed a two-year spell of exhibition matches across seven countries, including a 19-1 win over a Comedians XI that paid homage, of sorts, to Owen's previous career in stand-up. It has a social media reach approaching three million, beyond all but a handful of Premier League clubs.

All home matches, staged at the Len Salmon Stadium, owned by Isthmian League club Bowers & Pitsea, are streamed, free of charge, to a global interactive audience that builds, over time, from an immediate 45,000 to hundreds of thousands. The commercial principles are familiar: Owen organised a YouTubers' tournament at Wembley, including the Sidemen, which led to a 300 per cent increase in brand searches for its sponsor, EE.

Players are ahead of the curve. Mason Mount linked with Chunkz and Yung Filly on the Pro: Direct Soccer YouTube channel. Their video, in which Chelsea's England international was taught the 'Frankenstein' goal celebration he used against Everton, went viral. Similarly, Declan Rice, Mount's childhood friend, is a follower of Hashtag; Owen jokes: 'We have an official agreement that he will play for us in 2035.'

Spencer, who has Chelsea captain César Azpilicueta as a business partner, is a compelling commentator for the new generation: 'I've huge respect for proper members of the football canon, clubs who have been around for a long time, but they haven't got our dexterity to move and find newer audiences. Whereas they have a local following with fans whose dad was probably from the area, we've found people from all over the world to support our team.

'It's kind of reverse-engineering if you think about it. You have the club that does the traditional hundred-year journey; one day, it finds itself in the Premier League and starts to become a brand, doing all the travelling and the tours. We've done that bit, in terms of building global awareness, and are now trying to grow a local community.

'We've found a way of getting ourselves in the football conversation online. Our name creates an emotional response. When you hear it, you either love it or hate it, or want to know more. That's deliberate, to be honest. We are very different in the way we do things and I understand why that ruffles a few feathers, but we pride ourselves on impressing teams or individuals who give us a chance.'

The influence of newer platforms is mirrored by the acuity and expertise of many teenaged volunteers in quietly progressive environments in non-league football, such as a phoenix club like Bury AFC, where a multi-faceted social media programme conducts a mental health campaign in addition to selling merchandise to a small but responsive multi-national fan base.

Phil Young, the driving force behind the club, detects a new spirit: 'We've worked heavily on a digital strategy, doing all of our memberships online, because we've had no other choice. Covid has put everyone under enormous financial strain, but we've come out of it relatively healthily, without having to do enormous fundraisers. Others are now copying the way we charge.

'We are trying to inspire a different culture around financial sustainability, and being able to run things ourselves. There's a real bond and a lack of separation between the players, the manager, the fans, the volunteers, the people that are running the club. There's no real distance, no real gap between them. It's a tiring, emotional process, a source of immense pride.

'The days of sitting in a stand, tutting and shrugging your shoulders and saying "that was rubbish", are coming to a close. The culture of boom and bust that involves expecting a rich person to come to the rescue is changing, away from the bigger clubs at least. There's a spirit of activism among supporters, who have the nous to organise and solve problems within their own clubs.'

At the highest level, American investors, in particular, are conscious of more conventional media possibilities in a post-pandemic world. Their interest is nakedly financial; the Glazers have proved there are debt-leveraged fortunes to be made from English football. Other involvement, most notably from the Gulf, China and Russia, has a political as well as an economic dimension. They are united in using the game's global popularity, and the venality and incompetence of the governing bodies, for their own ends.

The mainstream media has become harsher, more subservient and expedient, because it is compromised economically. It remains vulnerable to proprietorial or ideological whim. Content is less lyrical, more analytical, and has acquired the nasty habit of sacrificing accuracy for speed. The tyranny of unpaid internships limits its field of vision; though budding talent has a way of forcing through the stoniest of ground, entry routes are contracting.

The Football Supporters' Association has 15 full-time staff, but the concept of collective fandom is still confused. The organisation seeks to impose common sense on territory stalked by cyber lynch mobs, swathed in club colours, who periodically wish ill on anyone impertinent enough to express an educated opinion. Their froth and fury is, quite literally, laughable, but they can cause real concern.

Football is a game of emotional connection, but can be defined by compassion, rather than confrontation. Again,

Leyton Orient are an instructive example of the game's humanity. They distributed 200 junior shirts, purchased by Spurs fans as a gesture of solidarity when a Covid outbreak led to Orient forfeiting a League Cup tie, to local children's hospitals at Christmas 2020.

Fans are not a homogenous blob. Supporters of the top six will resist the suggestion, but they are increasingly defined by sense of entitlement, expressed in differing degrees of delicacy. Manchester City fans, for instance, romanticise their status as a local club with a history of loveable ineptitude. The reality, that it is a state-funded global corporation, with Spanish senior management, is glossed over.

Followers of those making up the numbers in the Premier League tend not to be as jaded, but need little invitation to kiss the corporate badge. To be fair, some Leeds United fans recognise the absurdity of a superiority complex that dates back to Don Revie's team-building games of carpet bowls. Others, by contrast, responded to the club's promotion as if it was the Second Coming.

Tribalism is understandable, but dangerously unstable. The torrent of sexist and misogynistic filth triggered by the club's criticism of unguarded comments by pundit Karen Carney through an official social media outlet forced the former England player to delete her accounts. In expressing surprise at the predictable consequences of their actions, Leeds were rightly accused of being sanctimonious, hypocritical and unprofessional.

In accepting full responsibility for the damaging tweet, and identifying with its content, Leeds owner Andrea Radrizzani blurred the boundaries between brand building and rabble rousing. Blue collar clubs like Leeds, Cardiff, Millwall, Stoke, Portsmouth and Bristol Rovers are sustained by intensity of tribal loyalty, but traditions can be protected without emotional incontinence.

Speaking truth to power is perilous. Bob Beech, whose SOS Pompey movement successfully marshalled opposition to a succession of malign owners, was so preoccupied he was made bankrupt. Micah Hall, his close friend and colleague, lost his house and family. Iain McInnes, who became Portsmouth chairman under fan ownership, was one of several activists to be burgled in suspicious circumstances.

Actions have greater weight than words. Too many fans talk a good game without putting passion into practice. If they cherish football as a localised exercise that reflects where they were born and brought up, they must become more assertive. Supporters have unrealised economic power; they should reaffirm what they require from a sport that, at its best, holds a mirror to them. Let us not forget what football was like without them. The lack of a crowd sucked us into a void. Enforced voyeurism, through television's keyhole, felt wrong. It held its fascinations, most notably in stripping the game down so that the faults of players, coaches and referees became more apparent, but it was a poor substitute for the real thing.

My release involved channelling the positive energy of the evening of 27 May 2002, when Ivor Heller received a call from an FA contact, confirming what he had gleaned from several other sources. The old Wimbledon, his boyhood club, was dead and, as far as the authorities were concerned, deserved to be dumped in an unmarked grave. Heller and three friends faced a primal challenge: fight, or flight.

Kris Stewart was deputed to go to London the following day for the formal announcement, while Marc Jones and Trevor Williams remained with him in his now-defunct print works to sketch out plans for a phoenix club. Another ally,

Erik Samuelson, who would become the new club's first chief executive, was soon on board.

'I was very upset when I heard about the Milton Keynes situation for about two minutes,' Heller recalls. 'I just couldn't imagine life without football, and my club. That was quickly replaced by a determination to go again. Genuinely, none of us knew how to start a football club, but by the end of the following day, the 28th, we knew what we had to do. It was a lot, and we virtually had no time.'

David Fowkes, secretary of the London FA, acted as facilitator. Heller admits: 'Without his help, we would have been struggling.' Fowkes explained that, to start the following season, the new club would be required to secure senior status within a fortnight. The subsequent conversation, according to Heller, went something like this:

'So, what do we need for that?'

'Well, you need a three-year lease on a ground. You need a name, a badge, and colours. The ground has to have floodlights. And a bar. A bar is very important by the way.'

'Wow. Best get started then, hadn't we?'

Fowkes arrived at the print works the following day with the requisite forms. He didn't look up from his paperwork when told that they intended to name the phoenix club Real Wimbledon.

'No.'

Heller laughs at the memory of feeling like a naughty child: 'He gave us some ridiculous reason we couldn't do what we wanted, so we went through a couple of other names before we settled on AFC Wimbledon, which seemed as close as we were going to get to the old name. He asked us what year we were formed. It was massive for us that it should be recognised as 1889, the date the original club was set up. He agreed.

'It was so pioneering. Everything we did was completely and utterly by the seat of our pants. None of us had run a football club before, but we'd all had businesses, we'd all been involved in serious things. We knew what we were doing to a certain degree, but it was fuelled by righteous indignation. We'd had our football club taken away.

'One of the most important things in our lives, in fact the most important thing in some of our lives, apart from our families, obviously, had just been ripped out of our community and taken 80 miles up the road. Why would you stand for that? Why wouldn't you try and do something about it? What happened to us was, and will always be, completely wrong.'

The new club began in the Combined Counties League, the ninth tier of English football, and needed only nine years to return to the Football League. Their sixth promotion took them into League One. Fans raised an initial £2.4million for a new stadium, the site of a former greyhound racing track 250 yards from Wimbledon's old ground at Plough Lane, and underwrote a £5.4million bond scheme with loans of a minimum £1,000.

AFC Wimbledon is the exemplar of the fan-run model, but does that birthmark of rejection by football's establishment ever fade? Heller, a squat, jovial man known as The Flying Satsuma for his antics as a goalkeeper during half-time, fund-raising sessions for the High Path Centre, which caters for 80 local people with learning difficulties, is suddenly serious:

'Not to me, no, because it had never happened before and has never happened since. A lot of football clubs have gone through their problems, one way and another, but none of them have actually been ripped out of the heart of their community and taken away. That was a unique injustice to us.

'I feel terrible for the clubs who have got into trouble. Some of them, Bury being a prime example, have had to go right back to the beginning and start again. They've had hard times, but they've still got their roots, their community, and in some cases, like Macclesfield, their grounds. But we were violated as a football club. That's a wrong that can never be put right.

'What you're seeing around us here today is the result of all that righteous indignation. We are back where we belong. We have proved that the whole thing was a load of rubbish and they should never have taken the football club away in the first place. To me, a football club is all about its community, serving it, making it happy, making it sad. A community is always with its football club, and a football club is always with its community.

'The minute you break that bond, you start to destroy the fabric of that community, wherever it may be. We are living proof that a club is not just about what it does on the pitch for 90 minutes. It is not about what league you're in or how far up the pyramid you go. Never say die. Never ever say die. We never give up. We never stop. There is always tomorrow.

'We have fed our community through the Covid-19 crisis. We have raised money to look after people that can't look after themselves. This is all done in the name of this wonderful football club. We can actually affect the people who are around us.

'People talk about the Crazy Gang, but we're not the Crazy Gang any more. We do, though, have their spirit. We're never beaten. Yes, we might lose a football match. We might lose ten football matches. But we're never beaten. You pick our football club up, move it and tell us we're not in the wider interests of football? We tell you what we're going to do, and do it.'

Dave Bassett, an iconic Wimbledon manager, didn't realise the consequences of his actions when he leaped a fence during a testimonial match at the old ground to jokingly remove a glass of beer from the two-handed grip of a 13-year-old boy enjoying his first illicit drink. 'He actually nicked my pint,' exclaimed Ivor Heller, radiating the warmth of first love.

Heller acted as my guide around the new stadium, in which we wore hard hats, hi-viz jackets, goggles and borrowed boots to conform to the health and safety requirements of what was still an active building site. We paused to remember Les Varron, a life-long fan who was the club's guest of honour on his retirement after 52 years as a platform assistant at Wimbledon Station.

He cherished his present, a signed shirt, but passed away before he could witness the homecoming. His coffin was draped in an AFC Wimbledon flag and his cortege stopped the traffic. On this October afternoon, he offered a posthumous reminder of life, love and loss that matched the wistfulness of my mood.

I felt renewed affinity with the boy in that isolation ward all those years before. That boy now found joy in his grandchildren and, with God's grace, planned to emulate his parents by teaching them to have the courage of their convictions. He felt reconnected to the sporting landscape and, in particular, football's stripped-back version of humanity.

There could have been no more fitting place than Plough Lane to end a journey of rediscovery. Yellow and blue seats were still being installed, but as the AFC players underwent their first training session on a pristine pitch, a week before the inaugural game, a 2-2 draw against Doncaster Rovers, I was seized by a sudden sense of closure.

This was football's future. It will be sustained at local level by the love of the common man. It will be imperfect because life is imperfect, but it will be viable. It might be different, in context and culture, but it will continue to matter. Hearts will still beat faster on match day. Songs will be sung, loudly and discordantly. Arguments will remain largely illogical but purified by a fan's formative passion. The game they tried to kill will refuse to die.

Football doesn't belong to fossils like Greg Clarke, potentates like Sheik Mansour or speculators like Stan Kroenke. It belongs to a young boy or girl, holding a parent's hand as they walk into a newly sanitised stadium for the first time. It belongs to rheumy-eyed regulars with fast-fading memories. It belongs to Olly Goss and an army of friendly ghosts. It belongs to you, and me.

It's ours.

Acknowledgements

WRITING THIS book has been an occasionally uncomfortable process, like looking into a mirror at the height of a hangover. I recognise the figure peering back at me, and wince at the obvious imperfections. Such unease and discomfort reflects a professional premise, that the writer should never be bigger than the story.

I hope I have avoided that impression, despite the personalised nature of the narrative. If anything, this process has emphasised the debt I owe, both to colleagues, past and present, and to my family. They've had to put up with my prolonged absences and variable moods, either pining for or recovering from life on the road.

Thanks, first of all, to my wife Lynn, who picks up the pieces without anyone else noticing. My children, Nicholas, Aaron, William and Lydia, are a source of endless pride. They've brought Vasiliki, Jo and Joe into our family. I promise that my grandchildren, Marielli, Michael and Jesse, will know the goodness of their great-grandparents, Charlie and Margaret, Olly and Joy.

As ever, I value the insight and instinctive excellence of my literary agent Rory Scarfe, and the help of everyone at the Blair Partnership. This is my first book for Pitch Publishing, the

UK's fastest-growing sports imprint. Huge thanks to Jane and Paul Camillin, and their team. Designer Duncan Olner showed admirable patience in dealing with my whims. The editing of Nigel Matheson, the proof reading of Dean Rockett and the production work of Graham Hales was crisp and efficient. Promotional work is effortless, thanks to the professionalism of Laura Wolfe.

I was pleased to learn that Oli Phillips is enjoying retirement in France. I hope I've acknowledged his influence on me; his *Official Illustrated History of Watford FC*, published to mark the club's centenary in 1991, was of great assistance in my research, which also involved re-reading *More Than Just a Game* by Chuck Korr and Marvin Close.

I've raided the archive of the *Watford Observer*, and the online treasure trove that is oldwatford.com. My gratitude to Reg Hayter was renewed by the sudden relevance of his timeless advice that 'if you keep your cuttings, your cuttings will keep you.' I have attempted to acknowledge sources, but apologise for any unintentional oversight.

Thanks to the sports editors who put up with me down the years, Ted Barrett, Ron O'Connor, David Welch, Keith Blackmore, Dan Evans, David Walker and Neil Robinson. I must also acknowledge the help of BT Sport, and the specific support of Simon Green, Jamie Hindhaugh, Kim Fitzsimmons, Barry Andrews and Sally Brown. My work with the brilliant Tom Boswell, who produced and directed our third documentary, *Ours*, underpins the final chapter, in particular.

Books are immersive and addictive. If there is an Authors Anonymous out there, put me down for membership … You see, I've got this idea …

**Michael Calvin,
December 2020.**

Also available at all good book stores

9781785316548

9781785316869

9781785316463

9781785316531

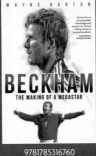

9781785316760

9781785316708

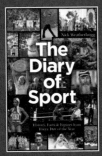

9781785316289

9781785315381

9781785316487

INGSIDE
PRESS

Lombard **rall**

PRESS

MEDIA

IBM AMERICA'S CU
MEDIA CENTR

Name: _MICHAEL CALVIN_
Country: _U.K._
From: _DAILY TELEGRAPH_

MC

2 NOVEMBER
19th~23rd
1989

WORLD
RALLY
CHAMPIONSHIP

FOR CONDITIONS OF USE PLEASE SEE OVER

HANIMEX FUJI FUJI FI
Official film and cameras

Michael Calvin
Daily Telegraph, The
Columnist

Sec. West	Row C	Seat 24

ISTORY IN THE MAKING

2 Rounds of Boxing for the WBC Heavyweight Championship of the World

LEWIS V BRUNO

Cardiff Arms Park Friday 1st October 1993

И Г Р Ы
XXII
ОЛИМПИАДЫ

МОСКВА
1980

E

E
E

SIGNATURE
SIGNATURE
ЛИЧНАЯ ПОДПИСЬ

NOM
SURNAME
ФАМИЛИЯ _CALVIN_

PRENOMS
FIRST NAMES
ИМЯ _Michael_

PAYS
COUNTRY
СТРАНА _GREAT BRITAIN_

FONCTIONS OLYMPIQUES
OLYMPIC FUNCTIONS
ОЛИМПИЙСКИЕ ФУНКЦИИ _GBR_

041307

**PALAIS OMNISPORTS
PARIS BERCY**

PRESSE

titre _Daily Telegraph_
nom _CALVIN_
CP _132000185_

CYCLISME

89-90

WAGE-DATA IDENT SYSTEM

XIII

COMMONWEALTH
GAMES SCOTLAND
1986

CALVIN

MICHAEL

REPORTER

ENG

XIII

**E
R**